The Woman Manager's Troubleshooter

Pinpointing the Causes & Cures of Today's Tough Supervisory Problems

VICKIE L. MONTGOMERY

PRENTICE HALL
Englewood Cliffs, New Jersey 07632

Library of Congress Cataloging-in-Publication Data

Montgomery, Vickie.
    The woman manager's troubleshooter : pinpointing the causes & cures
of today's tough supervisory problems / Vickie L. Montgomery.
       p. cm.
    Includes bibliographical references and index.
    ISBN 0-13-460080-0. — ISBN 0-13-460072-X (pbk.)
    1. Supervision of employees.   2. Women supervisors.   I. Title.
HF5549.12.M665   1996
658.3`02—dc20   96-38662
                                                 CIP

Printed in the United States of America

10 9 8 7 6 5 4 3 2 1

ISBN 0-13-460080-0 (c) ISBN 0-13-460072-X (p)

PRENTICE HALL
Career & Personal Development
Englewood Cliffs, NJ 07632
A Simon & Schuster Company

On the World Wide Web at http://www.phdirect.com

Prentice-Hall International (UK) Limited, *London*
Prentice-Hall of Australia Pty. Limited, *Sydney*
Prentice-Hall Canada, Inc., *Toronto*
Prentice-Hall Hispanoamericana, S.A., *Mexico*
Prentice-Hall of India Private Limited, *New Delhi*
Prentice-Hall of Japan, Inc., *Tokyo*
Simon & Schuster Asia Pte. Ltd., *Singapore*
Editora Prentice-Hall do Brasil, Ltda., *Rio de Janeiro*

This book is
dedicated to my sisters
Brenda, Linda, and Diane—
whose strength, individuality,
spirit, kindness, and perception
represent today's woman.
They have taught me much
and give me hope for the future.

Contents

Introduction

Why a book just for women managers? That is probably the question you are asking yourself right now. Do men and women really manage all that differently? And shouldn't management techniques be universal, not gender-biased?

Quite simply, the answer is at times yes, and at times no. *The Woman Manager's Troubleshooter* concentrates on those differences. Things can be different because you're a woman; sometimes your style is different, your tone is different, your words may be heard differently, all because of your gender. Sometimes it's not *what* you say but what you *didn't* say that counts. Other times your words may be respectful of another's feelings, yet be interpreted as weak, lacking authority, or even insulting. Men and women may not even see the problem as the same. Women are more likely to approach a problem from a macroperspective (seeing the big picture) while men manage in more of a microenvironment manner (assessing the most minute details).

This book will help you develop and use your feminine style to its advantage. You are not handicapped because you are a women, you are fortunate. Yet this book is not exclusively for women. I encourage men to read *The Woman Manager's Troubleshooter* as well. For men, in addition to learning about how women manage differently, they can also benefit from this book by learning more about their own responses to women in today's workforce. It helps bridge the gender gap, not reinforce it.

Did you know that:

- Over half of all women in the United States are currently in the labor force
- Nearly half of all working women regard their jobs as careers
- About 40 percent of all managerial, executive, and administrative workers are women
- Women now account for half of all undergraduate business students and about one-third of all MBA students

Yet despite these statistics, women are still rarely seen in the upper ranks of management or in board rooms. The glass ceiling continues to separate men from women.

The Woman Manager's Troubleshooter is divided into nine chapters, each representing a unique relationship or area of concern that managers typically handle. These relationships include those with staff, colleagues, friends, and senior management, not to mention those problems that involve only the manager herself. *The Woman Manager's Troubleshooter* is set up to incorporate both gender- and nongender-related issues because the same scene may be found for either case. After reading all probable causes, and their respective cures, you will have a better understanding of how to proceed in your own management approach.

Realistically, one problem does not have only one cause. Instead, you will find a combination of causes masked under a single scene. In your own work life you will need to determine which factors are playing more important roles than others. You will notice that frequently the cures suggest identifying your options and weighing the consequences and risk from each choice. Remember, women do have choices. This is a very liberating feeling, one they must not take for granted.

The first chapter, *Troubleshooting Personnel Problems with a Woman's Touch*, looks at how a woman might handle some common personnel problems. This kinder, gentler approach that is characteristic of the feminine style is one that seeks inclusion, compromise, and opportunities for everyone to win. Even when forced to terminate an employee, often one of the most dreaded acts required of any manager, women seek ways to lessen the pain and move quickly into the healing mode, as this chapter discusses.

Chapter 2, *Troubleshooting Problems That Occur Because You're a Woman*, focuses on incidents that are typically related to gender issues. These include when the staff looks at you as a friend, not as a manager; not being respected by female staff members; and managing a staff that prefers the previous male boss. Many of these cures include information about changing or adopting a style to fit a particular environment. This chapter also looks at identifying those things that you control (and can change) and those things that you do not control. You cannot change someone else; you can only change your perception, your understanding, your actions, and your words.

Chapter 3 looks at *Troubleshooting Personal Problems for the Staff*. Inevitably, personal problems do come into the work environment. Whether a divorce, childcare issues, or illness, how you manage these interruptions is key to building a strong and supportive work unit. Integrating personal problems, accepting family as a priority, operating with a flexible style, and handling each person's problem individually are all addressed in this chapter.

Chapter 4, *Troubleshooting Your Own Personal Problems*, is one of the most important chapters. It is centered around problems and situations that you yourself are facing. Your tone, style, image, and ability to handle day-to-day pressures and communicate effectively under duress are all discussed in this chapter. This chapter also looks at childcare problems, health issues, guilt, and emotional responses.

Chapter 5 discusses *Troubleshooting for Teams with a Woman's Touch*. It focuses on how to create, motivate, and manage a team as well as handling individual problems within a group atmosphere.

In Chapter 6, we look at *Troubleshooting Problems Involving Peers*. Whether these problems come from colleagues or friends, they can present some of the most difficult obstacles for women to overcome. Peer acceptance is critical for all of us; their actions and rejections can leave us second-guessing our decisions if we let them. This chapter discusses styles, competition, and knowing how, when, and what game to play.

Chapter 7 addresses *Troubleshooting Tensions from Superiors*. These frictions can make it difficult to go to work. Topics include promotions, the glass ceiling, sexual harassment, and how to gain respect. Many of these problems offer legal as well as moral and practical remedies. Knowledge allows women to become empowered and to carefully review choices and make informed decisions.

Chapter 8 discusses *Troubleshooting Tensions Between Upper Management and the Staff*. Sometimes you may feel like your hands are tied, that no matter what you do someone will not like your response. This chapter explores being caught in the middle, between employer and employee. Your actions and how you handle these situations are critical in maintaining a strong and dependable department.

The final chapter presents the biggest challenge for women: *Troubleshooting Corporate Policy Conflicts for Women*. Whether you are unable to hire your staff, restricted in your authority, or frustrated with the decision-making process, you must carefully review the situation, determine the cause, and evaluate your choices. There is great freedom and power in knowing that we do have choices along with responsibility for our actions. The chapter ends with accepting when it is time to leave and find another employer, which can sometimes be the best solution.

The research for this book has been both fun and enlightening. I surveyed over fifty women in a variety of management roles, to lend advice and comments. Women responded from coast to coast. These women included owner/managers, college administrators, as well as retail, service, and manufacturing managers. Some were new to their roles; others had years of experience. In addition, several survey respondents were interviewed personally. I want to say a special thank you to all the women who so graciously shared their thoughts and concerns, their excitement, and their frustrations about managing.

My personal experiences in management have also guided these pages. My first job as a manager placed me as the first female vice president and the youngest vice president in an Atlanta bank. The battle scars I earned during this time have been shared in several problems throughout this book. I lacked having a female role model or mentor with which to share my problems or learn the way to play the game. It made the journey lonely at times. Fortunately, women today have many opportunities to share and grow together, and networking is accessible to every woman.

My hope is that *The Woman Manager's Troubleshooter* will be a great source of inspiration and practical advice for you. You do not have to journey alone; let this book be your guide.

What This Book Will Do for You

The Woman Manager's Troubleshooter is designed to help you through the many obstacles you face as a manager. It is divided into nine chapters, so that you can easily find a problem similar to the one you are facing, then decide which cause or causes best fits your case and read the cures that follow.

Now more than ever, women need somewhere to go for advice, support, and understanding of corporate behavior, and to learn how to play the game. *The Woman Manager's Troubleshooter* is that place. It is a guide that provides insight into handling a variety of situations, in that no two problems will ever be the same. Understanding both the dynamics of people and understanding yourself will go a long way in your becoming the type of leader and manager you want to be—someone you'd enjoy working for—who will make a difference for all the other women who will someday follow in your footsteps. You will find that management styles are the combination of many factors, including regional traits, education, gender, and life experiences.

To use this book, first turn to the Table of Contents, and decide which chapter covers your problem. If you are having a problem with an employee, Chapters 1, 2, 3, or 8 are where you should begin. Then review the problems that are outlined in each chapter. Find the problem most like what you are experiencing, and go to that section. First will be an outline of The Problem, followed by a detailed description of the Scene involving this particular problem. Read the scene and decide if it is similar to your problem. If so, proceed; if not, then return to either the Table of Contents or the Chapter overview.

To solve a problem you must first understand its Possible Causes. After the scene is outlined, identify which causes may have influenced or led up to these events. You may find that more than one cause is contributing to your problem (which is often the case). Each cause will have a correlating Cure in that section. In this area you will be given advice and suggestions for handling the situation, based on a specific cause. Many times you will be referred to other sections for similar cures, additional information, or other ways of handling the problem.

The Woman Manager's Troubleshooter can provide you with many answers to today's most troubling problems.

- If you need information on ways to motivate and praise employees, especially nonmonetary methods, see *Sections 1.5, 2.1,* and *5.2* for suggestions.

- If you need to know how to fire someone (especially if this is your first time), *Section 1.7* outlines the steps to take as well as the necessary precautions, so that the department can return to normal with the least amount of disruption.

- If you are trying to rebuild trust after being lied to, *Sections 1.3, 1.4,* and *5.4* look closely at this dilemma.

- If you are concerned with the image you or the employees are presenting, *Sections 2.5* and *4.6* address those concerns.

- If you need to know the legal remedies for sexual harassment and pay discrimination cases, see *Sections 2.2, 7.2, 7.4,* and *8.4* for details including an 800 number to call concerning filing an Equal Employment Opportunity Commission (EEOC) complaint.

- If you were wondering about the glass ceiling, and whether it was being penetrated, see *Section 7.3* for some unsettling government statistics and recent trends.

- Other topics include: menopause, diversity, death, homosexuality, downsizing, and emotions in the workplace. There is never an attempt to ignore these tough issues that are continuing to make managing a challenging task in today's competitive atmosphere.

For a woman, family often remains the top priority, whereas men are still almost solely considered the financial providers of the household. Too few men help in substantial ways when it comes to responsibilities of home and childrearing. Equality has not been reached at home, and that inequality transfers to the workplace. Instead, mothers are faced with careers that become blended with both marriage and family duties, a position men rarely find themselves in. It is estimated that a mere 14 percent of all husbands contribute equally (50/50) to the housework, whereas an overwhelming 71 percent of married women do 75 percent of these chores. Is it no wonder why juggling these demanding roles is still associated primarily with women?

If you take the time to develop your management skills properly, stay focused on your goals, find the support system you need, and take time out for yourself, management can be everything you want it to be. Best of luck as you reach onward and upward.

Vickie L. Montgomery

Troubleshooting Personnel Problems with a Woman's Touch

Overview

Personnel problems affect all workplaces; no office is immune. The differences in styles between the genders is often shown by different approaches and solutions. Women analyze problems more through a macro approach, factoring in a lot of peripheral information, to gain what they sense is at issue. Men, on the other hand, use a micro approach, focusing more on the individual problem and less on outside factors.

As a woman manager, understanding the nature of the problem is crucial to how you choose to respond. A "woman's touch" refers to the kinder, gentler approach associated with a feminine style. Remember that we are concentrating on the differences in the styles of men and women in management, not the similarities. For the most part, women build while men conquer. Women are more relational, men more logical. Women more sympathetic, men more aggressive. Men are rewarded by status and power, but women seek support and acceptance.

This chapter addresses the following problems, possible causes, and cures.

1.1   *The Problem: Handling employees who continue to start work late.*

Possible Causes: Poor work attitudes may create lax schedules; people may operate on different time clocks; a lax policy was established by the previous boss; there may not even be a problem.

Cures: Create a positive work environment; how to handle employees with different time clocks; change a lax policy; don't create a problem when one doesn't exist.

1.2   *The Problem: An employee's personal time off request is putting an additional strain on the department.*

Possible Causes: These are interruptions from her personal life.

Cures: How to integrate life outside the office with work.

1.3   *The Problem: An employee lies to you to get a day off from work.*

Possible Causes: An employee isn't comfortable mentioning that she has a personal conflict; she is not concerned about her job or the ramifications of her disregard for the system; your previous actions may be part of the problem through little exaggerations, innocent lies, or bad examples.

Cures: Handle conflicting priorities; improve morale; lead by example.

1.4   *The Problem: A new employee lies on her job application form.*

Possible Causes: Issues that seem important to you may seem less important to someone else; some employees may feel above ordinary rules.

Cures: There may be differences of opinion; how to manage when patterns of lies are uncovered.

1.5   *The Problem: One employee continues talking about other employees behind their backs.*

Possible Causes: An employee is undermining your authority; the need for attention may cause an employee to disregard other people's feelings; she may be trying to improve her status in the company; some people have grown up thinking that talking about someone else is perfectly acceptable behavior.

Cures: Regain a sense of control; implement praise, thanking, and other forms of validation; understand when power comes with information; some may not know any better.

1.6   *The Problem: Handling a problem employee who has already been placed on probation, but hasn't improved.*

Possible Causes: Inadequate training may be adding to the problem; Tom may not understand what is expected of him; you may have an employee who is mismatched for the job; outside life may be affecting his daytime job.

Cures: Offer proper training; improve communications to understand what is expected; match qualifications and strengths; minimize the disruptions from personal problems.

1.7   *The Problem: This is your first time firing an employee.*

Section 1.7 suggests guidelines and other considerations in firing an employee.

It is important for both men and women to find balance in their management style, to be able to manage naturally, and maintain some sense of flexibility. As you read the various problems identified in this section, you will see how women may handle these problems differently than do men.

1.1 | The Problem: Handling employees who continue to start work late.

THE SCENE

You've been in the office since 8:00 A.M. The staff is due by 8:30, since that is when the night ring is released and the phone calls start coming in immediately. It is 8:40 and half the staff members are not at their desks answering phones. One is getting coffee; another is chatting somewhere in the building; others haven't even arrived. You are answering the phones along with a skeleton staff. However, you have a managers' meeting that starts in a few minutes, and you need to leave. Complicating the situation is the fact that you are new to the job, and the previous manager was extremely lax in discipline.

Several employees come in late frequently. You have discussed this matter with the employees involved, but see virtually no improvement. During staff meetings you have stated that employees should be at their desks and ready to start work by 8:30 every morning. Things improve slightly for a week after these meetings, but then return to the old routines. In your discussions with tardy employees, their excuses sound sincere and legitimate.

Other employees in the department have been abiding by the policy for starting work as scheduled. How should you handle those employees who are excessively tardy to work?

POSSIBLE CAUSES

Poor work attitudes may create lax schedules.

Employees may not care whether or not it inconveniences others in the department; they may see themselves as above the rules. Making exceptions may be their way of asserting power and authority over those who threaten them, including you as their manager. This is the most serious cause and needs your immediate attention.

People may operate on different time clocks.

Some people are just not punctual; others may not be morning people; and still others measure time by whether there is enough to get the job done, not what time it is. Understanding those differences is at the core of having employees work at their optimum. Listening to excuses and talking with employees individually should shed light on how each person views time.

A lax policy was established by the previous boss.

Unfortunately, when you inherit a situation that is disorderly, your options are limited in the beginning. Since the previous manager allowed (or tolerated) this behavior, you will have a tough time correcting it until you establish trust and respect within the department.

There may not even be a problem.

Is anyone in the department complaining? Is the work getting done? Aside from 10-15 minutes of busy phones, is the department running smoothly? Simply because someone is late does not mean there is a problem. If there isn't a problem, don't create one. Choose your battles carefully. And when things are operating smoothly, leave well enough alone.

Other Considerations: Some employees may be late because family or personal considerations take precedence over work and punctuality. If excuses are frequently centered around a family member or event, this is an indication of a conflict in priorities. Corporate institutions often dictate work as the number one priority for employees. Trying to change an employee's priorities is a losing battle. Instead, it is important to respect an individual's decisions, whether or not you choose to accommodate his or her needs. That does not mean that his or her choices come without consequences, only that it is the employee's choice to make, not yours (or the company's) to dictate.

CURES

Create a positive work environment

When you have an employee who consistently has bad work habits beyond just being late, handling this situation can be more challenging. This applies to those employees who don't care about when they come in or what they do while they are at work.

Deal with this problem immediately! It will only get worse if left alone, and potentially contaminate the remaining staff members. Your choices are either to create positive morale, or (as a final but necessary step), get rid of the problem employee(s). See Section 1.7 for suggestions on firing an employee, should that be your desired plan of action. Also, Section 2.1 may be appropriate if you feel employees are abusing your lenient style.

When an employee is asked why he or she is continually late and the response is, *"I don't know,"* the problem may well be one of attitude. Look for other indications such as work performance, the way the employee handles customers, complaints by either co-workers or customers, and negative comments made by the employee. Usually when you find someone with a bad work attitude, these tendencies carry over to other areas beyond punctuality. See Section 5.3 for more information concerning handling employee attitudes within a department.

Identifying the problem is only the first step. Creating positive morale takes time. You should be central in setting the tone for the office; work attitudes can be changed when work becomes fun. If you are having fun, others will respond in kind. However, if you are feeling frustrated, resentful, or ambivalent in your job, others will also take the lead from you. Make certain that you are not a part of the problem.

When the problem is isolated to one employee, talk directly with that employee to find out what his or her concerns are. Try to determine what is missing. Some employees may need more attention and praise; others may want more autonomy and authority. Ask the employee to suggest ways to make the office more fun, then listen to his or her comments and ideas, and respond accordingly.

Being understanding does not translate into being a weak leader—quite the contrary. It takes a lot of strength and courage to listen and admit that you may not have all the answers.

No matter what you do though, creating a fun work environment may never be achieved to some employee's satisfaction. Accept your limitations; you cannot make others change. Attitudes did not get created overnight, nor will they change overnight. Allow a reasonable amount of time before you evaluate the situation to determine if progress is being made.

How to handle employees with different time clocks.

Tardiness can be frustrating, especially if you are an extremely prompt person. Some people do not live or work by a standard time clock. Perhaps their internal time clock does not function properly before a certain hour; these are not morning people. Despite what time they rise, they move in slow motion before a certain mid-morning hour and are always arriving late wherever they go. Others may reach their peak performance in late afternoon, when you are winding down.

Some people have a different concept of time altogether. Time may not be a specific hour of the day. Cultural inferences, economic factors, and just a natural body response are all considerations. Time may be viewed in terms of having enough or not enough. When people have enough time to get the job done, then they consider themselves to be on time. When there is not enough time to finish a project, then they are late.

When excuses offered seem vague, like: *"No matter what time I get up in the morning, I always seem to get to work late,"* this is an indication that this employee's time clock is operating differently from yours. Managing different values of time may be difficult, depending on your particular job duties, how these differences affect other employees in the department, and your appreciation of nontemporal concepts.

If the company requires everyone to start work at a specific time, and does not allow for flexibility, then you must respond accordingly. Disciplinary actions include placing employees on probation for being late continually, documenting personnel files, or docking pay. Perhaps you can guide them into other areas of work that are more apt to accommodate or tolerate their continued tardiness. For example, smaller offices may allow for more schedule flexibility than larger companies, or maybe another department has shift work hours available that better suits their body clocks.

If the tardiness of some employees is affecting your punctual staff members, and resentment is building, then you need to mediate the situation quickly. You do not want one employee to alienate the other employees, or create a hostile working environment for everyone.

Change a lax policy.

When you're new to a position, it is generally better to wait before you change employee routines. This is especially true if you are new to a group, as opposed to being promoted from within that department. Change is often met with resistance, especially when it is implemented without a foundation of trust or an understanding of its consequences. See Sections 2.4 and 5.1 for more information about easing the tension caused by change.

If you feel that it is essential that employees follow this promptness rule, then explain this to the staff. Clearly establish what is acceptable and non-acceptable behavior as well as the correlating consequences. Exceptions may be allowed, but if this is an important rule, then it needs to be enforced.

You might say the following at a staff meeting:

> *We are continuing to start most mornings without a full staff, and this troubles me. I need your support to make this department run efficiently. I am open to ideas and suggestions for how we can achieve this goal. Let me be perfectly honest so that everyone understands the situation: I will not tolerate continued tardiness. It is not fair to those staff members who are at their desks on time taking calls; it is not fair to the customers who are being put on hold and waiting for answers; it is not fair to me. I want to operate fairly, but I can only do that if you will meet me halfway. If this seems like an unreasonable request, let's talk about it now. Otherwise, I assume that everyone agrees with the request and will abide by the rules. I'd*

like everyone's input for creating a list of acceptable excuses and what appropriate disciplinary action should be followed.

You can be caring *and* firm—the two are not mutually exclusive. Sometimes you may need to be more of one than the other.

Don't create a problem when one doesn't exist.

Now here's an interesting concept: Maybe there really isn't a problem after all. Could you be making a mountain out of a mole hill?

Talk to each employee in private, and then meet with the entire staff. Do not assume employees are resentful simply because others are overworked. The employees may be operating by an unwritten code that says: Some employees come in a little late, others take more breaks or longer lunches, or receive more personal phone calls. Each day the work gets done and everyone is happy. Maybe they have negotiated a system that works for them.

Again, the worst part of being tardy may be that it's irritating to you. In that case you may need to relax your own thinking about punctuality. If customers are being handled properly, and the production level is maintained, don't create a problem if one doesn't exist.

Conforming to rules doesn't guarantee positive results. Everyone must learn to work together for the good of the whole.

1.2 The Problem: An employee's personal time off request is putting an additional strain on the department.

THE SCENE

Recent corporate changes have caused the department to be downsized considerably, and everyone is absorbing the additional workloads. There never seems to be enough time in the day to complete that day's deadline tasks.

In light of this, a valued employee comes to you requesting time off to attend to personal matters. The employee explains the situation, and you understand. The problem is that her absence will put an additional strain on the other employees who are already working at their maximum capacity.

Should you allow the employee's requested time off, or deny it because it is unfair to the other workers?

> *Note:* The length of time off requested can change your response. There is a significant difference in needing three days off compared *to two weeks off*, or in requesting a one-month leave. You must weigh being fair to an employee with the amount of potential disruption to the office.

POSSIBLE CAUSES

These are interruptions from her personal life.

Realistically, an employee's life may interfere with his or her job duties. When this happens, you must be able to handle the situation as smoothly as possible for all concerned. Some people will be inconvenienced by whatever action you take. The best response looks beyond the immediate situation and assesses the long-term ramifications of each choice.

Other Considerations: If there is tension within the department, it may have more to do with management's recent changes and workload demands than with an employee's absence. Downsizing frequently creates significant amounts of tension in the workforce, and can leave employees feeling used and insecure. More work without additional pay is always a point of contention and anxiety for employees. To ignore their feelings may only add to the tension that has already been expressed. See Sections 8.1 and 9.7 for more information about handling the fallout from downsizing and rebuilding morale.

CURES

How to integrate life outside the office with work.

Personal problems generally cannot be left at home, no matter how hard one tries to do this. Therefore, it is important for the workplace to learn how to handle problems so they are acknowledged, accepted, and supported despite the interruptions to work life.

If a request for time off is legitimate, accommodating an employee's request may be the lesser of evils. This is a two-step process. The first step is deciding to grant the request, depending on its validity. The second step is creating or maintaining unity within the department as additional work is reassigned to the remaining staff.

As you listen to the employee's request for time off, ask him or her to suggest how the department can accommodate this need least disruptively. This will make the employee feel like part of the team, and pivotal to the process.

> *I understand your situation and want to help. How do you suggest we handle the additional work load that will result from your absence?*

The employee may not have any suggestions, so be prepared for that response. It is still important to ask and for everyone to understand that choices have consequences. However, she may provide you with some ideas that you had previously overlooked.

The next step involves handling the remaining employees. Make sure that the staff members are appreciated for their hard work plus the added responsibilities you are giving them. The process of valuing employees can never be taken for granted, so take time to explain the short-term needs to each employee. If you have some suggestions for redistributing the workload, discuss them now.

During a staff meeting, invite suggestions. Your tone sets the stage and establishes boundaries that are negotiable. This is especially important when a department has resentment about being downsized. You may say something like:

> *I agree that this department would run more smoothly if we hired additional workers, but that is something that is just not going to happen right now. Given that fact, how can we make workloads more comfortable for everyone? Should we centralize functions? Or decentralize them? Redistribute workloads? What about cross-training? We need to make some temporary adjustment and I'd like everyone's support and input on how we should do this.*

Listen carefully to everyone's suggestions, concerns, and comments. By describing the situation as temporary, often co-workers are more willing to pick up the slack. Frustration and anger may be expressed for a variety of reasons, including abuse of the system by one or more employees, a sense of unfairness about this situation, or fear of job security throughout the company.

Possible solutions include assigning the duties among several employees, adapting a flexible work schedule for the employee who requested time-off, or even allowing her to work from home. This, of course, depends on several factors: the reason for the request, the nature of her job duties, and the work involved.

What If: You are forced to say "no."

All requests for time off will not be accepted. There will be times when you will have to tell an employee that his or her request has been denied. Women must not be afraid of saying no. It is not easy, but not every request is possible, feasible, or in the best interest of the group. Many women come into management wanting to please everyone; this approach is one that is full of disappointments.

Your final decision may be influenced by personal convenience, policy, or popularity, and your response may be to decline the request. How well you maintain control over a potentially disgruntled employee can minimize or magnify future problems. In some companies, because you do not have complete authority over all decisions that impact a department, you may be forced to follow a policy that you feel is wrong. The result is still having to say "no" to the request.

While not all employees will become hostile, you should stay alert to this possibility. If an employee remains at work against her wishes, her production may be down, she may quit without notice, or she may sabotage the operation through deceptive and harmful measures. Although you may not be able to prevent these actions completely, how you set the stage can play a significant role.

Saying "no" doesn't mean that you have to be harsh in your approach. Being firm does not mean you don't care, but it does mean that you will not allow others to take advantage of you. Know your limitations, and let others know them too. This will help eliminate some conflicts that arise out of uncertainty.

As you evaluate the situation, consider the long-term effects on the department and staff if the disgruntled employee decides to quickly leave this employment. You must factor in things such as interviewing, hiring, and training time for a new employee, plus any lag time and clean-up work that may be required from the previous employee's work, especially if his or her performance had become unacceptable or sloppy. Depending on the skill level of the staff and local employment conditions, this could again place significant hardship on the rest of the employees who may already be overworked.

Still, sometimes you must say "no" to an employee's request. During a conversation with the employee, you may say something like:

> *I understand your request, and wish that I could grant it. Unfortunately, I cannot. However, I want to explain why I must say no at this time.*

Then continue with honest reasons for turning down the request, such as:

> *Our department is just not able to make the necessary adjustments that your absence would create. While this may seem unfair to you, I have to consider the effects on everyone else as well. This is not an easy decision for me to make, but we really need you to be here.*

By explaining why you are declining the request, you are establishing and communicating boundaries of control. It is important for everyone to stay within the boundaries you create, otherwise you may find yourself managing a situation that has gotten completely out of control.

When the staff trusts you, they may give you the benefit of the doubt. In the meantime do not talk negatively about management or the conditions under which you are confined in your decision making, no matter how frustrating or aggravating these conditions become. If you are feeling the pressure of managing through restrictive policy guidelines, see Situations 9.3 or 9.5.

1.3 | The Problem: An employee lies to you to get a day off from work.

THE SCENE

Susan calls in and states her mother has been taken to the hospital with a heart attack. Everyone in the department is sincerely concerned, and willingly covers the additional workload created by her absence.

Later in the day, however, another employee receives a phone call from Susan's mother wanting to speak to her daughter. Needless to say everyone is quite surprised she is calling from intensive care; when asked about her condition, the mother seems surprised. There is nothing wrong with her, she replies.

Trying not to jump to conclusions, you decide to wait until the next day and listen to Susan's response. You try to encourage the staff not to rush to judgment, but you know it is difficult.

> *Note:* None of the possible causes that follow justify the act of lying. They are offered to help you understand *why* someone has lied. It is through understanding why someone has lied that you can begin to build the bridge of trust again. Reestablishing trust can be much more difficult for women than for men. In general, women place more emphasis on personal relationships than status, information, or results, things that men are more likely to value. As a woman, unless someone is willing to meet you halfway, you are less likely to regain confidence in him or her.

POSSIBLE CAUSES

An employee isn't comfortable mentioning that she has a personal conflict.

Perhaps there was something Susan felt was important to do, but she knew you would not grant her the day off. You may have a track record of denying time-off requests. If Susan had previously asked for time off that had been denied, she might have felt that she had limited options available. She might have felt backed in a corner and responded with what she thought was in her best interest. Even though she was not being honest, she may have felt it to be a harmless lie.

She is not concerned about her job or the ramifications of her disregard for the system.

Poor work ethics can be revealed in a variety of actions. Reasons for negative attitudes could be the result of many things, including feeling unappreciated or undervalued for her contributions, or experiencing less than desirable working conditions, boredom, or financial hardships. When work isn't an employee's priority, many excuses or activities may take precedence over the office. Susan may be there for the paycheck, and simply biding time until she finds something she enjoys more.

Your previous actions may be part of the problem through little exaggerations, innocent lies, or bad examples.

Sometimes the line between right and wrong—truth and a lie—is not clear. What may appear absolute and precise to one person may be ambiguous and uncertain to another. Since you lead by your actions, not your words, sometimes you are not even aware of the inconsistencies. If, for whatever reason, you have not been completely honest in the past, employees may think lying is perfectly acceptable behavior. Whether these are lies by omission, lies supporting corporate behavior, or lies to presumably protect another, ultimately they may be viewed as a license to lie, whenever an individual feels justified.

CURES

Handle conflicting priorities

Although a particular request may not seem important to you, remember that you are not the one requesting the time off. When an employee makes a specific request, make certain that you understand why he or she wants and needs that time off before making a decision about the request. A quick decision to deny the time off may result in an employee calling in sick, making up a lie that fits your acceptable excuses, or just quitting. None of these actions address the underlying problem.

You do not want to appear unreasonable in your management style. When employees lose respect for you because of your rigid adherence to rules, they place themselves above the system. Lack of control may easily be the result. You also do not want to be a pushover. Abuse and lack of control could just as easily result from too lenient a management style. Instead, you need to create balance and tolerance.

One way to determine the importance of a request is by asking the employee to rate this particular request along with other common requests you often hear. For example you might say:

> *Susan, you have requested next Friday off. I know you realize that we are short staffed, and this is our busy season. I also know that your request is very important to you, or you wouldn't have made it. In trying to make my decision, I need to know more about how important this particular request is to you. If you will help me by ranking this request, it will make my decision easier. Is it as important as* (then give some examples such as a child's play or recital, doctor's appointment, picking a relative up at the airport, and so on).

Not all requests are top priority. But given the fact that importance is subjective, and like beauty, is in the eye of the beholder, you need to understand its relative importance to the other person.

Obviously if Susan is going for a job interview, no matter how much trust she has in you she may feel that honesty is not in her best interest. She may not want to alert you that she is unhappy with her present position; she may protect herself by lying.

However, if the employee has already taken the day off, or called in sick, then the previous conversation would be moot. Instead, you want to seek an explanation by creating a safe environment where someone can be honest without fear of repercussions.

> *Susan, I want to know why you took yesterday off. I will not punish you for being honest. But, I confess that I was hurt because you didn't come to me first. It appears that you don't trust me, and I am concerned about our working relationship. This now places me in a position of not trusting you, a position that I do not relish. We have a lot of work ahead of us to reestablish trust. Honesty is that first step.*

Next you must listen. Listen carefully to what she says. Listen carefully to how she says it. Respect her feelings. Respect her priorities. You do not have to agree with them, but they are hers to choose, not yours.

When employees feel justified in lying because you or the company are being unreasonable in their estimation, handling this situation is more delicate. They may be correct. Poor management often breeds contempt, mistrust, and disloyal employees. Hopefully, you are not strapped by an outdated, closed-minded policy that you must follow. Susan may say, *"But I had already asked for the day off and you said we were too busy. I really needed it, but it didn't seem to matter. You had already said no."* At that point, it is time for you to reevaluate individual requests and find a happy middle ground where the department doesn't suffer, where individuals are valued, appreciated, and respected for their contributions.

Improve morale.

If Susan's actions seem to be representative of her attitude toward work in general, address the situation immediately. Complacency, while not uncommon in the workplace, can be the rotten apple that ruins the bushel. Bad attitudes are contagious. They can bring down an entire department when ignored.

Depending upon the severity of the situation, you may be able to try different plans of action and evaluate her response; or you may need to immediately remove the problem, in this case, Susan, from the situation. See Section 1.7 for more information about terminating an employee.

Try not to judge Susan because of her actions, but try to see why she is so unhappy with work that she would lie. Susan may not enjoy her job duties. She may be mismatched for the skills required, and not know how to express her frustration. She may be unhappy in her personal life, which carries over into work. Or, there may be past incidents that created hostility between Susan and the employer, situations of which you may not even be aware.

Concentrate your time and energy on those things that you can influence. You can help create a positive work environment, but the employees must be willing to meet you halfway. When they refuse, your options are greatly reduced. Ask yourself the following questions: Is work a fun place to be? Are there personality clashes and tension among employees that have not been handled properly? Do employees have a voice in making decisions? Is there a lot of laughter in the office? Are employees allowed to have fun as well as work hard?

There is only so much that you can do. Once you have tried other, less absolute approaches, you may suggest that Susan seek employment better suited for her needs.

Lead by example.

You may be part of the problem. This is tough to swallow, but it could be a major factor nonetheless. In today's society it is becoming more acceptable to bend or even break rules. Society has relaxed its definition in many areas about what is right or wrong. Instead of seeing life's values in black and white, you now see the spectrum in shades of gray.

Little exaggerations, innocent lies, and bad examples are all lumped together. For some, the issue boils down to what is right or wrong behavior, whether it involves breaking the law, stretching the truth, lies by omission, or exceptions to the rules by which everyone else abides. These can all be considered value judgments. For some they are absolutes; for others they are much less clear.

What about speeding on the interstate? That is definitely breaking the law, but it is commonly done. What about telling an employee who asks about his status that his position will not be eliminated, but you know that it will be? In defending upper management's decisions, it may be necessary to avoid telling the truth. Sometimes the choice becomes telling the truth to one person while betraying another. This happens when someone tells you something in confidence that you are later questioned specifically about. What about taking advantage of company expenses for your personal gain? These do not have to be large expenses, they could be postage, long-distance phone calls, pens, stationary, or meals. It may be considered wrong by some, while others view these as *unspoken* job benefits. Where are the lines drawn?

Sometimes the lines between truth and justice become blurred and distorted. Even to the extent of trying to justify your actions by saying that you are protecting someone else's feelings, or by telling them what you think they will want to hear. You may assume, of course, that others do not want to hear the truth, or cannot handle it. (See Section 8.1.) A major reason for this behavior is not to protect the other person, but to avoid conflict. Truth may create conflict, something women typically avoid.

Fortunately, this is one area that *you* have a great deal of control over! It has to do with your own actions. While you are not responsible for the interpretations of your actions, there are still some very comfortable guidelines you can adapt that will prevent the illusion of impropriety.

First, identify the gray areas. This means stepping back from different situations and observing your own actions. Have you told "half-truths" before? Do you sugar-coat your answers because you do not want to hurt other people's feelings? Now may be a good time to clean your own slate and be honest to yourself and to others.

Being honest doesn't mean that you are not tactful. Actually, the best way to be honest is through tactfulness. Rudeness would result in the intentional hurting of someone else's feelings, whereas tactfulness and thoughtfulness allow for compassion and concern to also be expressed. These are honest emotions as well.

Ultimately, both you and Susan must mutually agree on how trust can be rebuilt. You must talk through this problem with an open mind. Hear the other side before you decide on the consequences. Being understanding does not mean that these actions go unpunished. It means that you are able to mutually come to an understanding through which you agree on what is right and wrong, and how to avoid this situation in the future. By explaining that her actions hurt you and diminished your trust in her, Susan can also gain insight into the fact that her actions had consequences. Creating dialogue will go a long way in mending this bridge.

Gender By-line: Trust is a big part of managing and achieving the desired results. Men and women handle trust issues quite differently. When trust has been lost it is more difficult for women to recreate than it is for men. Men are more likely to forgive and move on to the next issue at hand. Women may forgive when given a solid reason, but then will slowly and cautiously move to rebuild trust. For women, there often remains a shadow of mistrust and a reasonable doubt that continues to be a factor. Women may forgive but they do not forget.

1.4 The Problem: A new employee lies on her job application form.

THE SCENE

Ann was hired a few months ago. On her job application form she stated that she had attended college, but had not received a degree. You have learned that this is not true; Ann has never been to college.

Her job performance has been fine. Ann has caught on to her job responsibilities quickly, though it is still too soon to tell if she will work out in the long run. Since you continue to have a high employee turnover rate, you are always pleased when an employee appears to have potential.

Deep down inside of you, however, it hurts that Ann felt it was necessary to lie on her application. Can you ever trust her? Would you constantly go behind her back to verify her actions, her findings, and her words? Will you find yourself always waiting to catch her in another lie?

Note: You must have undisputed proof that an employee has lied—not a rumor, hunch, or assumption. Without proof, but a strong suspicion, you can try to draw out specific information through general conversation. *If you falsely accuse someone of lying who was in fact telling the truth, irreparable damage would be done to your own trustworthiness.* You would be responsible for breaking those bonds, and your ability to recreate trust and establish a strong foundation would remain an uphill battle.

POSSIBLE CAUSES

Issues that seem important to you may seem less important to someone else.

Ann may have felt pressure to put down college because she may have been denied employment opportunities in the past. She may be lying because she perceives that in the long run it is just not that important. Perhaps she feels that her production results will outweigh whatever methods she takes advantage of just to get the opportunity to prove herself. Some people feel the ends justify whatever means are used.

Some employees may feel above ordinary rules.

Ann may not see lying as a moral issue. Instead, she may believe she is justified in her actions; she may not feel she has done anything wrong. The problem is exaggerated when Ann does not concern herself with others' feelings and how her actions affect them.

CURES

There may be differences of opinion.

Whether the lie is about education, personal or professional references, or the past, you should address the problem immediately. While this lie may seem inconsequential to the one telling it, it may easily lead to more and more mistruths.

Talk directly to the employee to get answers.

> *Ann, I see on your application that you attended college.*
> *When I called to verify this information, I was told you had never*
> *been enrolled. This inconsistency bothers me. I would like you to*
> *explain the difference.*

A newly hired employee doesn't have an established bank of trust and respect built. This foundation is essential for women in building cohesive relationships. Because Ann lied in the beginning, she will be starting with a mark against her, a mark that may never be completely erased.

The gender differences here can often be illustrated by the need for information as opposed to the need to be connected. Men are primarily concerned with informational sources. If the new employee provides information, men are more likely to discount the lie and move forward. Women seek to be connected through relationships. Lying becomes very much a personal assault and destroys the foundation of trust and respect. In effect, it destroys the relationship; whether it can ever be repaired is questionable.

Some companies have very strict policies about inconsistencies, mistruths, or exaggerations that may be discovered on an employment application. In these instances, policy may dictate that personnel be immediately notified and action taken (often requiring the dismissal of the employee). Follow company policy and procedures whenever they are given.

If the company does not have such a policy, then your judgment becomes a major factor. You must determine the harm that has been done by this lie, the long-term damage to the department and company, often reflected through morale, and the time needed or even the possibility of ever reestablishing a relationship built on trust. After evaluating all these factors, you may feel termination is in the best interest of the majority; if so, move quickly to sever the ties.

If you decide to allow Ann to continue working, make sure that the boundaries and expectations are clearly established. Avoid adding to the problem by being vague, too nice, or inconsistent in your words and actions.

How to manage when patterns of lies are uncovered.

One lie could be the beginning of a pattern. This pattern could always cast a shadow of doubt over an employee's future work, results, and participation.

For those individuals who feel above the truth, for whatever reason, your role as leader is to establish ground rules and a sense of fairness for all. Ground rules include mutually respecting others. Without ground rules, fairness becomes irrelevant.

You might say the following:

> *Ann, I understand that you lied on your application. I will be perfectly honest and up front by stating that I have no tolerance for lies. I want to move beyond this obstacle, but I need your help in building an avenue of trust. It will take time. If I find you lying again, we will have a very serious situation on our hands which will require immediate action. Two strikes and you are out. Because our bond of trust has been damaged, I will tell you now that I will periodically go behind you rechecking your work, until I feel we have reestablished trust. Do you have any questions, comments, or concerns?*

You must also be willing to enforce your actions, otherwise they become empty threats which dilute your authority. You may decide to cut your losses, and be more thorough in the interviewing and hiring process in the future. See Section 1.7 for more details on firing an employee.

1.5 | The Problem: One employee continues talking about other employees behind their backs.

THE SCENE

Sharon has been with the company for years. Her reputation as the office gossip has preceded her wherever she goes within the company. Everyone knows that she maintains strong ties in some very influential places.

Sharon constantly talks about other people in the office. She knows who is dating whom, is having an affair, or having problems at home. She knows who's about to get promoted, fired, or placed on probation. She is rarely wrong, as she likes to brag. Unfortunately, Sharon wants everyone to know that she is the source of such explosive information. She keeps the office wars going by adding fuel to the fire.

You've spoken to Sharon about this situation before. Generally, she just denies it. Because she does not include you in her loop, it is hard for you to prove. No one will go up against her; she wields too much power. Even you are somewhat intimidated by her knowledge and connections. What she knows never ceases to amaze you. Obviously there are some connections to people in high places, otherwise she wouldn't know as much as she does.

The friction continues to build within the department as well as within other areas of the company. Her lack of respect for other employees and her insensitivity toward what is private and public information continue to embarrass you and hurt others in the workplace. What should you do? What can you do?

POSSIBLE CAUSES

An employee is undermining your authority.

Sharon may want to show her authority within the company by controlling information. Perhaps the only way she knows how to do this is by talking behind your back about you and others. This may be the result of being overlooked for promotions in the past, or because she simply resents authority. Sometimes people do not play games to win, but only to see their opponents lose. Proceed cautiously and quickly.

The need for attention may cause an employee to disregard other people's feelings.

Sharon may have a poor self-image and be looking for ways to gain attention, no matter how extreme. Her fifteen minutes of fame may not feed her insatiable appetite. In Sharon's mind, another person's feelings may be inconsequential to her need to be noticed.

She may be trying to improve her status in the company.

Many organizations still silently or even publicly advocate that power is given to those who control information. They often base promotions on those with power. For Sharon, gossiping may be her way of asserting to you and to other employees that she is a powerful individual. Sharon may be so focused on her personal goals that she doesn't care who she steps on or how she manages to reach those objectives.

> ***Some people have grown up thinking that talking about someone else is perfectly acceptable behavior.***

Sharon may not know any better. She may just be communicating what she knows, and she may feel that sharing information is not harming anyone, especially if it is true. This becomes the most difficult problem to change because Sharon may not admit there is even a problem.

CURES

Regain a sense of control.

If you sense that Sharon resents you and your position of authority, deal with this situation immediately. This has the potential to become an even greater problem if left alone. Other employees may soon sabotage anything you say or do. Her actions may create many, many more problems for you, the least of which is a department that doesn't listen to or respect you.

First, meet with Sharon individually. In a nonthreatening manner, let her know that her talking about others has to stop because it is hurtful to those involved. Discuss what the terms *privacy* and *respect* mean to you, then ask her to explain what they mean to her. Together try to find how the office can operate more smoothly without talking about others:

> *Sharon, I am continuing to hear that you are the source of gossip around the office. I have spoken to you about this in the past and you have denied it. However, it is coming from too many different people for me to overlook. We have a very big problem that must be addressed. For me, gossiping is a matter of discussing personal information that does not concern you, with people other than those involved. It has become very hurtful to many individuals around this office. I want to hear your feelings about this. I am here to help; but I need your help as well if this is going to work.*

You may be surprised how many problems have been resolved by meeting them head-on. Sharon may not realize that her actions are hurtful to others. When you face her directly, you are confronting the problem, not ignoring it, and not letting the situation control you.

There may not be an easy solution to this problem. The victory comes in creating boundaries that are acceptable to both parties, and in your willingness to create dialogue and reach a compromise. Should Sharon deny these allegations, and should the situation continue, then you need to review your options. Probation, transfer, or termination are all potential solutions. Proceed cautiously though, because Sharon may have people of great power and influence under her control as well. Protect yourself against possible backlash.

Implement praise, thanking, and other forms of validation.

Each of us has different needs, yet all women have a need to be liked. Once you have determined that the need for attention is the primary issue, look for more appropriate ways to encourage contributions. This situation did not occur overnight; it will take time to change.

Results will be slow. Offer praise for positive actions, give special recognition for jobs done well, and provide more responsibility to deserving employees. Sending a thank-you note for completion of a special project can go a long way in gaining results. All these techniques can make a difference.

Set boundaries and expectations between Sharon and yourself as to her performance. Let her know specifically what you will reward and what you will not tolerate. If these escapades are getting in the way of work, say so. Once Sharon understands her parameters, she is better able to meet these expectations or at least know the consequences if she chooses not to.

Understand when power comes with information.

Power can mean control. Within many corporate structures, those with certain information may be given power, and thus be in control. Promotions may be given to those who have a great deal of power and who control information.

How does the company value information? Is it held only by those with power? Is shared knowledge considered to be threatening to those who have power and control over information? You can answer these questions by looking at the company's financial information, budgets, or marketing plans. Who is allowed access to information and when? Are various levels of employees, not just selected managers, involved in the process? Does senior management make the decisions, and expect lower levels of management to implement these plans? Do all employees have access to company financial statements?

When senior management sends the message that power is control and those with information get promoted, Sharon may see information and power as steps toward advancing her professional career. Whether her interpretations of events are accurate may be overshadowed by her own perspective.

Talking with Sharon directly will help in determining her professional aspirations. Then, together you can offer positive avenues for her to achieve those results.

> *Sharon, where do you see yourself in a few years? What are your career goals? I would like to help you achieve those goals. If I know what positions you are aiming for, then together we can make your dreams become a reality.*

Realize that Sharon may feel that she is ready for a promotion now. She may feel that more learning is not needed. In fact, she may be after your job. As a mentor, boss, or role model, it is important that you communicate to the employees how their actions might be interpreted by others. For example:

> *Sharon, gossiping is seen as an inability to keep secrets. When someone is not viewed as trustworthy, promotional opportunities are much more limited, and often denied.*

The final decision is Sharon's; your role is to offer guidance and direction. Don't give up too soon, though. Keep hope that she will change.

Some may not know any better.

Some folks just like to gossip. Women prefer private talk; men prefer what is referred to as public talk. Gossiping falls into the private category. Organizations typically do not tolerate such behavior, especially when it interrupts work productivity. And eventually it will interrupt the office; it always does.

Office grapevines are very different from office gossip in both intent as well as content. Grapevines allow general information to be transferred quickly, without the need for meetings and other distribution channels. The nature of gossip is malicious and hurtful to the ones talked about. While the grapevine may transmit new product information or upcoming company changes such as extended hours or staff reductions, the gossip line would likely discuss personal issues not related to the job or the gossiper such as divorces, financial troubles, and so on. Sometimes the lines get blurred, but generally a distinction can be made clearly.

If no one has ever discussed the negative effects of gossiping, Sharon may not know any better. As her boss, you will need to explain to her the benefits and hazards of her actions. While it may be an obvious hazard to you, you must remember it is Sharon's understanding that you are aiming for, not your own. She must realize what repercussions her actions have and find other ways to communicate and share her ideas and concerns.

Be patient but firm. Let everyone know what you will and will not tolerate, and why. Changing old habits is a difficult and slow process. You cannot change other people; they must want to change themselves. However, you can explain how their actions affect others as well as yourself. You can provide opportunities for change. And you can explain the consequences of their actions, whether it is limited career opportunities, being placed on probation, being demoted, or terminated.

Realize that once you discuss this situation with Sharon, she may have difficulty changing her old ways. Change may be difficult not because Sharon doesn't want to, but because others may continue to come to her for information, as they have in the past. Stopping something that has been allowed to go on for years takes time as well as the cooperation of everyone working toward the same end.

1.6 | The Problem: Handling a problem employee who has already been placed on probation, but hasn't improved.

THE SCENE

You are new to supervising. Unfortunately you have inherited a problem employee, Tom. Tom's job performance does not meet the company or department standards. He continues to submit sloppy work with numerous errors. His ineptness reflects on the whole department, and has created tension and bad feelings among the staff. Other employees resent carrying the additional workload created by his carelessness. Several co-workers have recently complained to you about this.

Tom received two verbal warnings before you arrived. You have already placed him on probation for poor job performance, yet nothing has changed.

Personally, you like Tom. Things have not always been easy for him, to say the least. He has had many difficulties in life to overcome. He's a single father struggling to make ends meet; his mother is very ill and not expected to live long; his spouse is suing for custody of their son. How should you handle this situation? What about the other staff members?

POSSIBLE CAUSES

Inadequate training may be adding to the problem.

Whether the company has a standard training program or on-the-job training, Tom may not know how to do his job well. It is not fair to assume that he has been trained properly simply because everyone else is performing at an acceptable level. It is not fair to Tom, or to the department. Each person learns at a different pace. Standardized programs may not incorporate these variances. Placing someone on probation does not address the problem of training.

Tom may not understand what is expected of him.

Miscommunications or poor communications often add to a bad situation. Even with warnings and probation, Tom may not know what he is supposed to do at his job. Are performance evaluations done on a subjective or objective basis? Subjective evaluations make it more difficult for employees to evaluate their own progress and realize when they are not meeting expected standards.

You may have an employee who is mismatched for the job.

Tom may be a good worker in another position, but just not right for what he is doing. It could be that Tom's skills have not been properly matched for this job. This improper fit may be adding to the tension everyone is feeling. Can you help Tom identify his skills and where they can be better used?

Outside life may be affecting his daytime job.

The two worlds are intertwined, no matter how hard you try to keep them separate. There is a great deal of turmoil going on in Tom's life, as you are already aware. This may be just the tip of the iceberg. Personal problems can create unusual situations at work, and the results could easily be poor job performance. See Chapter 3 for a variety of topics on personal problems with employees.

Other considerations: It may be time to help Tom and the company, by letting him go. Tom may need a push to get out the door and find employment better suited to his own needs. He may be afraid to take the first step. Firing him may be your best solution. Section 1.7 provides guidance on terminating an employee.

CURES

Offer proper training.

Uniform training programs may not be sufficient for all the employees; individuals learn at different rates. To assume that everyone learns the same information in the same time period is too presumptuous. Tom may not have received adequate training.

Realize that some people need reviews of training programs from time to time as well. Poor performance may be an indication that a review is needed. Your problem may go much further than with just one employee; this may be the beginning of a much greater problem, such as an entire staff that is not well trained. Look into retraining all staff members so that consistency is maintained and assumptions are eliminated.

Talk with Tom in private. You might say the following:

> *Tom, we have talked in the past about your job performance. There seems to be confusion because you have not improved. I'd like to start at the beginning, though, and have you explain what your job duties are. Also, do you see any problems within the department? Is there something that I have overlooked or am not aware of? Do you have any suggestions for ways that your job performance can be improved? You understand that your performance is still not at an acceptable level right now, and that must change.*

Tom may feel uncomfortable saying he doesn't understand what he's supposed to be doing, or how to do it. Instead, he may find fault in other areas. Wanting to place blame on others is a common way of avoiding responsibility.

It may be too late for Tom. Tom may not be willing to be retrained, feeling embarrassed or humiliated by what he doesn't know. Even if Tom does not stay, you need to review the current training programs and see how they can be improved. Training can always be improved. Stagnant attitudes lead away from growth, potential, and opportunities.

If he stays, make sure Tom gets the training he needs. No matter how long Tom has been with the company, start at the beginning; train him thoroughly.

Improve communications to understand what is expected.

Assumptions breed confusion. Tom may not understand thoroughly what is expected of him; nor may he understand why he is being placed on probation. Instead, everyone may be going along assuming that Tom is clear on all of these issues. This only adds to the lack of clarity in the entire situation.

When you give verbal warnings and probation reviews, be certain to communicate specifically what you expect of Tom, how he can improve, and what will happen if he does not meet those standards.

Your meeting might go something like this:

> *Tom, your job performance has not been up to acceptable standards. I understand that this has been discussed with you before. I am starting with a new slate, and I want to make sure that we agree on what is expected and how to achieve those results. The number of calls you handle is well below the department average of 175 calls a day; you are averaging 92. I need your call average to be over 125 a day by the end of next week. And I need to see the progress continue. Also, I have had 5 complaints in the past two weeks that you were rude to customers over the phone. It wasn't what you said, so much as how you said it. When customers irritate you, and I don't deny that they can, try to put them on hold; take a breath before you speak. You may consider transferring the call if it is too volatile. Just be careful of what you say. Don't argue with the customers; they only call back and complain when that happens. Do these results sound achievable to you? To be sure that we*

agree, and to eliminate any confusion, I want you to repeat them
back to me.

You can be nice and still be direct and firm. By asking Tom to repeat your discussion, you know he understands what is expected of him, in his own words. This eliminates assumptions.

Match qualifications and strengths.

Tom may have many talents and qualifications that are not being used in this particular job setting. Look at his strengths. Everyone has both strengths and weaknesses. Be objective as you list his strengths and his talents. Is Tom more creative than the company allows? Does he need more discipline and tighter controls? Is he a people person who is being confined to the back office? Are there other departments where his talents can be better used?

Talk with Tom to see what he is interested in. You may be surprised by his hidden talents that are being overlooked or underused. Decide if there are interests and talents that can be utilized; if so, incorporate them into Tom's job duties. For example, if Tom is great with numbers, perhaps he can help out with some of the accounting responsibilities you have in the department.

When you talk with Tom, you may both decide that he is limited or poorly matched to perform in the company. Look for the win-win solution. A career move may be in everyone's best interest. By taking time and helping Tom, everyone can be a winner.

Minimize the disruptions from personal problems.

The problem may be much greater than you perceived initially. Poor job performance may be the result of numerous personal problems taking Tom's attention and energy away from his job.

Personal problems affect work, whether or not they are shared with others. Getting to the source of the trouble may be difficult. Many people do not want to talk about their problems.

Still, you should try. By talking privately with Tom, allowing him a place to discuss the issue without repercussions, you can be a better manager. For Tom to open up to you, he must trust you, and must feel that what he says will not be used against him. If you have not already established a foundation of trust, it is doubtful employees will be honest in these conversations.

If Tom is unhappy at home and bringing his tension to the office, it would be difficult for him to function as expected. Finding out what the underlying problem is may justify other remedies including flexible hours, part-time work, counseling, or legal advice. Adjustments may be necessary as a short-term solution.

If this is the case, refer to Chapter 3: Troubleshooting Personal Problems for the Staff.

1.7 | The Problem: This is your first time firing an employee.

THE SCENE

Peggy's performance is still not acceptable, even after receiving sufficient warnings, numerous personal discussions, and being put on probation. She is bringing down the entire department through friction, petty fighting, and sloppy work. You've tried everything to improve her performance, but no progress has been made. Now it is time to cut your losses.

If you must fire an employee.

Sometimes firing an employee cannot be avoided. It may be in everyone's best interest. If the consensus is that Peggy does not have the potential or lacks the desire to succeed, then you must proceed quickly with this next step. Once you have come to terms with the decision to let her go, do not put off the inevitable. It does not get easier with time. Procrastinating only makes life more miserable for everyone, including Peggy.

If this is the first time you have had to fire someone, make sure that senior management is aware of the situation and agrees with your recommendation. Seek input and guidance if you are unsure about procedures. Even though you are firing an employee, you don't have to be cold and impersonal.

Women have more difficulty in firing employees because the act is interpreted as a personal assault on their own inability to motivate each employee to his or her potential. Women may believe that firing an employee is the ultimate sign of failure as a manager.

Firing someone does not have to be an ugly scene. Being soft and caring does not translate into being weak. When you are firing an employee, consider his or her feelings. Try to create a win-win situation, if possible. Try to minimize the hurt and pain; be professional and polite. Do not get in a screaming match if an employee tries to entice you. Instead, stay calm, and always remain in control.

GENERAL GUIDELINES TO FOLLOW FOR FIRING AN EMPLOYEE

Be sure to document everything concerning the employee's performance, including verbal warnings, observations, probation, customer complaints, and individual talks.

Peggy's personnel file should include an easy-to-follow outline of talks, results, and disputes. Complete the paper trail.

Talk with Peggy, and explain why you must let her go.

Being direct does not mean you cannot also be kind and caring. Offer suggestions for other employment, perhaps better suited to her particular strengths. If additional schooling would be helpful to her career, point her in that direction.

Quickly move into rebuilding strength and unity within the department.

Don't ignore the possibility that other employees may be hurting or fear for their own job safety. If you believe it is appropriate, then explain the situation and use this opportunity to reestablish acceptable boundaries and to share concerns openly.

What If: Other employees are worried about being fired as well? When one employee is fired, others in the office may likely fear being fired if they fail to understand the dismissal. Talk openly and honestly with the remaining employees about the situation, but never gossip or put down another employee in front of his or her peers. Reassure the staff that their positions are not in jeopardy.

What If: During the firing process Peggy begins to scream and yell loudly at you so that other employees can hear? Do not counter her attacks, especially if they are personal digs at you. Listen and try to calm her down. Be sensitive to her feelings; being fired is a devastating event. Often individuals do not want to accept responsibility for their actions. Remain in control, and limit her contact with other employees.

Should you allow the employee to finish the day or ask her to leave immediately? Realize that you are firing an employee; he or she is not tendering a resignation. You should remain in control of the situation. Given that the situation resulted in an employee's termination, I would *not* recommend allowing her to stay any longer then is absolutely necessary. Allow her to clear off her desk and remove personal items. Some managers prefer taking this action late in the day, even after the other employees have gone home to avoid interaction and disruption in the office. That is a personal choice. It is important to know your options, minimize the downside risk (including corporate sabotage, or disruption to the workplace), and proceed in the best interest for the majority.

Chapter Summary

A woman's touch might be identified as a kinder, gentler touch, more indicative of caring about people above the implementation of justice, status, or the following of rules. A woman's touch builds relationships instead of simply creating policy, winning at all costs, or moving toward the desired end results with little regard for morale. Women traditionally seek the connection of others, whether colleagues, superiors, or staff. It is not the sense of approval by others that is needed as much as it is the unity achieved when everyone works together.

The need for connectedness contributes to how men and women manage so differently. It is through this connectedness that women become linked or bonded to the world around them. And it is through this connectedness that women respond to situations in a different way. It is through this connectedness that women understand the conflicts in priorities and time made upon them with work and family.

As managers, women are learning to accept those areas that they control and influence, to respect the decisions of others, and are trying to improve communications, tolerance, and diversity. Two very important lessons can be learned through this all: No one can change unless that person is open to change, and if you can't change something then simply change the way you look at it.

For a woman to succeed in business, she is expected to mimic the masculine models that surround her, a charade she frequently can't master, nor would want to, even if she could. Today, with the acceptance of some feminine qualities as positive influences in the workplace, women are still not judged by the same standards as men. Where men are assertive, women are labeled aggressive. Where men seek to be heard, women are thought loud, abrupt, or whiny. Men are considered caring fathers when childcare issues arise, while women are unable to handle the demands of combining a career and family. Obviously, the same models *do not* fit both genders.

There are downfalls on both sides of the equation though. For men, hierarchies often alienate employees. They can be too restrictive for the creative worker, instead keeping employees stuck in a specific position because that is where they are needed. Hierarchies can also create unnecessary red-tape and convoluted methods for decision making. The competitive nature within some organizations creates a win at all costs atmosphere, even against other employees.

But women's styles of leadership also have problems. The need to be connected often translates into a need to be liked. Reprimanding someone, placing them on probation, or firing an employee are difficult tasks, especially for women, because these scenarios appear personal in nature and are often associated with a personal failure. Many times these actions do not leave you in a very well-liked position; in fact, you may be the target of much anger and frustration.

At times the two styles seem worlds apart. Either style can achieve positive results, but the inherent difference is in the implementation. Women today, to their credit, have gained some freedom and flexibility in adapting styles with which they are comfortable. Men have clearly modified the male model to suit their own, and their employees' needs.

Troubleshooting Problems That Occur Because You're a Woman

Overview

Remember the saying, *"Mother never said life would be fair?"* She was right; often it isn't fair. You may ask yourself, why is it so unfair on some days? Does gender always play a role in the workplace? Or why aren't women accepted, appreciated, and valued for what they contribute instead of who they are? The answer to all these questions is, quite simply, because gender is an issue; there is no denying its effects. Sometimes things are different *because* you are a woman.

The pendulum also swings in a woman's favor, and her gender can become a benefit. Society still allows women greater range in expressing emotions. Women are more likely to hug an employee while men are more concerned with misunderstandings and cries of sexual harassment. Women have more tolerance and compassion for understanding personal problems, and allow for flexibile solutions, while men want work to be the main focus in the office, with little regard for personal issues.

This chapter addresses the following problems, possible causes, and cures.

2.1   ***The Problem: An employee continually abuses your lenient style.***

Possible Causes: An employee does not work well under your lenient style; he may not know or understand what is expected of him; he may be feeling unimportant, undervalued, or unappreciated; he may be bored.

Cures: Adjust your style to the staff's needs; improve communications; value employees; ease the boredom.

2.2   ***The Problem: A male worker complains about being abused by his female co-workers.***

Possible Causes: Sexual discrimination and harassment can happen to men just as it can to women; personality conflicts can wreak havoc on an organization; there may be a power struggle going on; he may be complaining when there really is not a problem.

Cures: Handle sexual discrimination and harassment charges; manage personality conflicts; minimize power-plays; listen to the complaining.

2.3   ***The Problem: A female worker does not respect your authority, especially in front of other employees.***

Possible Causes: She may be disrespectful of all female authority figures, not just you; she may be seeking attention; the problem may be with you.
Cures: Gain respect; provide positive attention; change your style.

2.4   ***The Problem: The staff doesn't accept you and prefers the previous male boss. Production has been declining since you arrived.***

Possible Causes: The staff may feel threatened by a female boss; change is often met with resistance; the staff may just need time to adjust to your style of managing; they may be going through a period of mourning.

Cures: Use gender as a benefit; ease the tensions caused by change; time is on your side; allow for a period of mourning.

2.5   ***The Problem: A female worker continues to wear inappropriate clothing to work.***

Possible Causes: She is seeking attention; you may have an employee secure enough with her body to wear fashionable styles; she may not know any better.

Cures: Provide less disruptive attention; transfer strengths into job skills; offer guidance as a role model.

2.6   The Problem: You are seen as a friend, not a manager, by several employees.

Possible Causes: You may not have communicated your role as manager; you may be sending mixed signals about your role.

Cures: Communicate your role as manager; send the right signals.

2.7   The Problem: You are feeling watched and scrutinized by other women in the organization.

Possible Causes: You are seen as a role model for all women; you may be feeling unprepared for your new position; jealousy may be a factor.

Cures: Become a role model; be prepared for your new role; respond to jealous females.

2.8   The Problem: A pregnant employee needs special consideration, including a reduced work schedule.

Possible Causes: Employees will question actions when they perceive a situation is unfair; unpopularity may be an issue; poor communication and vague expectations hurt everyone.

Cures: Create fairness and equity; take the focus away from popularity; communicate expectations beforehand.

2.9   The Problem: A problem employee happens to be the granddaughter of the CEO.

Possible Causes: You may be dealing with a spoiled brat; you may be expecting too much from her; she may not be trained properly.

Cures: Handle office politics and favorites; create realistic expectations; retrain employees.

Your role, as manager, is to work within the given parameters. You must evaluate each situation on its own merits, and treat every employee with respect and dignity. Some days this role may seem impossible to perform. Always do the best you can do.

2.1 | The Problem: An employee continually abuses your lenient style.

THE SCENE

Your style is one that allows employees to work out the details of their daily schedules. You feel that imposing too many rules and restrictions treats employees like children instead of adults. Everyone seems to enjoy this approach, respecting each other's special needs; all that is, except Phil. Phil continues to test your limits and abuse your generosity.

Just last week a customer called for the second time in an hour asking to speak to Phil. Another employee told the customer that he should have been back from lunch by now. Since he hadn't returned when expected, no one knew when he would actually be back or if he had an appointment away from the office. The customer was getting irritated, but wanted to speak to Phil only because Phil was aware of this particular problem.

You are not sure what is going on with Phil. He has begun challenging your authority. Lately, he has been returning later and later from lunch, has been making more personal calls, and has been late starting work. How should you handle this problem?

POSSIBLE CAUSES

An employee does not work well under your lenient style.

It could be that no matter what you say or do, Phil will continue to take it a step further than the rest of the staff. He may not accept your authority nor fear repercussions for his actions. No one else is pushing the boundaries; Phil may need help setting limits to work at his full potential.

He may not know or understand what is expected of him.

Phil cannot be expected to operate under boundaries that he does not know. There may be some confusion or miscommunication about what should happen in the office or what is acceptable behavior. There is more to a person's job than completing specific duties; everyone must agree on what needs to be done, and the best way to accomplish it.

He may be feeling unimportant, undervalued, or unappreciated.

These feelings could lead Phil to create attention for himself, either consciously or unconsciously. By not being present when a customer calls, Phil has made himself appear indispensable, at least for the moment. His absence has called attention to him; it has worked.

He may be bored.

Phil's job may have become so routine that he lacks the enthusiasm and drive he once had. His job may lack challenges because he has mastered his duties. If Phil is producing quality work, your job is to bring enthusiasm back into the office.

Other Considerations: There may be personal issues in Phil's life consuming his time and controlling his attention; things of which you are unaware. As mentioned previously, personal and work life are intertwined, and problems from one area often affect the other. Phil's phone calls and long breaks could be the result of attending to personal matters that can only be done during work hours. Chapter 3 provides additional details on handling staff personal problems.

CURES

Adjust your style to the staff's needs.

It is not uncommon for women to manage in a style that produces fewer rules and restrictions. Women often prefer building relationships and valuing individual contributions, while men are more likely to adhere to policy restrictions and take recognition for the department's accomplishments. While some employees may not respond well to one style, other employees will respond positively. Knowing when an employee needs more control and confinement to reach his or her individual potential is like looking into a crystal ball, so expect to make some mistakes. Your best defense is to remain flexible and to be willing to adjust if your style is met with resistance or abuse.

Your options are to either treat an individual problem independently, or respond with a change that everyone must follow. Ultimately, your solution will depend on several factors including how well employees adjust to these changes, how they are perceived, and what effect these changes will have on production.

Deciding to deal with the problem individually can only work if the group as a whole does not resent special or separate treatment. If it supports the notion that each employee is motivated differently, then the group may adjust well. Since this situation is being created by one person, only one person may need to be the focus of your change.

Talk to the employee privately. The conversation may go something like:

> *Phil, until now I have allowed the staff to work their schedules around each other. I usually do not like placing a lot of restrictions on employees, but prefer giving them the flexibility to adjust to individual needs. This style may not be one that everyone responds favorably to, as I am well aware. I have decided to make some short-term changes in your scheduling routine. I feel it is in everyone's best interest if you would schedule your lunch times and breaks so that I (and others in the department) know where you are and when you will return. This change is not meant to be a punishment, but to create better work flow. Please know that I am aware of your contributions and appreciate all that you have done. You are a valuable employee. I would like to hear your comments about these changes, and if you have any other suggestions, I'd like to hear those as well.*

It is not uncommon to find the need to manage different people in different styles, but often managers do not have the courage to do it. Creating specific rules or conditions to meet individual needs helps everyone do their best. This is a major test in managing a diversified workforce. It takes more skill and time for you as the manager, but it is a situation whereby everyone can win. Unfortunately, it may be met with resentment or jealousy and it does not always work.

Your other choice is to change from a lenient style and adopt a more rigid format for everyone to follow. There will be times when this is the best solution because changing the routine for one person may create excessive tension and not be in the group's best interest. A group meeting would be the time to discuss these unilateral changes.

> *My objective is to create an environment where everyone works at their top performance level. I have been very lenient in the past by not asking for schedules. However, now I feel it is necessary to make some changes around the office, and I ask that everyone*

*abide by these changes. Everyone can win when we improve com-
munications and have fixed schedules. There have been times when
a customer needs a specific employee, but because we do not have
set lunch times the customers do not know when you will be in or
out. While I realize exceptions will occur, I would like us to create
a routine lunch schedule so that everyone in the office as well as
customers knows who is in and out, and when.*

Announce other changes at this time and why you are introducing them.
The best way to sell new ideas is by concentrating on the benefits and positive results others will receive. If these changes are not permanent, then let
the staff know that too.

Your objective should be to operate with a management style you are
comfortable with, and one that produces the greatest results. By maintaining
a sense of flexibility you are able to respond to individual needs quicker.

Sometimes, no matter what you do, someone complains that the
changes are not fair. Expect the balance of fairness to swing in one direction
or the other, depending on the actual situation. You may need to rely on your
inner strength, intuition, and best judgment; there may not be an easy solution.

Improve communications.

It is dangerous to assume that employees know or understand their
roles. It is not what you understand a role to be that is at issue, but what they
perceive it to be. Employees need to know their job descriptions and your
expectations in order to reach those goals.

In talking with Phil, you may say the following:

*Phil, I am reviewing each person's job description and role in
the department. I know that job descriptions rarely tell what a person does each day, so I'd like for you to explain what your functions
and duties are.*

This request may be for either a written description or verbal understanding, depending on the depth of the problem and the amount of details
involved.

Listen as Phil states his role within the department. Does he spew out
expected answers without knowing the natural flow of the department or
how duties overlap? If so, your job will be to help him integrate those words
into a meaningful plan of action. Is Phil doing work of which you are not

aware? Maybe his duties have expanded without additional responsibility, authority, or recognition.

However, if Phil does not know what is expected of him, make sure that he learns it. If Phil is to reach his potential, you must both agree what his potential is and how it can be achieved. Ultimately, Phil must want to reach that plateau for himself.

Value employees.

Everyone wants to be appreciated for his or her contributions. Everyone enjoys feeling important in the process. Everyone wants to be noticed.

As manager, you can express positive sentiments through your words as well as your actions. Doing your part may not be enough; corporate philosophy may contradict your style and negate personal recognition. When a person feels unimportant, he or she may abuse your kindness because he or she doesn't fear the consequences.

Women typically excel in appreciating employees but fall short when it comes to reprimanding them. Many new and creative methods for showing appreciation are being introduced. Nonmonetary rewards can be as well received as monetary rewards. Special measures can be taken when employees achieve high levels of performance, complete special projects, or produce unusually high quality. This can include both individual achievements as well as group rewards.

Some methods for showing appreciation include writing individual thank-you notes, sending a balloon bouquet, having a special party for the department (ice cream Friday, celebrating a great sales month, and so on), taking employees out to lunch for specific accomplishments, giving comp time (additional time off) for extra time worked, certificates of appreciation, and giving prestigious assignments to those employees who are most deserving. Statements like, *"thank you, you are doing a great job"* and *"I really appreciate what you are doing"* can go a long way in showing the staff how much you value them.

Ease the boredom.

Employees become bored when their position is stagnant, routine, or appears to be a dead-end. If you suspect Phil is bored in his present position, look to see how his job has grown or changed over time. If the position has remained the same, it may be time to rewrite job descriptions or move Phil to another position that is more challenging for him.

Talk privately with Phil to determine his interests as well as satisfaction with his current position. Do not assume he is bored. Ask:

> *Phil, I'd like to know what you like or dislike about your current position. I realize that some jobs have a tendency to become boring if we do not continually change or modify them. Are you bored with your present position? It's only natural not to like everything about a job; perhaps you are looking for different assignments or a transfer to another department? I'd like to know what you want so that we can make the necessary changes.*

By discussing this matter directly with the employee you are able to hear his feelings, see his strengths, and understand his ambitions. It may be a matter of recommending additional training for Phil to get into another position. Your role as manager is to challenge Phil to achieve his peak performance. You can only provide opportunities for growth; Phil must be willing to accept the challenge.

2.2   The Problem: A male worker complains about being abused by his female co-workers.

THE SCENE

The department is an all female staff, except for Bill. Yesterday Bill came to you complaining that "the girls," as he refers to the rest of the staff, were making it impossible for him to do his job.

As Bill explained it, they make him feel alienated and embarrassed, and at times even dirty. During this conversation, Bill used terms such as "verbal abuse" and "harassment" in describing the situation. He noted several incidents, including when they commented about his private body parts to him, talked openly about female problems and sexual fantasies, intentionally left him out of conversations, and gave him the worst times for breaks even though he had earned more seniority. Bill also complained about getting stuck with the dirty grunt work, that he referred to as menial tasks.

Bill asked that you talk to the staff but said he doubted anything would change. He has never appeared to be a troublemaker before; Bill's a hard worker who likes his job. However, he has threatened to take legal action. If things do not improve quickly, he has said he would leave.

Note: By reversing the situation, if a female were in the minority and the object of these comments, how would you proceed? Sexual harassment is always a very serious offense; gender is not an issue. There have been many more cases filed by women then by men, but that should never lessen a man's claim.

POSSIBLE CAUSES

Sexual discrimination and harassment can happen to men just as it can to women.

Although with less frequency, it is still just as serious a situation. It is imperative to respond to these allegations quickly before they escalate. Bill's complaint may have legal ramifications; therefore this problem needs immediate attention by you as well as senior management.

Personality conflicts can wreak havoc on an organization.

Whether antagonistic or threatening, these clashes can increase the tension so much so that no one can perform his or her job well. Some personalities conflict no matter how hard you try to defuse them. You may not even be aware that these personality clashes are in the department.

There may be a power struggle going on.

Female staff members may feel threatened by a male co-worker. The presence of a woman manager may make these employees feel more powerful, as if you will take their side no matter what the circumstances. This could be another chapter of the war against the sexes, one that causes you to be the mediator and reconciler.

He may be complaining when there really is not a problem.

Bill may enjoy creating a little trouble. His discomfort with women may reflect on his relationship with his female co-workers. His threat of filing an EEOC harassment complaint may be in hopes of stirring up resentment in the department, thus adding substance and credibility to his claim.

Note: With regard to allegations of sexual harassment, give this matter your immediate and full attention. Sexual harassment, and all forms of discrimination for that matter, are serious claims. Most companies have an established and written policy for handling these delicate situations. Contact the necessary departments, then proceed per their instructions. Since much of the information is one person's word against another, trying to determine what actually happened may be a slow process, if not impossible. Until these allegations have been completely eliminated, proceed as if the discrimination charges were true. Other possible causes should not be considered until discrimination and sexual harassment have been ruled out.

CURES

Handle sexual discrimination and harassment charges.

If the company has an established policy for handling sexual harassment charges, follow it closely. Notify the appropriate departments and officials about the potentially volatile situation. This is not intended to alarm anyone, but instead to make sure that the necessary individuals are aware of the situation in a timely manner and that the proper procedures are followed.

For your part, document everything—this includes any meetings, observations, interviews, allegations, and so on, that you have witnessed, overhead, or been informed about. A written record will be your best defense. As the manager, you are responsible for the working conditions of the department and for allowing such behavior.

In some situations you will be interviewed, but not directly involved with gathering information or determining the appropriate disciplinary action needed. If this occurs, make sure that you are clear about how you are to handle the remaining staff members, and what changes should be provided to protect Bill.

In other instances you will be asked to gather the information and make some determination as to what actually happened. When you interview each person, do so privately. Try to remain fair and unbiased until all information has been collected. Admittedly, this may be hard, especially as you begin to learn more and more about the situation. Talk to witnesses, if there are any, to see what they observed.

Frequently, sexual harassment charges boil down to one person's word against another person's understanding of the same event. Often there are no witnesses. Do the best you can to understand these events.

For men who make claims of sexual harassment this situation is made more uncomfortable because they are often ridiculed by their male colleagues. Snide comments like: *"What, you can't handle it? I'd love to be in your situation. Be a man and give those women what they want,"* are often made. These comments aggravate the situation and leave the victim with a feeling of even greater despair. Be sensitive to this situation, and respond appropriately.

Sexual harassment continues to be difficult to prove. It is about power. Are there women in the office who have power over other staff members, and in particular over Bill? If so, look closely into those relationships first. Having power does not mean they are abusing it; withhold judgment until all the facts are in.

If suggestive comments and crude jokes have been repeated in the office, and no one denies their existence, ask that they stop. This may be the time to educate the staff about discrimination, harassment, and creating a diverse workplace. These verbal attacks and comments can create a hostile work environment. Hostile work environments constitute sexual harassment by law.

While you don't want to overreact, always take these allegations very seriously.

Manage personality conflicts.

Personalities are a part of group dynamics. Work is not immune to its power or its pitfalls. Sometimes personalities do not mesh well, no matter how hard you try. Two strong personalities may butt heads on even the smallest of issues. Instead of working together, you may find these personalities creating turmoil and disrupting office routines.

As manager, you will need to learn the personalities of those you manage in order to create a positive and productive work environment. Know the strengths, weaknesses, and little quirks of the employees; know which personalities work well together and which do not. If you identify a problem, manage it quickly. If left alone, personality conflicts can be the source of many other conflicts.

You will have several choices in how you handle this situation. You may choose to separate the personalities, find some common ground that is acceptable to both parties, or try to force the employees to work together. Ignoring the problem is the most hazardous choice of all; it doesn't go away on its own.

Finding common ground is the most desirable solution, but it cannot always be achieved. In an attempt to create mutual respect for one another, bring the feuding parties together. Set out the ground rules and your objective in the beginning. The ground rules may include that no one leaves the table until everyone completes the exercise, and your objective may be to focus on positive characteristics about the other person. It is important to get everyone to agree with these points before you begin. If not, you may find yourself dead in the water very soon. Start the exercise with something like: *"I would like both of you to list 10 things you admire about the other person."* Anticipate resistance, but with the ground rules established everyone knows what they must do. You may decide to reduce the number if listing 10 things seems to be too difficult. Give everyone time to reflect, but use your judgment to make the necessary changes. *"Now I would like you to list 3 things you find annoying about the other person, and 3 things about yourself that may be annoying to someone else."* It is important to stop after each section and let everyone have enough time to respond completely before moving ahead. Sometimes we expect more from others and forget that we may be hard to get along with ourselves. *"Finally, how can we work together, respect each other, and leave the personal conflicts aside?"* Let everyone know that they do not have to be friends, but while at work it is important to create an atmosphere where everyone is working for the good of the group.

There are no guarantees. If this does not bring positive results, then try to create combinations where these two personalities avoid butting heads.

Keep them apart, if possible. In case this situation becomes a detriment to the entire work environment, you will still need to maintain a watchful eye over the staff and be prepared to quickly jump in if needed.

Minimize power-plays.

The female staff may feel threatened by Bill's presence. This may be a factor whether or not Bill was the first male to work in the department. Bill may represent a career path they feel has not been accessible to them, no matter how well they have performed. The battle lines may be drawn on the issue of gender, and they may expect you to join their side.

As the manager, try to instill a sense of fairness within the department. Even though the company may have acted differently in the past, it is important for you to reassure everyone that you will be fair and equal to everyone based on performance, not gender.

> *In this department, I will treat everyone fairly. Each of you are equally valuable to this organization. I can assure you that I will recommend promotions and raises based on individual contributions, not gender. But I ask in return that you treat each other with a similar respect and appreciation. I will tolerate nothing less.*

If, in fact, there are gender biases within the company, then proceed as best you can. Do not lie to employees by stating they do not exist. That would cause you to lose credibility and create distrust among the staff.

Listen to the complaining.

The problem may be Bill. He may just be a complainer, an employee who needs attention and wants to voice his resentment, no matter what. Bill may expect special treatment because he is the only male.

Try to determine what is going on in the department. Other employees may have very different stories to tell. Listen, and try to get to the root of the problem. Then talk privately to Bill.

> *Bill, it seems that you are unhappy here. You have a lot to offer, and I think you're doing an excellent job. However, I will not tolerate the tensions and frustrations that are being created. Everyone needs to work together and respect each other. I have spoken with everyone in the department. I have heard their com-*

ments and I have heard yours. I have also observed numerous exchanges between all parties. Bill, the bottom line is that I need you to be more of a team player. Together let's create a game plan to make that happen. Are you willing to join the team?"

When you talk with Bill, reassure him that he is appreciated and valued, but that you will not tolerate constant complaining and unfounded threats. Make him feel a part of the process. Perhaps you can even give him a voice in the final decision. Be careful not to reward negative behavior, otherwise it will continue to haunt you. Section 5.2 addresses problems involving one employee disrupting an office. You may also want to review that information.

2.3 The Problem: A female worker does not respect your authority, especially in front of other employees.

THE SCENE

The monthly staff meeting is the time to share concerns and introduce new ideas or programs. One employee, Sandra, is determined to create dissension whenever she can. Sandra often speaks up during meetings and contradicts your comments. As you are getting everyone excited about the upcoming changes by kicking off a new program, Sandra dampens spirits by complaining that it won't work.

It is not that Sandra is negative as much as she is always defiant and disrespectful. You have spoken to her about her attitude before, but nothing has changed. Other employees have confirmed that Sandra doesn't respect you or your authority. Behind your back, Sandra makes a mockery of staff meetings and your mannerisms. You try not to take Sandra's actions personally, though sometimes that is difficult. Her actions have become disruptive to the department, and it's time to step in.

POSSIBLE CAUSES

She may be disrespectful of all female authority figures, not just you.

Sandra's preference may be working for male bosses because she feels more comfortable answering to men, pleasing men, and having men dote over her. Sandra's disrespect could stem from either a negative relationship with her mother or lack of self-respect. Whatever the reason, Sandra does not respect you.

She may be seeking attention.

Sandra may feel that no one is listening or responding to her ideas. She may be right. Sandra may be so starved for attention that even negative attention will do, just as long as she gets noticed.

The problem may be with you.

Sandra's perceptions may be correct; her approach may be what is really at issue. While these programs or changes may sound good on paper, they may be flawed in implementation or practicality. Your defensive posture may be because you are interpreting Sandra's actions as undermining to your authority, while all she really wants is what's best for the department.

Other Considerations: Your presence may be coincidental to the problem. Sandra may be a victim of abuse, feeling lost in her own personal struggles. She may be crying out for help. Victims of abuse often seek attention to compensate for the neglect they have had to endure. There may be personal problems at home, such as domestic violence, that Sandra is afraid to admit to herself, let alone to you. When a person feels controlled, she may try to gain balance in her life by asserting her control in another area.

CURES

Gain respect.

To gain respect you must earn it, not demand it. To be able to earn Sandra's respect though, requires knowing what it is she is looking for. Then you can decide if you want to make the necessary changes to your own style.

Women have been trained at an early age to compete with other women. Whether for the affection of another man, as in a beauty contestant, or to be the most popular, women play different games with other women.

When this competition is transferred into the workplace, it becomes an even greater problem.

There may be other factors affecting the roles women maintain among themselves. For example, if an employee did not have a good relationship with her mother, you cannot change her feelings or replace the void. Make sure she knows that *you* are not her mother, and do not treat her like a child. Talk openly to Sandra about how to work through this dilemma. Encourage her to share her concerns.

> *Sandra, I sense some tension between us. Every idea I offer, you shoot down. For the department to run smoothly, we need to be able to work together. You have had good reviews in the past, and you continue to do an excellent job. I appreciate your contributions, abilities, and dedication, but I would like to know if there is something about me that is troubling to you. Have I done something to offend you? Is my style one you feel uncomfortable with? I am determined to make this work. I need your honest feedback so that we can get to the bottom of this.*

Reaffirm to Sandra that you are not criticizing her. Approach it from how you feel and how you interpret her statements and actions. Avoid accusing her of any wrongdoing.

Continue to be fair, honest, and keep communications open. If Sandra prefers working for men, you may want to try to have her reassigned to another department if she likes this idea. That does not mean that you are throwing in the towel; it is merely a viable solution to this particular problem.

Provide positive attention.

Sandra may be causing disruption in hopes of gaining attention. She may need more attention than you have been offering, and her needs may be different from the rest of the staff. The need for attention and appreciation is universal. What is different is the amount and the type of attention to which each person responds.

Look for ways to give Sandra additional attention without causing hardships or resentment with the remaining staff members. One way to achieve this is through the occasional, private compliment. Another, assuming her work quality warrants it, is to increase her responsibility. You may consider assigning her a special project where she can take the reigns and run, one that will garner her a great deal of attention in the process.

Change your style.

Part of the problem may be that your style is not in the group's, or Sandra's best interest. It may not be what you say, but how you say it. Whether your style is seen as too aggressive, bold, strong, lenient, passive, friendly, or visionary, the department may not respond to these measures. You must be able to evaluate how your style is received by others, as opposed to what you meant by your words or actions.

Sandra may serve as an indication that communication needs to be improved. Other employees may not have the courage to speak out, at least not yet.

You maintain control over the input of your message. Adjustments may be necessary to reach a particular audience. The same words spoken by a man or a woman are received differently. While gender is always a factor when discussing style, the degree changes with each situation.

In addition, your ideas may not be as wonderful as you perceived them to be. Maybe Sandra's comments are correct. Women become very defensive when they are criticized. They assume an *"if you don't like my ideas, than you don't like me"* attitude. It is not a personal strike against you. Be a strong leader by showing your willingness to be open to other suggestions and ideas. Admitting you were wrong may be just what the staff needs to hear. Everyone makes mistakes; not everyone admits them.

See Sections 6.3, 6.6, 7.1, and 7.7 for advice and suggestions on how to adjust your style to fit a particular audience or situation.

2.4 | The Problem: The staff doesn't accept you and prefers the previous male boss. Production has been declining since you arrived.

THE SCENE

You have recently been promoted to supervise an all-female staff, replacing a very popular male manager. He remains in the company, in another position. The staff continues to remind you of his wonderful ways, his style, generosity, and humor.

The department was running problem-free before you arrived. Since you have taken over, production has steadily declined. Other departments are complaining about the poor quality and slow results this department is producing. They are also reminding you that this is a recent event, that it started after you took over as manager.

Staff meetings have produced little insight into this problem, with the exception that employees are constantly reminiscing about how things were before you came, and how much they miss the previous boss.

> *Note:* Try to maintain the previous manager's routine in the beginning. Your style will be different from your predecessors. No two styles are ever the same. After the initial shock has worn off, judge the routines and make necessary adjustments. If possible, make your changes slowly; they will be met with less resistance. Once production is affected, it is time to take immediate action.

POSSIBLE CAUSES

The staff may feel threatened by a female boss.

You cannot discount the possibility that the previous supervisor may have won his popularity by being lenient or easygoing. Everyone enjoys this. Yet, these are things that you cannot recreate. Staff members may fear the changes a female manager represents, fears such as trying to prove yourself to superiors without regard for their feelings or concerns. These fears may or may not be justified; it's their perceptions that are important.

Change is often met with resistance.

The staff may be experiencing the discomfort of change; you may represent that change. Without their approval, trust, and confidence, as manager there is little that you can accomplish. Change does not always produce improvements, so listen carefully to the concerns of the employees and proceed cautiously.

The staff may just need time to adjust to your style of managing.

Gender differences and individual style differences cannot be separated; instead, your total style, which includes gender roles and nongender-related attributes, contributes to how you manage. Some styles work better within certain groups, while other styles may work better in a different setting. You must determine if your style needs some time to be accepted or if it should be changed.

They may be going through a period of mourning.

Every loss, including those caused by transfers or promotions as well as death, creates a void and emptiness in routines. Depending on how long the previous manager had been in that department and his approval rating, you may be running up against a combination of popularity and resentment. His popularity combined with the employees' resentment toward you can make the situation more difficult.

Other Considerations: How would this situation vary if the previous boss had been a woman? This factors out gender favoritism, and allows you to concentrate on personalities and styles. There may be other factors besides gender that contribute to how people respond to you. If you feel you are blinded by the issue of gender, view the previous boss as the same gender as you, and see what differences you discover.

CURES

Use gender as a benefit.

There may be resistance simply because you are a woman. While you'd like to ignore this factor, it is still there. This is more likely to occur if you are the first woman manager an employee has had, or if the previous female managers had been poorly received.

The first thing you want to do is create your individuality. For example, if the staff had a female manager that they disliked, you want to make sure they know you are not that manager. Ask them to judge you for your accomplishments and failures, not against someone else's history.

Then, find ways to use gender to your advantage. For example, women are able to give hugs much more freely in the workplace, whereas men are having to reserve contact for fear of being misinterpreted or sued for harassment. Women seek the connectedness of employees (involving the staff in more shared responsibilities), are more nurturing (take time to develop employees more fully to reach their individual goals), and can be more caring (offer a variety of ways to show appreciation).

Nothing will change in the beginning until you have established a foundation of trust and mutual respect. Trust is a two-way street, however, and since you are new, you will need to take the first step. As results begin accumulating, slowly the staff will divulge signs of trust. Building a strong and successful work environment becomes easier once a foundation of trust has been laid. Mutual respect will then be a natural by-product of trust.

To create trust, always keep your word. Make sure that your words and actions are consistent, and be honest to yourself and others, and always be fair. If you say you trust the employees but then check up on them regarding the status or results of an assignment, you may be sending mixed signals. A signal that you may not completely trust them or their judgment despite what you say.

These inconsistent messages can set you back a great deal. Be consistent in what you say and what you do. It takes time. And once damaged, trust can be very difficult if not impossible to rebuild.

Ease the tensions caused by change.

Change is often met with fear and resistance. Fear because the results are unknown, and resistance because you may not be building a better mousetrap. Once the quality of work declines, the problem must be addressed quickly.

Since you are new, try to limit the amount of change you implement in the beginning. Ask the employees about which routines they enjoy and why, or what changes they would like to see. Employees are a great resource for ideas, but are frequently overlooked in the process. In a group meeting you may say the following:

> *I am new to this department and I need your help to make this transition a success. This department has an excellent reputation; I do not intend to fix what is not broken. However, I would like to hear some ideas from each of you that might allow us to improve on what we already have. I will schedule individual times so that you may share your concerns, your ideas, and the strengths of the department. In the meantime, please remember that my door is always open if you want to talk. You don't need to wait for an appointment.*

After you understand the work flow, job assignments, and duties, then you are in a better position to offer suggestions and make the necessary changes. Allow enough time to adapt to these changes before ruling them a success or failure. It is common to be faced with some resistance to change initially, but once routines get adjusted change is usually easier to accept. Be prepared to make additional adjustments if necessary. It may take several tries before a program that works in theory is accepted and promoted within any group. No one factors in the side variables, yet they can make or break a change.

Even if you have not changed any routines, but production and attitudes continue to decline, ask the employees what differences they perceive since you started:

> *I have noticed in the past few months that the production levels have dropped significantly. I am not aware of any specific changes that may have contributed to this situation. We are also getting a lot more returns, showing our quality is not what it used to be. Why do you feel production and quality have decreased lately? What can we do to bring it back to its previous levels? I am open for suggestions.*

If the response is because they worked better with their previous boss, reassure them that you can be a team player too, but that you must be given a chance. Positive reinforcement and encouragement will produce better results than threats. Do what you can do, as quickly as you can. Production and quality are measurable results. Your concern should be with the immeasurable factors that may also be affected.

Time is on your side.

Your style is reflective of you, your life experiences, gender, and personality. You will be different from your predecessor. Often what is needed is time to adjust to these changes and differences. How much time is needed will vary from situation to situation. During this period of adjustment try to minimize tension by maintaining as many of the same routines as you can. While waiting, make sure that you are doing all that you can do to ease the transition and support the staff.

Showing employees that you care about them may bridge this time gap. These signs can come in the form of validating their feelings, responding to their frustrations, and listening to their concerns. Your willingness to share and talk openly will encourage the staff to do the same:

I realize that my style is different from what you were used to. I am depending on you to maintain the strong image of this department. Your contributions to this department and company are very much appreciated; they do not and will not go unnoticed. I am looking forward to working with each one of you. It will take both of us adjusting to each other to make this department a success. I ask that you be patient while I learn. Unfortunately, I will make some mistakes and those will be the times when I need you the most. Together we can do this.

Reassure the staff that you are listening to them; and that they are not speaking to deaf ears.

Allow for a period of mourning.

Every loss produces a normal mourning period, and the departure of a popular boss is no exception. He is not dead, but he has left the role he once maintained in their lives. Providing avenues for remembering him does not mean you should eulogize him or immortalize him. Respect that the employees miss him and let them grieve.

Talk openly with the employees about their past experiences and what they enjoyed. Are these things that you want to incorporate? Can you incorporate them? Maybe yes, maybe no. Now you will be creating new experiences for them. Remember, competing with the past is a no-win situation.

2.5 | The Problem: A female worker continues to wear inappropriate clothing to work.

THE SCENE

Heather is young, attractive, talented, and single. She is new to the company and continues to receive a great deal of attention, especially concerning her attire. The company has set a very conservative style which most employees follow.

There is no formal dress code, but everyone abides by the understood policy. Everyone, that is, except Heather. Heather wears short, tight skirts and flimsy blouses. Days that she doesn't wear a bra continue to be a primary topic of conversation around the office. Some days she looks like she is ready to go out on the town instead coming into the office. Your boss feels that Heather's work attire is inappropriate, and according to him, *"in bad taste."* He confronts you with his concerns and asks that *"you speak to Heather about this situation."*

You feel awkward, as if you are being put in the middle. She has not broken any rules, but others find her clothing objectionable. Talking to her about appearance seems rather trite though, since she is becoming one of the company's top producers.

Other Considerations: Inappropriate to whom? Assess the situation objectively and determine what harm if any is being done because of what Heather wears. Are the personal preferences and agendas of some individuals creating policy standards? Is it time for the company to get into the nineties and relax its dress code? Could Heather's style actually hinder her professional career advancement?

You may want to review Chapter 7 if you are experiencing upper-management tensions, while Chapter 9 looks at policy conflicts. Both may be factors to consider in this situation.

POSSIBLE CAUSES

She is seeking attention.

Heather may enjoy being the topic of conversation, even if it is office gossip. Her flamboyant style may be a game she plays for attention. She may not care what you think about her attire; noticing her means that she has won the game. As long as she continues to be noticed, she continues to win.

You may have an employee secure enough with her body to wear fashionable styles.

Heather may have the confidence and shape to take fashion risks and win. She may be perfectly comfortable expressing her individuality and style through her clothes. Are other women jealous? Is the boss' wife complaining the loudest? Is management old fashioned in its clothing standards?

She may not know any better.

If this is Heather's first career position, she may not know what appropriate work attire is. Unwritten rules are often the most difficult to understand. What Heather may need is advice and mentoring from a successful woman manager like you. She doesn't need to be a clone of you to succeed in the office, but some pointers and encouragement may help. Women are judged more on their outward appearances than men are; that is a fact that Heather may not have learned.

CURES

Provide less disruptive attention.

If Heather enjoys attention simply for attention's sake, she may actually have low self-esteem. Her way of dealing with her low self-esteem may be to solicit constant reaffirmations from other people. Part of her image may be linked to the attention she receives from males swarming over her, and the jealousy this creates in other females.

Try to build Heather's self-esteem in positive and healthy ways. For example, make a special effort to compliment her job performance and contributions; remind her how important she is to the department and company; that she is smart, intuitive, capable; that she is a valuable asset.

If you decide to discuss this matter with Heather, do so carefully. It has the potential to explode if not handled gently.

Heather, I have been asked to speak with you about how you dress at work. Senior management feels that your attire is not appropriate for its corporate image. You are doing an excellent job; I really do appreciate your contributions and I understand that you want to move into management one day. You have the potential to make that move, if you choose. Your work contributions are only a part of what is evaluated for promotions; the image you project is equally as important. Customers see us as representatives of the company. It is important to maintain a consistent image, according to what management wants to say. It is the company's right to choose and promote a specific personality or style. We choose to agree or not by whether or not we stay and uphold it.

Honesty is the best policy. Not that it will be easy; often it is the hardest solution to undertake. Try to reach an agreement that both you and Heather are comfortable with, and that conforms to the *acceptable* unwritten dress policy. Stress the importance and long-term benefits of creating such an image. Heather does have the choice of finding another employer who is more liberal in its dress code. She may prefer an employer that values her results over its image.

Transfer strengths into job skills.

This situation becomes more challenging if Heather enjoys dressing stylishly, feels comfortable with herself, and does not see anything inappropriate in her clothing. It is further complicated if you agree with her.

Without a strong belief in what you are doing, hesitation could resonate in your voice and easily be detected. If you feel senior management is being unreasonable, discuss this situation with the appropriate parties (senior managers) and get resolution on the issue before talking with Heather. You may suggest that a company policy be written so that everyone understands what is meant by acceptable attire, eliminating the need to enforce a vague, unwritten code.

Heather has many strong characteristics and talents that could be developed and utilized within the company. By identifying and utilizing them, everyone becomes a winner. If Heather is a self-confident person, are there other career avenues available to channel that confidence? For example, her confidence may make her a candidate for leading internal seminars or workshops or perhaps she could develop a sales relationship with a specific market that values individuality and creativity. Look at other attributes she has and identify correlating job skills that the company can benefit from. If these are not existing positions, you may want to suggest creating a new position designed around her strengths. Since she is already a top producer for the company, salvaging that relationship seems a worthwhile investment.

Offer guidance as a role model.

If she is young and new to the working world, the concept of appropriate business attire may be completely foreign to Heather. You may be her guardian angel. By discussing this matter with her, you are making yourself available to be a mentor for her future. Remember that she chooses her mentors and role models; your job is to be available if she chooses you, and to offer your services if she requires them.

Approach the topic by sharing the benefits Heather will receive by conforming to these codes. Then guide her to more appropriate attire. You may wish to remind her that women are still judged *more* by their outward appearances at work than their male colleagues. Extravagant styles could work against her by causing her to constantly prove herself competent and capable, not pretty and stylish. Not that these situations are fair, only that they are.

> *Heather, I want to share a little friendly, unsolicited advice. I too had to learn about what it means for a woman to succeed in the workplace. Women are judged more by their physical appearances than men are. Clothing is like an extension of our personalities and images. Personally, I love that; we have a lot more flexibility and choices. No longer do I always have to wear dark, boring suits; I can be just as professional in a dress or even in a pant suit. Great strides have been made in what women can wear to work today. Thanks to women in previous decades who broke through the glass ceiling to change those standards, now I, and other women, have some flexibility in what we wear to work. However, there are still some restrictions and expectations as to what is appropriate to maintain the corporate image. Heather, what that means for you is that success may be denied to you early on because of your appearance. It is not right; but that is how businesses operate. My advice for you is to find a style you can adapt, and that fits into the confines of acceptable business attire for women. It will make your chances for business success much easier.*

Reiterate the advantages she will see in her long-term career by conforming. Later on, once she has achieved a certain level of status, she may be able to widen the definition of acceptable work attire for future women entering these ranks; but for now, with this company, her options are limited.

Gender By-line: When it comes to clothing, men are generally perceived as *unmarked* while women are *marked*. In other words, you rarely notice what a man is wearing; whereas the woman's attire adds to your perception of who she is, her credibility, delivery, and style. A man has fewer fashion choices to obstruct your ability to listen to what he is saying, while a woman's endless array of colors, prints, styles, and lengths can complement or interfere with her message. Men have great latitude in going unnoticed, but for women there is no margin. Choosing not to wear make-up, for example, doesn't leave a woman unmarked; instead she is *marked* as plain, simple, or even conservative.

2.6   The Problem: You are seen as a friend, not a manager, by several employees.

THE SCENE

As a single woman, you frequently join the other single women on your staff for lunch, after-work social parties, or weekend get-togethers. On a personal level, everything is fine. However, on a professional level there seems to be some confusion about you as an authority figure. These friendly employees are unable to accept you as their boss, instead treating you like a member of the gang. These same employees have verbally trashed the company in your presence, and have tried to pry confidential information from you. Even against your objections, they have continued their comments.

You have worked hard at showing these employees that you care about them personally and professionally. You value their friendships, but not at the expense of compromising your authority or your position. You feel that you are being taken advantage of and it hurts. Will you be able to maintain these friendships? How can you regain control of the situation? Have you lost control completely?

POSSIBLE CAUSES

You may not have communicated your role as manager.

In fact, the role may be somewhat ambiguous to you. Women seek the connectedness of others, which can blur their positions of friend and boss, often leaving them in a state of limbo. You may assume the role of manager is the dominant position; while the staff may view your friendship as being more important. These employees may resent your authority and want you to be just a member of their tribe. They may not even realize that they have crossed over any lines, or that you feel uncomfortable.

You may be sending mixed signals about your role.

Your camaraderie may be adding to the problem and complicating everyone's ability to establish ground rules. These relationships may be so close that boundaries have not been established, or it may be difficult to establish them. While our work lives and our personal lives are intertwined, there remains a private life we all maintain. Once you have interfaced with the private person, it may be a challenge for you to manage the public person. You may not view the staff members as the professionals they really are because you have seen their other side, and vice-versa. You may question their answers because you know more about the situation than a manager generally does. In fact, you may be expecting more from them because of your friendship. Likewise, they may not respect you as manager because they know your personal side.

CURES

Communicate your role as manager.

To achieve communication involves three elements. It takes a message, someone to deliver that message, and someone to receive that message. Any one of these three levels can stop or hinder the communication process.

The first step involves knowing precisely what the message is before you can communicate it. If the role of manager seems unclear to you, get clarity on it. Talk with personnel or a supervisor for some guidelines and boundaries. You cannot deliver a message and expect others to understand it, if you are not 100 percent certain what that message is.

Some organizations allow for flexibility in how you define your role; other organizations have very specific and detailed descriptions already written. It is important for you to know exactly how much flexibility there is so that you do not overstep those boundaries or fail to deliver what is expected.

The terms *role* and *style* are often used synonymously, but they have very different meanings. Role has to do with your duties and authority, and style is the manner in which you carry out those duties or act on that authority. Style is unique to each person. Roles are more likely to be defined.

The following steps will help you start the discovery process:

1. Do you fully understand and accept your role as a manager?
2. What does the staff understand your role to be? (Ask your staff directly, don't make assumptions.)
3. Clarify any inconsistencies between numbers 1 and 2.
4. Establish new and healthy boundaries where needed.

Then talk with the staff. If you feel the problem is only with a few of the employees, then you may want to talk to them separately either one-on-one, or in a small group:

> *I sense there is some tension or confusion with my role as manager. It is important for me to know your feelings about me as your manager. It seems that our friendship can make the situation difficult for all of us. Is it difficult to accept suggestions or advice from me? Do you feel that I am a fair, equitable manager? Does our friendship get in the way of work? How exactly do you see the role of manager? Do you have any suggestions for how we can establish some boundaries between our personal friendships and our work relationships?*

Look closely at the demands and the conflicts of the roles as friend and manager. Is it hard for you to manage a friend? Do your friends find it hard to be close to their manager? Share your concerns and uneasiness by discussing specific incidents in which you were troubled. Together create boundaries that everyone feels more comfortable with. It is important to accept that this duel relationship may not work; differences may remain unresolved.

There are times when you must choose one role over the other. Your choices include asking for a transfer for either yourself or those employees involved, depending on skill levels, opportunities, and the least disruptive option, relinquishing your role as manager, or ending the friendships. There may not be an easy solution, but creating open communication will benefit everyone.

Send the right signals.

You may be the primary source of the problem. By participating in these activities, you may be sending a signal that this behavior is acceptable, or you may be sending a signal that you are first of all their friend who just happens to also be their boss.

The easiest things to change are those things that you control yourself. It may be difficult for you to accept responsibility for creating or adding to a problem, especially one that involves your professional future. Instead, you may identify the weaknesses in others, hoping to downplay your own involvement.

Try to evaluate your role within the scope of the problem. If you find that you are the one who needs to change, ask yourself several questions: Is it difficult for you to supervise friends? Do you need help in managing? Are the boundaries clearly set in your mind as to what is acceptable behavior and what is not? Have you communicated these boundaries to the staff?

Don't feel embarrassed or ashamed to ask for help. This is a very difficult time.

Male colleagues may be oblivious as to why this is a difficult or troubling situation for you. Men are more comfortable maintaining a stage presence in public situations, while women seek the connections of others. Intimate friendships are less common among men, and rarely interfere with work. A man may suggest that you prioritize your life (decide what is more important) or simply gain control of your emotions; a woman will resolve this situation quite differently. She will try to find a way to have both.

2.7 The Problem: You are feeling watched and scrutinized by other women in the organization.

THE SCENE

In the company cafeteria you have seen women watching every move you make, including what you eat, where you sit, and with whom. Nothing you do goes unnoticed. It's as if you were working in a fishbowl.

You are the youngest and first female promoted to this position. You remain in awe of the responsibilities and realize what a triumph you have gained. Despite the fact that the company employs 75 percent women, few have broken through these gender barriers.

All of the hard work, time, and dedication have finally paid off. It has been a tough fight; nothing was just handed to you. You have tried to take advantage of every opportunity that presented itself.

Your promotion has separated you from the other females in the company. You feel isolated, alone, and even scrutinized. They expect you to be perfect and to pull them up the ranks with you. But you still have to prove yourself competent and capable of handling these responsibilities. It's all so overwhelming; you'd like for these women to cut you some slack.

POSSIBLE CAUSES

You are seen as a role model for all women.

Because you were the first to achieve such success, you do stand alone. You are a role model, whether officially or not, for women who want to break through those same barriers. Circumstances have caused you to be elevated to such stature. You did not choose this role; it is because of your position. You must realize, however, that how you handle the situation has a great impact on the future roles of women within the company.

You may be feeling unprepared for your new position.

Needless to say, this new position can be overwhelming, even scary. You have to prove your abilities to senior management, the employees, not to mention to yourself. Feeling the pressure of other women watching and admiring you may seem too much unless you are confident enough to handle the pressure. It is important to have realistic expectations and to keep everything in its proper perspective.

Jealousy may be a factor.

Women compete with other women in very covert ways. Some female co-workers may feel threatened by your promotion, and they may feel they deserved it, not you. Perhaps they would like to see you fail. They may feel that now, promotions will be scarce. While this may sound farfetched to you, it doesn't stop these feelings from arising.

CURES

Become a role model.

You have been singled out by management and elevated to a new position. You are now a role model for other women. Everywhere you go women may be watching you, hoping to learn from someone who has done it right and is reaping the rewards.

Being a role model has more to do with timing and circumstances than it does with performance and results. You do stand alone; you will be noticed and observed more. Learn to accept this role along with the responsibilities it carries. Role models are not perfect. They are individuals who have succeeded against odds and are willing to share their insights with others.

Many women find this role difficult to accept, because there is a great responsibility surrounding it. This pressure is one few men understand since they rarely stand alone. Men are supported by a lot of other men in similar positions, and there is both safety and anonymity in numbers.

You can offer support to these women through a variety of measures. First, talk to senior management about matching women with other women in the company. These personal relationships can allow women to have other mentors and role models to learn from and share with, which will lessen the direct pressure on you. The company may be willing to offer a women-in-management training program so that women can learn what it takes to succeed and get promoted. Women are more comfortable sharing with other women, although it may be objected to as being preferential treatment. Finally, outside organizations are another great resource that provides support for women. Finding an environment where women are comfortable sharing their concerns, and a place where they feel respected, heard, and appreciated will do a lot toward positioning these women for success.

Be prepared for your new role.

If you are reluctant or hesitant about your new position, feeling watched can add additional pressure you do not need. It can strip away your confidence.

Being prepared may have more to do with personal self-confidence than it does with experience. You may be afraid to try because you are afraid you will fail. A woman's fear of failure often leaves her believing she has only one opportunity to prove herself—if she blows it, she will not get another chance. All you can ever do is your best. Sometimes that will not be enough, but no one can ever expect more than that. If you believe in yourself, continue to learn from every experience, and are open to change when change is needed, you will be a success whether or not you lose a battle here and there.

If your fear is based on your lack of experience, then seek additional training. Accept responsibility for your choices and your actions. Evening courses and community or continuing education classes offer excellent learning opportunities at very reasonable prices.

Respond to jealous females.

Some women will be jealous of you and your status. You may be the target of their hostility and frustration, no matter what you do. They may be looking for you to make small mistakes, hoping that these signal your potential demise. How you manage these women can make your transition more meaningful or more challenging.

First, recognize the underlying cause of the problem. Second, move to build a better work environment for all women.

Do what you can with what you control, and let the rest go, otherwise it will consume a lot of energy unnecessarily. If someone else is resentful about your promotion, that is her problem, not yours. You cannot change her feelings. Remember, management is not a popularity contest; at times you may be viewed as the opposition by co-workers. Focus your attention on doing the best job that you can and try to share your knowledge about what it takes for a woman to succeed in management. Beyond that, it is outside of your control.

Look for ways to create opportunities and programs within the company for women to learn, share, and grow. These may be either formal or informal programs. Some women may take advantage of these opportunities, others may not. It is important to provide everyone with a chance.

2.8 The Problem: A pregnant employee needs special consideration, including a reduced work schedule.

THE SCENE

Less than six months after returning from an extended maternity leave, Cindy has announced she is pregnant again. Her doctor has suggested that she reduce her work schedule because of problems she is already having. Cindy's financial obligations and loss of insurance benefits make part-time work an unacceptable alternative.

Cindy has asked you to consider letting her work from her home. When word got out about this request, tension immediately began mounting in the department. Cindy is not well-liked, which makes selling this exception an uphill battle. In addition, the company has not offered telecommuting before; this would be a first. Some aspects of the job will be easier to adapt to telecommuting than others. The files will remain in the department, but computer hook-ups and the telephone can accomplish many duties.

There remains a great deal of confusion about what she will be doing as well as how much work Cindy will actually be able to accomplish at home. Should you allow this exception? What factors should you consider? What are your other options?

POSSIBLE CAUSES

Employees will question actions when they perceive a situation is unfair.

When you handle a situation individually, it will appear unjust to one side or the other. Therefore, the issue of fairness needs to be looked at from a wider angle. Fair to whom? It is important to minimize resentment at its earliest sign, and to maintain control through your authority.

Unpopularity may be an issue.

Because Cindy is not as popular or well-liked as other employees, there is not an automatic reaching out to embrace her needs by co-workers. You cannot make Cindy liked by her peers. Why she is not liked isn't the issue, assuming there is even a reason. But her unpopularity does make your job a lot harder.

Poor communication and vague expectations hurt everyone.

You and Cindy may not agree on what her results will be at home. Cindy may not be expecting to work much from home while you may expect Cindy to produce more because there are fewer interruptions. Everyone loses when communications break down and assumptions are made. Cindy must know exactly what is expected of her, and what the consequences are for not maintaining those standards. Together with Cindy, you must establish reasonable expectations given her present condition. Working from home has the potential to produce better results than being in an office, but it does not work well for everyone.

Other Considerations: Setting precedence may be a factor. If you view this situation as an isolated event, but feel others may ask to participate later, proceed cautiously. What is the downside if precedence is established? Talk to senior management about this possibility and seek its input. However, if this is the only reason you are declining working from home, it is a weak position. It may be a factor, but should rarely be the primary basis for your decision.

CURES

Create fairness and equity.

Deciding whether or not to allow an exception to policy is a difficult role for a manager. It is usually impossible to maintain a sense of fairness for everyone at all times. The scales of justice will be unequal, and appear to be unfair, from time to time. Sometimes conformity is the best solution; other times it is not. If you say no to this request, the majority of the staff will be pleased, but it is not fair to Cindy. If you say yes to the exception, Cindy will be happy and the company may actually gain a more productive employee, but other employees may consider this action unfair.

Evaluate each situation on its own merits. Consider the goodness, fairness, and equity about each solution. Look at the quality of work produced by the employee requesting the change, the disruption to the remaining staff members, the reason for the request, the ability of work to be redistributed, and the long- and short-term gains or losses. There will be times when the disruption of the department is not worth the small gains achieved by granting this request. Other times will exist where making an exception is worth the risk.

Talk with Cindy about your concerns:

> *Cindy, you are asking me to make an exception to our policy; no one has worked from home before. I will take your request under consideration, but I am not sure if your job can be done at home. I would like you to prepare a formal written request, outlining the reasons for this exception as well as what duties you will be able to perform at home and those that will need to be reassigned. I would like for you to include in this report your projections as well as different ways to measure your productivity and progress. Then, after I have reviewed your formal request, we can talk again and work on details and feasibility.*

Women are more comfortable managing individual situations separately. However, policy may not allow for flexibility to be considered. If policy precludes exceptions, talk to either your supervisor or personnel for a final ruling, and follow their directive.

If you choose to make an exception, how you handle the remaining staff members can make or break the success of the deal. See Sections 3.2 and 5.6 for suggestions on how to handle other employees.

Take the focus away from popularity.

While Cindy's popularity can make your job a lot easier, it may not be a luxury that you are afforded. Her unpopularity can complicate the situation greatly. While her popularity should not be an issue in deciding whether or not to grant the exception, it will be a factor in how you sell the idea to the remaining staff members.

The best way to sell an idea to someone is to share with them the benefits they will receive, if any. For example, senior management may consider companywide telecommuting if this pilot program is a success. Telecommuting is growing in popularity as more and more companies are finding ways to allow employees to work part time or full time from their homes. Not every position translates into a telecommuting job; some work cannot be done at home. If you have no indication from the company that this may be under future consideration, do not mislead the employees.

Change is often met with resistance. See Section 2.4 for ways to ease the tensions caused by change. By ignoring staff members' concerns, you are contributing to the problem. Meet, talk, listen, and get them involved in helping to redistribute the workloads. Accept responsibility for the final decision—it rests on your shoulders alone.

Communicate expectations beforehand.

Before you can determine expected results, you and Cindy must have all the facts in front of you. There must be enough information to evaluate the situation thoroughly.

> *Cindy, I have reviewed your request to work from home during your pregnancy, but I still have some questions. Do you know if you plan on taking the full maternity leave time after you give birth? How long do you plan to work? How many hours do you think you will be able to put in each day? Making this exception, even though it is temporary, means reassigning the workloads. It helps if I know approximately how long we are looking at for these adjustments. I'd like to know which job duties you feel you will be able to perform and which cannot be done at home. Also, if you have any suggestions for redistributing the work, I'd like your input.*

Employees need to know what your expectations are, and how their meeting those goals will be measured. When a job position changes so drastically, or is newly created, the expectations may need to be reviewed and altered to better fit the situation. At this point, both you and Cindy are basing these decisions on guesswork. After a few weeks, the plan may need to be reevaluated to see if the goals and expectations are too high or too low.

Try to establish measurable ways of monitoring the progress whenever possible such as the number of calls handled each day or week, or a sales quota. Some positions necessitate a person be in the office one or two days a week; other jobs require less office time. Review possible outcomes, problems, or complications from this arrangement and have a back-up plan of action in place. Be willing to make the necessary adjustments when a situation is not working out.

Is your objective to buy some time until the situation improves? Or is your objective to maintain the same amount of output from all employees? Keeping your objective in mind will help you decide on a reasonable and acceptable approach.

2.9 | The Problem: A problem employee happens to be the granddaughter of the CEO.

THE SCENE

Staci, a problem employee, continues to cause tension and disrupt the office routine. You have tried numerous times to focus her attention on doing her job, but nothing seems to work. At times she has become belligerent to you, defying the authority you have.

Staci has a blatant disrespect for policy and rules. With total disregard to the consequences, Staci does whatever she wants to do. Staci knows no one would dare fire her because her grandfather is the CEO of the company, and she constantly taunts you with reminders.

Your boss has been less than supportive of you in this situation. Whenever you've complained about her performance, he has said to do the best that you can. He continues to reiterate that you are stuck with her. While you can discipline Staci, you are not allowed to put her on probation. You know her actions are beyond probation, and she should be fired.

POSSIBLE CAUSES

You may be dealing with a spoiled brat.

Handling someone who always gets her way, and who has the clout to demand it, can be tricky. However, allowing Staci to get by with these actions is in no one's best interest, least of all Staci's. You would like to handle this problem as you would any other problem employee, but it appears you do not have that authority. Company politics can create complications for your professional future. Is it no wonder that you feel stuck?

You may be expecting too much from her.

You should be creating an environment which rewards and encourages employees to work toward their optimum performance. You may be expecting more from Staci because of who her grandfather is than what she is capable of contributing. Have you been completely honest in your evaluation of the situation? Have you penalized Staci because of who she is, trying to avoid appearing too lenient?

She may not be trained properly.

Everyone may assume that Staci knows what to do. They may even bypass many of the basic training steps that other employees have gone through because she is part of the "family." Staci may not be aware of her duties, yet she continues to be penalized for poor performance.

CURES

Handle office politics and favorites.

When an employee acts like a spoiled brat, managing him or her can be difficult. When you factor in nepotism, it becomes an even more fragile situation. A spoiled brat expects others to respond to her whim, while she sees herself above the rules that restrict others. She not only expects to be treated differently, she demands it. She will challenge you on every issue.

Usually a spoiled brat is forced to change when she enters the workforce. She learns that others will not cater to her every whim, often placing her career in jeopardy. At that point, a spoiled brat must sink or swim on her performance. When family ties restrict your authority, these lessons are more difficult, if not impossible to learn. A spoiled brat with family connections and political power may continue to exist in the workforce with little chance of remedy. There may be little that you can do because of who she is.

Try to gain Staci's respect. Focus on her actions toward you and others while at work. The best solution is to directly confront conflict and minimize its effects.

> *Staci, there seems to be some tension between us. It seems that you feel you do not need to follow the same rules as the rest of the department. Other staff members resent your actions. We need to honestly share our concerns and reach an agreement. This department will be run with certain rules and boundaries that everyone must follow. This seems like a good time to reestablish those boundaries. The current situation is not working well, and I think you realize this, too.*

This scenario assumes that you have already had several meetings discussing Staci's performance, but nothing has changed. Short of firing her, your next step is to reestablish boundaries or enforce those that already exist. Your solution must be something that you both agree on, otherwise nothing will change.

Create realistic expectations.

Everyone may be responding to Staci as if she knows more than she really does. Some people may be treating Staci as if she were special because she grew up in the business. They may be expecting more from her than she is capable of producing.

Review your expectations of her against your expectations of the other employees. Look primarily at those employees with similar backgrounds and experiences to see how they are doing. If you determine that you are guilty of expecting too much from Staci, then cut her some slack.

> *Staci, I would like to reassign some of your workload. I realize that I have expected too much from you for the short period of time you've been in this department. Perhaps if we work together, we can establish a load that is more within your abilities. How does that sound?*

In this situation you are managing those things that you can control. This solution also works when you have limited other options and must keep Staci employed in the department, despite her abilities. Find a way to make it work. Remember, work with what you have, not what you don't have.

Retrain employees.

When the situation is the result of improper training, then concentrate on getting that employee trained. By discussing job duties with Staci, you will be able to determine the amount of knowledge she has about her job responsibilities and functions. This may be the time to retrain the entire department to make sure that everyone is up to the current standards and expectations.

> *Staci, as you know there have been some problems with your work performance lately. What I have decided to do is retrain all of the department so that everyone agrees on what needs to be done and the appropriate way of doing it. Before I can establish a training program, though, I need for each person to write out a detailed description of their current job duties. The more complete this is, the*

easier it will be for others to follow. Can you have that done for me by Friday? I want to start putting together a plan very soon. Thanks.

Once you have reviewed the job description outline from Staci and other employees, then you can determine where the training is needed. If everything seems to be in good working order, you can still offer a departmentwide review of training. A review can only help the department to run better—even though your original problem may still be there.

Other Considerations: When all else fails, you may need to talk to Staci's grandfather about terminating or transferring her. A transfer doesn't solve the problem, it only moves it to someone else to handle. But because of her kinship, letting her go may not be an option. Do not assume that her grandfather will tolerate her behavior. He may be looking for a strong leader who will deal directly and firmly with the problem at hand. If you have gotten no help from your supervisor, you may consider talking directly with the CEO. It is a risky move, but one that may bring some relief in this situation.

Chapter Summary

Your style will be influenced by more than simply gender. But there is no question that gender will play a role. If that role is not in how you deliver the message, than it surely is in how the message is received. As a woman, your communication and style are often very different from your male colleagues.

Communication, an important element in any person's style, involves three primary elements: a message, someone to deliver that message, and someone to receive that message. Open communication means that you listen as well as speak. As you improve on communication, be sure to address all three elements.

Women have promoted a more inclusive style, valuing and appreciating employees with greater frequency. Some methods for showing appreciation include writing individual thank-you notes, sending a balloon bouquet, having a special party for the department, taking employees out to lunch for specific accomplishments, giving comp time for extra time worked, certificates of appreciation, and giving additional assignments to those employees who are most deserving. Statements like, *"Thank you, you are doing a great job"* and *"I really appreciate what you are doing"* can go a long way in showing the staff how much you value them. Private compliments are also wonderful.

Many women often have different priorities than men. Women continue to be the primary contributor for domestic chores and child rearing. Women who work outside the home typically work 90 hours each week while men work on average 50 hours a week. Is it no wonder, then, why women are often more overstressed and show greater tendency toward depression?

Women manage in a kinder, more caring, and less bureaucratic style. Women are more apt to allow the emotions and personal lives of their staff to be integrated into their work lives. In general, women build relationships between people, while men evaluate life in terms of status and hierarchy. The relationships women build can lead to friendships, that, at times, may get in the way of managing, and these friendships can call your authority into question as well. Becoming a friend to the employees can create obstacles for women managers; they may find that relationships interfere with their authority on the job. They may feel criticism and comments on a very personal level. Because of these reactions, many women have a difficult time when it comes to terminating an employee, and take this action very personally.

Caring about employees is a natural response for women. When an employee is hurting, you will share his or her pain. Encourage the employees to let you know about those things going on in their personal lives that could affect their job performance. This will help you to make the necessary adjustments to schedules or workloads. Remind the staff that you are there for them.

For a woman to show and share pain, she must admit to herself and others that she cannot fix the problem alone. A woman manager must be sure to handle her own problems and needs first, in order to be able to nurture her staff properly and create effective solutions. She must then work with them to come up with synergistic plans that will benefit all concerned.

Troubleshooting Personal Problems for the Staff

Overview

On any given day you will be confronted with a variety of problems, many having nothing at all to do with work. Yet everything about work life will be affected. Even if you do not want to deal with the personal problems of the employees, you cannot make them go away. Their presence will be felt. Personal problems do not simply stay at home.

Work routines can become disrupted because of personal issues. Employees may have feelings of sadness, happiness, depression, frustration, or fear all because of what is going on away from the office. These problems stem from a variety of sources including childcare issues, divorce, separation, sickness, or death.

Your leadership abilities will be tested during these tumultuous times. Providing a cohesive environment for the staff may mean fostering a safe place to work, creating feelings of mutual respect, and showing gestures of compassion and caring. At times, it may be enough to simply be with someone and show you care; other times routines must be adjusted and exceptions made to accommodate temporary needs. It is never easy.

This chapter addresses the following problems, possible causes, and cures.

3.1   The Problem: An employee requests time off next week to handle childcare problems.

Possible Causes: Situations outside your control affect work; an employee may place family concerns ahead of work.

Cures: Address limited childcare issues and work; accept family as an employee's first priority.

3.2   The Problem: A secretary's divorce is affecting her job performance and disrupting the office.

Possible Causes: A divorce can affect job performance; it may be more than a divorce she is worried about; her problems may be medical, not psychological.

Cures: You can deal with a divorce at work; you can handle a variety of problems; you can work with mental disorders.

3.3   The Problem: An employee is being stalked by her ex-boyfriend.

Possible Causes: While there may be side issues, the focus should be on the stalking; respond to unreported cases.

Cures: Understand the crime of stalking; handle an unreported case.

3.4   The Problem: An employee has offensive body odor and other employees are complaining.

Possible Causes: Cultural differences can create tension; bad hygiene may be a problem; his body may be omitting natural odors.

Cures: Understand there is diversity in the workplace; deal with the poor hygiene; work around offensive natural body odors.

3.5   The Problem: An employee's companion is very sick. Does it matter if the employee is gay?

Possible Causes: Issues surrounding sexual preference must be addressed; you may feel loyalty to two forces colliding.

Cures: Manage homosexuality and workplace stereotypes; juggle conflicts in loyalty; what if this were a heterosexual couple?

3.6   *The Problem: An employee's father has been diagnosed with terminal cancer and the employee has requested extended paid leave time.*

Possible Causes: Family crises require special consideration; handling stressful situations can be overwhelming; there may be other problems in the department.

Cures: Manage extended family issues; handle overstressed employees; resolve problems within the department.

3.7   *The Problem: An employee returns to work too soon after her spouse's sudden death, is emotionally not ready to work, and disrupts the office.*

Possible Causes: Healing takes time; the staff may feel uncomfortable; fear may be a catalyst.

Cures: Allow enough time for healing; find the right words to say; understand fear and the need for security.

3.8   *The Problem: A terminally ill employee wants to keep working as long as possible but his productivity continues to decline.*

Possible Causes: Communicating and managing are much more important than the cause.

Cures: Have a conversation with Mark; have a conversation with the staff; have a conversation with his customers; have a conversation with senior management.

Your challenge will be to make the workplace as normal and nondisruptive as possible. Some days that may be a much greater challenge than others. In fact, you may feel that it is an impossible goal. Your objective on these days may be just to get through them, and hope that things will be calmer tomorrow.

3.1 | The Problem: An employee requests time off next week to handle childcare problems.

THE SCENE

Emily comes into your office, visibly upset and frustrated, to inform you that her baby sitter cannot watch her child two days next week. She has already called around and is unable to find anyone to keep her on such short notice. She looks up at you, exhausted, and asks for those days off next week without pay since she has used all of her vacation and sick days for this year. This is not the first time childcare problems have been an issue for Emily; last month she was out three days.

It could not have come at a worse time. You have two employees scheduled to be out for vacation and another out for jury duty. The department is already operating on a minimal staff. Another person out would place significant pressure on the few remaining in attendance. Is it time to say no to her request? Is it the request or the timing of the request that concerns you the most?

Note: The good news is that Emily has given you advance notice. She could have called in that morning to tell you she wasn't coming in; instead she has asked your permission a week ahead of time. The bad news is that the rest of the staff suffers because of her situation. There may be resentment building among co-workers, especially by those who do not have childcare problems. Sometimes being fair does not mean being equally fair to all parties. Try to be as fair as you can, realizing the scales may tilt in one direction or the other. Make sure you do something special for those workers who are carrying the additional workload. This could include verbal appreciation, having lunch catered, and so on, to release the stress.

POSSIBLE CAUSES

Situations outside your control affect work.

Actions by a third party, the baby sitter, have caused you to make adjustments. Much like the game of dominos, these actions have a ripple affect.

Emily may have an unreliable baby sitter who takes off at a whim, or the baby sitter may have a legitimate request, such as a medical appointment, family concerns, and so forth. Whatever the case, the actions of the baby sitter have placed additional pressure and concern on the department. Assuming that Emily is unable to find a reliable back-up sitter, there may be little that she—or you—can do, except grant her the days off.

An employee may place family concerns ahead of work.

Each person establishes his or her own set of priorities for life. Working moms continue to feel the heaviest pressure as they juggle these demanding roles. When forced, mothers overwhelmingly choose family needs over their career demands, something few fathers are ever forced to do. Workplaces are slowly making adjustments, finding ways not to penalize career-track working mothers for these conflicts.

Other Considerations: Guilt can be a factor for working mothers. Unless there are other identifiable signs of guilt that Emily has exhibited, do not assume guilt is a major factor. Does she seem sad while at work? Does she have frequent crying spells, especially when her child calls during the day? Does she talk about her child, and then sound distant, wishing that she were with her? Does Emily feel that she cannot be a good mother if she puts her child in daycare? Guilt can be a contributing factor, the source of great pain and turmoil.

CURES

Address limited childcare issues and work.

Actions caused by the baby sitter are affecting Emily and therefore affecting the office. You have no influence over the actions of the baby sitter; instead, you are forced to respond to a problem beyond your control. Do not penalize Emily for something she, too, cannot control. The problem was initiated by the baby sitter. Blame does not solve the problem, and benefits no one.

Because there remains a shortage of qualified childcare options in most areas of this country, there may be few backup choices for Emily to consider. Emily's options may be further impeded by such things as limited financial resources, unusual working hours, or a sick or hard-to-manage child. Primarily you have two choices: deny her request or grant her request.

The first choice, denying the request, is generally not recommended. Emily may be putting you on notice about her absenteeism; not really asking your permission. By denying her request you are sending the message that family is not as important as work, that you are the one in control, and that personal problems have no place in the office. The exception would be for those cases where you feel Emily is abusing your kindness and taking advantage of the situation. (See Section 2.1.)

Your second alternative is to grant the request, perhaps even conditionally. Ask Emily how she recommends accommodating this request given the fact that the department is already short-staffed. She may even come up with suggestions that you had not considered.

While Emily has asked for the time off without pay, she may consider working part time from her home for those two days. Both you and she will need to determine if some of her job duties can be done at home, and if her particular circumstances will allow it. While her child is napping she may be able to return phone calls, sort files, type letters, or proofread reports. This depends on the nature of her job duties, as well as her accessibility to a computer, calculator, fax machine, or other office equipment. Sometimes it is not a realistic option.

Talk with Emily to see what her suggestions are:

> *Emily, this is a tough situation for you, I know, and I want to be fair. You are a very conscientious, loyal employee and I appreciate your contributions. As you know, we will already be short-staffed next week, with two on vacation and another out for jury duty. Do you have any suggestions for how we can handle your request with the least amount of disruption to those employees who will still be here? I don't want to penalize them. I understand your dilemma and wish I had a reliable backup sitter to suggest, but I don't. Thank you for coming to me early with it. This gives us some time to make the necessary preparations.*

Another option may be for her to bring her child to work. Again, this doesn't work for every office, but it may be able to solve two problems with one solution. It is worth a try. Of course, this depends on the age of the child, the amount of customer contact, and the type of office you manage.

Remember, we still live in a society where the majority of domestic chores and childrearing activities are performed by females, whether or not they work outside the home. Depending on the frequency of this problem, you may want to provide some direction for finding a backup childcare provider. You may consider allowing some time off from work for Emily to interview and search for affordable, reliable, and dependable childcare.

Accept family as an employee's first priority.

Corporate America is slowly beginning to make adjustments for mothers who choose, or are forced to maintain careers outside of the home. Childrearing, in this country, is primarily the mother's responsibility. Working fathers are seen as providers of the family, while mothers remain the nurturers.

Share your concerns and understandings with the employee:

> *Emily, I know it must be tough juggling both a career and raising a young child. I realize situations outside of your control are affecting your life. Your family responsibilities should and do come first; I respect that decision. And I appreciate the fact that you have given me some advance notice. Do you have any suggestions for how we should distribute your workload in your absence? I will already have three employees out, not counting you.*

This dialogue may sound soft, but it is exactly the kind of dialogue that is needed in the workplace today. It may not be so simple, especially if the corporate policy prohibits such exceptions and flexibility.

While you may agree with Emily's priority to her family, the company may not. In some company policies, unexcused absences may be grounds for probation or dismissal. You may need to find a middle ground until the company becomes more open and flexible to these present-day realities. If you are operating under constrained rules and procedures, be perfectly honest with Emily. Promising something that you are unable to deliver benefits no one.

Gender By-line: Working mothers still have different considerations than working fathers do. Adjustments have to be made to balance this inequity. Corporate America must actively participate in making these adjustments, which primarily involve making allowances during company time for family needs.

3.2 | The Problem: A secretary's divorce is affecting her job performance and disrupting the office.

THE SCENE

You manage a busy office comprised of three secretaries and several support and sales personnel. Kim, one of the secretaries, has been in the department almost three years. Everyone has been pleased with her performance.

Lately, though, Kim's personal life has been affecting her job performance. Kim filed for a divorce after she found out her husband was having an affair. She has become very emotional at work, and is often seen crying at her desk. Her performance continues to decline as she leaves projects unfinished and doesn't answer ringing phones while she makes her personal calls. Kim has been late several mornings because of meetings with attorneys, court dates, and therapist appointments.

Other employees in the department, while initially supportive of Kim and her turmoils, are becoming less tolerant. Several co-workers have complained openly to you about Kim's sloppy work habits and the fact that they continue to have to "cover" for her. What should you do?

POSSIBLE CAUSES

A divorce can affect job performance.

Kim's life at present is in a state of turmoil. The fact that the divorce was brought on by an unfaithful husband may have added to feelings of low self-esteem, insecurity, or guilt. No one will deny that Kim is under a significant amount of pressure. It would be impractical to expect Kim to leave her personal life at home, but that doesn't mean it should overpower everyone else.

It may be more than a divorce she is worried about.

Being divorced, facing the single lifestyle, and the financial insecurity of being on her own may be the beginning of a lot of personal issues for Kim.

Kim's closet may be full of skeletons and demons that she has never faced. It is common for one major life trauma to open the door for many other crises to come through the flood gates. Problems such as a bad childhood, physical or emotional abuse, medical complications, or codependency can make handling a divorce more intense. Concentrating on work may be impossible right now.

Her problems may be medical, not psychological.

Kim may be suffering from mental disorders, complicating her ability to reason and function. Mental disorders are considered diseases of the brain, not weaknesses of the mind. This important distinction is one that many in society have failed to recognize. It is not uncommon for lack of sleep and poor eating habits to add unnecessary pressure to an already unbearable situation. By knowing the signs of a nervous breakdown, depression, panic attack, and so on, you can direct Kim toward the professional help she needs.

CURES

You can deal with a divorce at work.

Be patient with Kim; every person heals on his or her own timetable. By reassuring Kim that she is needed in the department, and with this company, you are providing a safe and secure place for her to be. This is something that may be missing from other areas of her life right now.

Keep communication lines open by encouraging Kim to inform you of her time off needs as soon as possible. She is emotionally wounded; try to reward her and work with her as much as possible. Because of Kim's state of mind at present, do not expect her to meet you halfway. Instead, you should take the initiative by opening dialogue, frequently checking in with her, respecting her feelings, and making Kim feel needed. Realize that the healing process is different for each person.

Talk privately with Kim to see how she is doing:

> *Kim, I understand that you are under a lot of pressure right now. We are all trying to make adjustments to ease some of your work load. I hope you will feel comfortable talking to me about situations that may affect your job performance. If the work load becomes too much, or you feel too exhausted, I need to know. Let me assure you, we are here for you. We want to know how we can help, but we need you to guide us.*

You can minimize the effects of an employee's personal life at work, but it cannot be eliminated. Encourage others to be patient and tolerant of Kim during this difficult time. You do not want to lose a good employee, nor do you want to disrupt the entire office.

Determine if Kim is abusing privileges offered to her by taking advantage of your kindness and patience. If so, try to regain your sense of control and authority, but do so gently. Let Kim know beforehand how much you are willing to bend for her particular circumstances before you break. It is unfair to hold her responsible when you have not communicated those boundaries.

You can handle a variety of problems.

It is not uncommon for one major life crisis to open up the cesspool of many, many other problems that had been previously ignored, tolerated, or masked. These hidden skeletons may be adding additional pressure to an almost intolerable situation. These may include other problems that you did not even know she had.

Don't underestimate the power of showing you care, of simply being there for someone:

> *Kim, I know this is a difficult situation for you. You are doing a great job. You are holding up well under such enormous pressure. If you ever need to talk, feel free to come in. Or if you need to just come in and get away, I understand. My door is always open. If there is anything I can do, please let me know.*

Healthy, healed individuals make the best employees. By giving Kim the encouragement she needs, you are helping her to become a healthy, healed employee. If she is already in therapy, offer her the support she needs to continue, which may include additional time off. Be patient. The healing process is slow and bumpy.

You can work with mental disorders.

You, in all likelihood, are not trained in diagnosing mental disorders, nor does anyone expect you to be. Mental disorders can reveal themselves through a multitude of symptoms. If you suspect someone has a mental disorder, guide him or her toward professional treatment.

> *Kim, you know I care for you and your well-being. I know this is a difficult time and I am very concerned. Have you seen a medical doctor?*

A medical doctor can prescribe medication that can eliminate or control chemical imbalances that may be causing or intensifying Kim's disease. A psychiatrist is a medical doctor who is trained in this specialty, whereas a psychologist or therapist is someone who works through the emotional issues. Both treatments may be needed for her total recovery; both may impact her work schedule.

Recovery for mental disorders takes time, as recovery does for any illness. Treat Kim's illness as you would someone with cancer or heart disease. Encourage her to share her concerns, frustrations, tears, and anger with you.

Note: It is not uncommon for there to be residual effects on the staff caused by focusing on only one person's problems. There may be times when other employees feel left out, forgotten, or ignored. Some employees may show signs of jealousy or resentment because of the attention given to the employee. While you may choose to continue providing the individual attention, it is always important not to forget the remaining staff members. It doesn't have to be an either/or situation. The following are some suggestions for keeping those lines of communication open.

1. *When you hear disruptive comments being made, have a group meeting and dispel these frictions.* Are any employees complaining? The voice of dissent begins with one employee but can quickly spread to others. Deal with this as soon as possible.

2. *If you hear (or suspect) comments are being made behind people's backs, put an end to them immediately.* Keep conversations open, honest, and fair; gossip should not be tolerated.

3. *Talk about your decisions with the staff to keep them informed.* You do not need to seek their advice or approval for this situation. Other employees may have gone through a divorce and handled the situation quite differently. Respect their different manners in handling the situation, and ask that they respect how Kim is handling her problems.

4. *Listen carefully to everyone's opinion.* This means do not talk; do not plan your rebuttal while they are talking; do not dismiss their comments as inconsequential. You do not have to agree, just listen.

5. *Build unity by trying to find a common ground where everyone is happy.* Since every person may not agree, adapt a consensus each can live with.

6. *Show your leadership skills by making the tough choices.* Realize that not everyone will agree with your direction. This does not mean that you should become a dictator, only that group decisions are not always in a group's best interest.

If only one person adamantly objects, you may prefer to talk to that individual privately to try to reach an understanding. Be sure to listen to his or her feelings and respond accordingly. Perhaps one employee is getting hit the hardest by Kim's poor work performance.

By sharing your concerns within the group, you are showing the members that you respect each of them. As manager, the decision and responsibility ultimately lies with you.

3.3 | The Problem: An employee is being stalked by her exboyfriend.

THE SCENE

Kathy comes into your office shaking and sobbing uncontrollably. After closing the door, you try to comfort her, reassuring her that it is all right to cry and that you will listen whenever she is ready to talk.

Finally, she composes herself enough to tell you that her former boyfriend has been harassing her. He has been writing, calling, and following her, despite her pleas to leave her alone. Kathy is scared for her life. Sometimes he follows her when she is going to work; other times he watches from across the street at lunchtime, waiting to see where she goes. She had just received a phone call from him begging her to meet him after work so they could talk.

He was insanely jealous while they were dating. That was a major reason for their break-up. It has gotten worse since he has learned that Kathy is seeing someone else.

A restraining order was filed several months ago. Most of the time he manages to keep his distance, though she knows he is always "out there." Kathy is afraid to go anywhere, afraid of what he might do. The police do not feel her life is in danger, so until he breaks the restraining order there is little they can do. You knew none of this was going on. What can you do? What should you do?

POSSIBLE CAUSES

While there may be side issues, the focus should be on the stalking.

Stalking is a controlling behavior with obsession as its underlying foundation. It should always be taken seriously. Because the number of stalking incidents being reported is on the rise, all 50 states and the District of Columbia have passed stalking laws. They continue to be revised, making stalking an even more egregious crime.

Respond to unreported cases.

You have a responsibility to Kathy as well as to the rest of the staff to provide a safe place to work. Your actions, or lack of actions, could jeopardize other employees' physical safety, so this must be carefully evaluated.

Other Considerations: Side issues are generally not of great importance when it comes to stalking, although side issues may heighten the fear and make a situation become much more life-threatening. For example, if Kathy is being threatened by a former boyfriend who happens to be a drug dealer, the situation could become even more intense. If there is a history of domestic violence in their relationship, again the current situation becomes even more frightening because of his violent past.

CURES

Understand the crime of stalking.

There are two issues at play here: one is the law; the other is how to deal with an emotionally shattered employee. Both are equally important and should be handled simultaneously. The first requires notifying the appropriate authorities, while the second involves more of your time, attention, compassion, support, and leadership skills.

Kathy needs to feel secure. She is seeking a safe place where someone can offer her protection. Your office may be the safest place around her right now.

First things first. Kathy needs to release her emotions so that she can regain control of herself. This may take some time. Your role is to just be there for Kathy, to comfort and support her until she is ready. Once she has regained control, then you can proceed in a more strategic manner. Encourage her once again to contact the police so that accurate records are maintained and the appropriate authorities notified. You should also notify any building security staff and receptionist so that internal safety precautions are put in place.

> *Kathy, are you feeling better? You may stay in here as long as you like, there's no rush. You stated that you'd already filed a restraining order, and you believed he was in violation of it by calling you this afternoon. Why don't you call the police from my office and let them know? It is important for records to be maintained and the appropriate parties to be notified. Maybe the police can do more this time. Do you feel like calling now?*

The number of stalking cases reported each year continues to increase. Some stalkers like to harass individuals; others seek complete control. In the extreme case, when stalkers are unable to get what they want, they seek revenge. Death is the ultimate sacrifice, signifying *"If I can't have you, then no one will."*

Stalking is a very serious situation; do not take it lightly and do not try to handle the situation alone. Realize that other people may also be in danger. Notify your superiors to see how they recommend that you proceed. The safety of all workers must be maintained.

Handle an unreported case.

Encourage Kathy to go to the police, especially if she hasn't already done so. Unfortunately you cannot force her to go. It is ultimately her decision. If she is unwilling to press charges against him, for whatever reasons you must respect her decision.

> *Kathy, this really must be a living hell for you; I cannot even imagine. Let me assure you that my first priority is for your safety. I wish you would go to the police, though, so they could offer some protection for you. There is very little that I can do here, and noth-*

ing that I can do once you leave here. If you like, I can go with you to the police station, so that you're not alone. Or perhaps you can call from my office and an officer can come out here and take the report.

Try to determine if she is in any immediate physical danger. While you may want to go to the police and file the paperwork on Kathy's behalf, if you have promised her that you wouldn't go, review your next step carefully. The question becomes weighing her trust in you versus weighing the safety of one individual (or maybe even the group). Your reaction may be an overreaction; it may only be a perceived fear. The situation could even become aggravated by involving the police.

Sometimes there are no easy choices. You may need to follow your heart instead of your head. By keeping senior management informed about the volatile, and potentially dangerous situation you are experiencing, you are using the resources that you have available.

3.4 | The Problem: An employee has offensive body odor and other employees are complaining.

THE SCENE

Two employees, Sharon and Ross, ask to speak to you in private. Once behind closed doors they complain about the offensive body odor of the new employee, Jamal. Because these two employees sit closest to Jamal, they are the ones most affected by the smell. They say the odor makes them nauseated and it has become impossible to sit at their desks and concentrate on work.

Jamal is not originally from this country and you do not know what "normal" hygiene is for him. While you had noticed the odd smells, you were somewhat insulated in your office. How do you handle this delicate situation diplomatically?

> *Note:* Different nationalities follow different hygiene rituals. What seems normal and acceptable to Americans has not always been so rigid even in this country. Not everyone agrees that it is necessary to bathe daily to maintain good hygiene. Weekly baths were the acceptable norm in the United States just a few decades ago. Americans are known for their obsession with cleanliness, something not shared with other nationalities.

POSSIBLE CAUSES

Cultural differences can create tension.

You may be straddling the line between accepting or integrating diversity into the workplace, and maintaining peace through traditionally accepted behavior. Simply because you are not accustomed to his body smells do not necessarily make them bad. Since there is not a universally accepted routine that all cultures follow for hygiene, this becomes a more delicate situation.

Bad hygiene may be a problem.

When you factor out cultural differences, there may be a more serious or uncomfortable problem remaining. You may have an employee who has bad hygiene. There are several things presumed necessary in order to achieve good hygiene, including bathing with soap and water and using a deodorant. When these routines are not followed, the result may be unsettling for those who work closely with this person. While there may not be any good way to handle the situation, there are definitely bad ways that should be avoided.

His body may be omitting natural odors.

Jamal's problem may have nothing to do with hygiene, but is still offensive. Even if he uses a deodorant, bathes frequently and uses soap, there still may be odors emitted. The foods he eats can affect his body odors; even a medical problem could aggravate the condition. Daily baths may not lessen the smells. How you handle this delicate situation is crucial.

CURES

Understand there is diversity in the workplace.

As Corporate America diversifies its workplace, there remains some tension and uncertainty about how much to accept and how much to change. This tension and uncertainty produces questions such as: When is enough, enough? or Who exactly needs to change?

The fact remains that most cultures do not share the same obsession with cleanliness that Americans promote. Still, some employees are finding it difficult to work when Jamal is around because of these smells. It is a situation that cannot be ignored—something must be done. Whether or not they agree with Jamal's right to follow his own cultural hygiene rituals, Sharon and Ross feel their rights have been violated. They feel that they do not have a choice in the air they breathe.

The first step is to learn about Jamal's culture, rituals, and routines. It is important to determine if there is a difference. If there is, then try to understand its heritage and roots. This research can be found in the library or obtained from local community experts.

Assuming that this research has uncovered cultural differences in hygiene which explain his body odors, then what is your next step?

Seek the support and guidance from professional advisors who are trained in areas of cultural diversity. Understanding diversity requires educating everyone on these differences. Before anyone can be expected to accept diversity, he or she must first understand it. Most cities have business professionals who are trained in creating a cohesive work environment and integrating cultural differences into the workplace. Local universities, religious leaders, or the local government may also offer additional assistance as cultures learn more about each other.

Senior management may not share your openness and tolerance of differences. When management feels outsiders should conform, your job will be to educate yourself away from the office. In the office, talk privately with Sharon and Ross to see what their concerns are and discuss various ways to meet their needs. Sharon and Ross may have personality problems with Jamal and be using the odor as a diversion. Try to enlist their patience and indulgence as everyone works to create a diversified and tolerant workplace. Understanding is the first step toward reaching that goal.

Focus on the benefits the staff will receive. Ultimately the company, as well as all its employees, will benefit from such a varied background of experiences. Each of us has more in common with others than we think, no matter what our gender, race, nationality, or culture. As the world becomes more global, it is very important that workplaces learn this valuable lesson.

Education about diversity doesn't lessen the smell. For those employees who are unable to continue working next to someone because his body odor makes them sick, you must address the problem head-on. Ignoring it creates more conflict. You cannot force change on people who do not want to change.

In the end, you may need to talk privately to Jamal, explain the situation, and seek suggestions from him about how best to find a resolution. A compromise takes concessions on everybody's part, and it may not be easy. Unfortunately, someone may quit in the meantime. Do the best you can with what you have, as you wade through the turmoil.

Deal with the poor hygiene.

The above situation was complicated by cultural differences. It could just as easily have been presented with someone from the American culture, completely eliminating diversity as a factor. Instead, the underlying tension could arise when one employee has poor hygiene habits.

When offensive hygiene is the result of poor bathing rituals, you must address the problem quickly. Because of the delicate nature of such a personal topic, discuss this matter in private.

> *Jamal, I know this is a very personal matter, but we need to discuss it openly together. It does affect everyone you work with. Several people have complained about your body odor. I want to help. This may be an uncomfortable conversation, at least it is for me. You are a hard worker, Jamal, and I want you to continue working here. Is there something going on personally with you that I need to know about?*

This conversation could still have some lingering ramifications. Jamal may feel lonely, and your comments may make him feel even more isolated. He may be homeless and too ashamed to tell you. He may feel embarrassed that you have mentioned this topic and retaliate with anger toward you or someone else.

It is a tough situation, with tough choices. But you must feel comfortable enough to discuss it frankly, honestly, and compassionately. Trying to avoid conflict only makes the situation worse.

Work around offensive natural body odors.

Assume that you have spoken with Jamal, and have determined that he has no control over these odors, that they are natural. What is your solution? He bathes daily, uses soap, scrubs thoroughly, and uses a strong deodorant, but still has offensive body odors.

You and the staff will need to make some adjustments. This won't be easy; there may be some resistance. As a manager, your role will be to handle both sides of the equation as peacefully and tactfully as is possible.

There are three primary avenues for resolving this dilemma. First is to penalize Jamal for something that he cannot control. Second is to penalize the rest of the staff for something they cannot control. Or third, the best solution, is to find a compromise agreeable with everyone.

While I do not like the idea of penalizing Jamal, in this situation it is actually something that you must consider. Penalizing the remaining staff members seems completely out of the question. So, if those are your only two choices, Jamal would probably lose. Otherwise you run the risk of having a mutiny with the remaining staff members, risking that several may leave at once.

Finding a middle ground is the best solution. It may be challenging, if not impossible, to reach such a solution. Reaching a compromise may involve job reassignments, assuming you have that ability within the company. Many of your choices will be dependent on how the company operates. For example, are you able to separate Jamal from the other employees? Can he work in an office without co-workers feeling jealous? Will these changes be met with resistance from Jamal, because he wants to be treated just like everyone else, not separated from others? Is a transfer possible, where Jamal can work in a more isolated surrounding, but not feel like he is getting special treatment?

Again, much of this resolution will be dependent upon how the company is set up, and in light of the work distributions, as well as the willingness of all parties to make concessions.

Talk with Jamal privately about the situation and offer suggestions and solutions that he may not have considered.

Jamal, I know this is an awkward situation for both of us, but I need to speak honestly. Several employees have commented about your body odor. I know you are a clean person, and I am not questioning your hygiene. Have you seen a doctor about this? Perhaps stronger deodorants could help, or maybe using deodorant pads is an option. As a person with a lot of allergies, I realize that foods can cause a variety of reactions, including body odors. Have you seen an allergist? Jamal, what I'm saying is that I very much want to help. I realize that the other employees not wanting to work around you has got to hurt your feelings. Working together, I believe we can handle this problem. You're a great employee; I want to find a way to make this work!

If Jamal is interested in exploring any of these solutions, provide the support as well as any time off he requests. Talk openly with the remaining staff members; ask their patience and indulgence while together you try to find a solution that is both fair and sensitive. This problem may not have an easy answer, and the conversation may make Jamal feel embarrassed, ashamed, or uncomfortable, so approach it tenderly.

3.5 | The Problem: An employee's companion is very sick. Does it matter if the employee is gay?

THE SCENE

Albert is a good employee, easy-going, amiable, with many years of seniority in the company. Although he has not felt comfortable coming out, everyone in the department assumes he is gay. Out of respect for Albert's privacy, no one broaches the subject.

Albert rarely goes to company parties since most are centered around family activities and spouses. There are some old-fashioned employees who would cause a ruckus if he were to come to a company function with his companion. Albert feels uncomfortable coming alone so instead he makes excuses and avoids socializing with co-workers away from the office.

After lunch, Albert comes into your office to ask for some leave time from work. He knows he needs to explain why, but seems reluctant, almost embarrassed. You try to offer him a safe place, and start by saying, *"Albert, whatever you tell me will be kept confidential. I want to assure you of that."* Finally, he tells you that his companion is very sick, and he needs to take care of him for awhile. The company policy allows for family leave time (both paid and unpaid), but only includes the traditional forms of family.

You know you will need to get this exception approved by human resources. You also know that it will not be easy. For fear that he will be penalized professionally, Albert has asked that you maintain his confidentiality about many of the details. He has stated that he also fears for his personal safety.

POSSIBLE CAUSES

Issues surrounding sexual preference must be addressed.

This remains a controversial topic within many workplaces. For some people the homosexual lifestyle is a moral issue. Whether Albert has personally been denied advancement in the past, or simply knows of friends who have, his knowledge of the professional gamble he would be facing by admitting his sexual preference is a major factor. In addition, personal safety issues must be considered. There may be both real and perceived risks associated with divulging too much information. Since you cannot guarantee to Albert that nothing will happen to him, proceed cautiously, and only with his blessings.

You may feel loyalty to two forces colliding.

Issues of loyalty and trust are at the foundation of every relationship. As a manager, you will be circulating in several different plateaus that may from time to time be in conflict with one another. Your relationship with the company and senior management may be just as strong as the relationship you have with the staff. When these two forces collide, you must evaluate your choices and consequences carefully.

CURES

Manage homosexuality and workplace stereotypes.

Same-sex relationships deeply offend some people. That is the reality of our culture, not a judgment valuation. These individuals consider homosexuality a moral issue. When these viewpoints are shared by senior management, company policy is often shaped along these lines. Allowances for exceptions under such circumstances will rarely be granted with such a conservative management philosophy.

You may even agree with these conservative viewpoints, making it difficult for you to stay objective in this situation. It is important to understand your own motives, prejudices, and moral code when evaluating problems, especially those that are of such a controversial nature.

Creating and incorporating a diverse workforce means a lot of different things. In essence, it means accepting those who are different from yourself, respecting their differences, and asking that in turn they accept and respect you. It is not always that easy when put to everyday use. Sexual preference is a protected right in few states. Some companies openly fire employees because of their lifestyles, even when it has no bearing on work performance.

The physical or financial risk to Albert may be real or it may be perceived. When you offer confidentiality, you must maintain it, otherwise trust is broken and disingenuous actions produce privileged information. You offered Albert confidentiality, and by speaking he accepted that offer. He has revealed a very personal part of his life to you because he felt safe. He has asked that you not elaborate on his reason for requesting leave time with senior management. To break that bond of trust may result in irreparable harm. While you may not be able to approve the leave, you should not discuss this matter with anyone else inside or outside the company.

> *Albert, I have promised you a confidential environment. I respect what you have shared with me, and will proceed how you decide. I do not know how management will respond to this situation. I realize that some people strongly disapprove of your lifestyle*

and thus it could carry damaging repercussions for your future career here. But right now I feel very limited in what I can do. No one has ever asked for family leave time for a companion. Until someone tests the policy, I do not know how it will be answered. Human resources must approve any request for time off, with or without pay. A reason for the request is part of the form. I know the importance of your request, or you wouldn't have made it; but my choices are limited. First I can go to human resources without complete information, and in all likelihood get the request denied. Or, my second choice is to go to human resources with sufficient information, be ready to defend your request, and hope that it gets approved. Neither are guarantees, but the chance of the first request being approved is nearly zero. Do you have any other suggestions? Any advice for how I could proceed?

Although you may not want to discuss it, Albert does have the choice of finding employment elsewhere. However, changing jobs and finding a paid leave of absence immediately is unlikely. Albert may choose to quit his current employer, stay home for as long as he needs to, and then seek new employment at a later time, assuming that he isn't requesting paid leave time.

If the company allows for rehiring of former employees, you may keep the door open to him as a rehire. Not all companies allow you to rehire former employees which may eliminate this option.

Juggle conflicts in loyalty.

Conflicts in loyalty, stemming either from different philosophies or different levels of commitment, are not uncommon in the workplace. Women experience these with more intensity than men because of women's need to be connected. Sections 9.3 and 9.4 provide additional information for handling these philosophical conflicts.

Seeking a common ground may be impossible. At times there may appear to be different objectives, methods, and reasons—all for the same events. Some may even produce different results. For example, if you work in a place where you are penalized for not revealing what you know, then do not promise what you cannot deliver. Do not promise confidentiality if you are not able to keep your word.

If there is a degree of confidentiality that you may keep, then it is important to communicate those boundaries up front. This will help you avoid situations where you feel that you must choose between your loyalty to the company and your loyalty to an employee.

> *Albert, I understand your dilemma; now I am also in an uncomfortable situation. Senior management has asked to be kept informed of any personnel problems or potential situations that each department anticipates. As a manager, I have a responsibility to both the staff and to the company. They appear on a collision course here. I want to be fair to you, but I also must be fair to my employer. How much of what you have confided to me may I share?*

The answer may well be *"nothing."* It is at that pivotal point that you must weigh the information given along with your management responsibility, and make a decision. Sometimes it may feel like you are weighing your heart against your head. Situations such as these are never easy. They require evaluation of all events, consequences, and repercussions.

What If: this were a heterosexual couple?

Factoring out the issues surrounding sexual preference still leaves you in a situation of seeking an exception to the company's definition of traditional family. Are you better able to evaluate the need for an exception when other perhaps less controversial circumstances are not impacting your decision?

Decide if you are willing to challenge the company's definition of family, with the consent and approval of the employee. If so, then present your arguments before human resources. Many companies are not open to broadening their definition of family. If the company maintains a conservative view, it is unlikely that it will change.

Even though the odds are against you, you may still decide to try. When you take on these risks, make sure they are *calculated* risks. While you may win one battle, you may lose the war and damage your career future. That would be a great travesty. First, talk to Albert:

> *Albert, I know you need this time off, however the company family leave time is very specific about who it covers. I am afraid that your request does not fall under that category. I will meet with human resources to see if there is something that can be worked out, although there are no guarantees. I'll get back to you as soon as I hear something. I am very sorry to hear about [insert name].*

The best way to affect change is by creating meaningful dialogue. It works to your advantage if Albert is a valuable, well-respected, and knowledgeable employee. While it should not be a factor, oftentimes exceptions are more readily made for key employees, for those employees management personally likes. Once the mold has been broken, then perhaps policy can be rewritten. See Section 2.8 for handling issues of fairness and equity.

3.6 The Problem: An employee's father has been diagnosed with terminal cancer, and the employee has requested extended paid time leave.

THE SCENE

Debbie has requested an extended paid leave of absence to be with her ailing father. He was diagnosed with terminal cancer earlier this year and his health is rapidly declining. Her request is for an unknown period of time. She wants to be with her father while he is still alive, and then spend some time with her mother.

Debbie's position is important to the department. Her absence leaves you in a difficult position; you will need to request hiring a replacement worker during the interim. However, you are not too optimistic about finding someone because of the detailed nature of the job duties and the amount of time required for training. Redistributing the work doesn't seem feasible either since everyone is already working to their capacity.

Because Debbie is single, without any other source of income, an unpaid leave is not practical. Her family cannot support her with the enormous medical and financial hardships they are facing. Exceptions have been made in the past for granting limited paid leave time from the company, although there is no formal policy. Even if you recommend this leave, the approval process will be long and difficult. Approval with pay will mean that you cannot hire anyone during her absence. Plus if she takes leave time, you must hold Debbie's job open for her in case she returns.

POSSIBLE CAUSES

Family crises require special consideration.

Family is not just limited to your spouse and children. Society is having to look at the roles extended family now play. Baby boomers are dealing with sick or aging parents in record numbers, and feeling squeezed by the added pressure. Balancing or juggling these roles may seem awkward. It may require more attention be given to immediate situations. As with any balancing act, the scales of justice may temporarily lean in one direction or the other at any given moment in time.

Handling stressful situations can be overwhelming.

Debbie may be absolutely exhausted from everyone wanting part of her life, from everyone needing her, and leaning on her for strength. She may be experiencing the pressures of her life being out of control and need some time to herself as well as time to give to her family. For Debbie to accept that she cannot change these circumstances may be very difficult.

There may be other problems in the department.

The disruption caused by an employee's absence may be intensified when a department is not running smoothly, efficiently, and at its optimum. An unexpected crisis should not immobilize a department. If it does, perhaps the department needs to be realigned and built based on teams, so that cross-training and filling in can be part of the everyday operation. Even for the most technical positions, the work still needs to get done.

Note: Factor out your needs and inconveniences from Debbie's request. These are two different issues. Even though they become intertwined, each issue should be handled independent of the other. Simply because you are inconvenienced should not weigh on the decision of whether or not Debbie should be granted her time off. Whether or not she is paid during her absence is a separate issue from your ability or constraint to hire a replacement worker.

CURES

Manage extended family issues.

Working women continue to be squeezed from a variety of sources. If they are mothers, they must leave their small children; if they are married, they attempt to integrate their career and family duties under one act. Added to the many stresses that women face is the fact that more women are caring for aging relatives, including in-laws. Any one of these roles can be overwhelming. They chip away at the small amount of time women have set aside for themselves.

Debbie's needs do not seem unreasonable. However, because of the nature of the illness, Debbie does not know how long she will be gone. This makes planning more difficult. If you feel uncomfortable completely granting her request, you may consider placing parameters on it:

> *Debbie, I am very sorry to hear about your father. I under-stand your need to be with him right now. You had requested paid leave time, and I will do my best to get that approved for you. Unfortunately, I do not have the final word, so I cannot make any promises. We will have a better chance of getting it approved with specific time frames. I know that may be difficult, but is that some-thing you would consider? It helps if I know some areas that are more negotiable when I formulate my request. Perhaps we should evaluate all the possible outcomes together, and see what choices are left. I know this is difficult, but with some careful planning our chances are greatly improved.*

The kinder, gentler style women may adapt could mean that you are temporarily short-staffed, that you may not be able to hire a replacement worker, or that everyone must carry the additional workload. These are, in fact, separate issues from Debbie's request. They should be evaluated and handled on their own merits, not in conjunction with penalizing or reward-ing this individual request.

Handle overstressed employees.

Sometimes life is complicated by a lot of stress and pressure points. You may be completely overwhelmed by everything. The staff is no different. No one is immune to these realities. See Section 4.1 for ideas on handling and eliminating stress.

Needing some time away seems not only realistic, it also seems very healthy. If you respond by belittling her request (perhaps out of your own selfish needs) then your feelings can easily be transferred into guilt.

In talking with Debbie, you may say the following:

> *Debbie, my heart goes out for you during this very difficult time. If there is anything that I can do, please let me know. You have requested time off; I will submit your request, and recommend its approval to human resources. The final decision is theirs. In the meantime, I want you to know that I am here if you need me.*

Be patient and gentle with Debbie; time is on her side. Talk openly to the staff. Most will be supportive of her struggles. They may offer to pick up the slack; don't underestimate their compassion. See Section 3.2 for ways to handle the remaining staff members.

Resolve problems within the department.

This problem could be compounded because of a poorly run department. Every department should be able to react to an unexpected crisis with minor interruptions. Although some departments may require more training and technical expertise, there should still remain an ability to continue operations with few snags. When this doesn't happen, it is important to determine exactly why not.

Decide if the situation you are facing is intensified because of temporary or outside conditions. For example, have you recently gone through a company or department downsizing, and the staff is still adjusting to those demands? Has an employee recently been terminated, and left you understaffed or in the process of training an employee who would eventually be Debbie's backup? Is the company experiencing rapid growth and placing an enormous amount of pressure on all workers?

When the situation is compounded by outside circumstances, handle those circumstances in conjunction with this problem. In other words, look for the opportunities to reorganize or rearrange positions so that the work flow is maintained. Communicate directly with the staff to encourage its input and suggestions. Use boundaries as a springboard for new ideas. If you are unable to hire a replacement worker, state so unequivocally, then seek other solutions.

Many offices have been able to meet high production goals when reaching a quota meant leaving early that day. These incentives must not be used to set higher standards, but instead used to reward great accomplishments. In the meantime, do not forget to give praise whenever appropriate. Everyone likes to be noticed.

3.7 | The Problem: An employee returns to work too soon after her spouse's sudden death, is emotionally not ready to work, and disrupts the office.

THE SCENE

Lois has been with the company for 20 years and is a loyal, cheerful, and knowledgeable employee. After her husband's sudden death, Lois decided to return to work the following week. She said that she needed to stay busy and get out of the house.

Her first week back was chaotic for everyone. During the day you could see her crying at her desk. Her smile was gone, she looked exhausted, and was even short with customers. Her work was uncharacteristically sloppy and full of mistakes. Other employees in the office are feeling uncomfortable as the tension thickens. Should you talk to Lois? Should you suggest she seek counseling or should take some vacation time and get away?

POSSIBLE CAUSES

Healing takes time.

There is no magic formula for how to heal, when to heal, or where to heal. The process is different for each person. While there are some commonly identified stages to healing, most people experience a variety of bumpy roads in the process. Though it is a challenge to balance a constructive work environment while offering an employee a safe place to be; it is not impossible. The fact that other people are affected by this event will require more of your time and attention.

The staff may feel uncomfortable.

Employees may not know what to say to Lois. They may be looking to you to guide them with the appropriate words of support and acts of concern. Often this tension is complicated by denial; Lois may not want anyone to mention the word death, say how sorry they are, or show acts of consideration. Lois may want to pretend that her life is the same as it was before her husband's death. While you may not agree with Lois' decision to return to work so soon, it is still her decision to make. Your role is to ease the tension by creating open, honest, and caring dialogue with the staff as well as with Lois if appropriate.

Fear may be a catalyst.

Lois' house may seem empty without her husband around. Family and friends may serve as constant reminders that she is now a widow. She may no longer feel comfortable going to the places where they used to go together. In fact, she may not even want to see the friends that were their friends before. Work may be the one constant in her changing life. Disrupting her safe haven seems unfair, not to mention unhealthy. Understanding Lois' pain and fears can go a long way in meeting her needs.

Other Considerations: Does it matter if the death was last month, six months ago, or last year? Would you still handle the situation the same? Can you accept that each person heals on their own individual timetable? Or do you feel more sensitive to the immediacy of this situation?

CURES

Allow enough time for healing.

The healing process varies for each person based on his or her particular circumstances. For some, the process may be achieved rather quickly; for others, there may be stages of grief consisting of denial, anger, bargaining, depression, and acceptance.

Support Lois' decision to return to work. It may result in some short-term complications, but staying busy and feeling useful may be key to Lois' healing process. The long-term benefits may outweigh any short-term obstacles.

When Lois goes home she is faced with the reality of an empty house. Getting out of the house can do her a lot of good. Staying busy may not mean denying what has actually happened; instead it may mean that she is just not dwelling on it all day long. Respect her decision to return to work, but stay aware of her vulnerable phases and changing needs. Share your concerns and your willingness to respond to her needs in a private conversation:

> *Lois, I want you to know I am here if you need anything. I understand your need to return to work. If things get to be too much around here, please let me know. Everyone wants to make this as easy and safe for you as possible. We will make some adjustments if you think that may help. You may not want anything changed right now and I am perfectly comfortable with that. However, later on if you ever feel the pressure mounting, please feel free to come and talk to me about it. Lois, I am truly sorry about your loss.*

Denial is a common stage in the healing process, as is anger. If you know of some local support groups for widows, you may offer them as suggestions. For right now, though, Lois needs to feel needed. Your patience and concern will show her how much you care.

Find the right words to say.

Issues of mortality often leave people feeling awkward and uncertain of what to do or say. While you want to express your concern and sadness, you are afraid that your gestures will be misunderstood or you are not sure just what someone needs to hear right now. All too often, faced with this dilemma, you may say nothing.

The employees may be just as unclear as you are about what appropriate signs of concern and grief to show. Appropriate to whom? It is important for everyone to recognize the loss as well as to allow for awkward moments to pass.

Talk to the department, perhaps before Lois returns to ease some of the anticipated tension. Reassure the staff that they are important to this whole process, and that their fears and anxieties will be honored.

> *Tomorrow Lois will be returning to work. She needs our support during this very difficult transition time in her life. I came across a Bill of Rights for those Grieving, that might help us all to better understand her pain. I'll pass copies of this around so that everyone will have it as a reminder. The rights include: Let me cry;*

> *allow me to talk about the deceased; do not force me to make quick decisions; let me act strange sometimes; let me see that you are grieving too; when I am angry, do not discount it; listen to me, please; forgive me my trespasses, my rudeness, and my thoughtlessness; don't put a time limit on my grief. This may be difficult or uncomfortable for all of us, but we need to be here for Lois. If you don't know what to say, that is fine—say nothing. Just give her a hug and let her know that you are thinking about her, and that you care.*

You may also have a similar dialogue with Lois present. Although you should talk to Lois privately beforehand, share your list, and get her blessing. You do not want to make her feel any more uncomfortable than she already does.

Understand fear and the need for security.

The fear of the unknown can be frightening. When lifestyle changes are forced upon us unexpectedly, we often do not know what to do or where to turn. It is during these times of transition that we seek places of solace where nothing seems to have changed.

Lois is facing many changes in her life, the extent to which she may not totally know yet. Decisions such as: Does she want to stay in the same house? Perhaps she did not handle the maintenance problems in the past, but with a car in need of repair she may have to. What about insurance? Who will do the taxes? How will the death affect her tax filing? The list of questions could be endless.

During these tumultuous times, it is common to seek some place where you feel safe in your routine, a place where you know the answers, and where you feel needed. Seeking support during such transitional times cannot be overemphasized.

> *Lois, I just want to let you know that if there is anything, anything at all that I can do, please do not hesitate to let me know. We are glad that you are back at work. Nothing has changed here while you were gone. We'll try to keep everything like it was. And I am deeply sorry for your loss.*

Lois may be seeking a safe place where she knows the routine without thinking about it. If she fails to respond appreciatively to your signs of warmth and openness, do not take offense. The healing process is difficult.

Facing these fears may be extremely scary for her. Acknowledging you would, in essence, mean that she is accepting them. If she is not ready to do that just yet, be patient. Time is on your side. Don't expect too much, too soon, or you will be disappointed.

3.8 The Problem: A terminally ill employee wants to keep working as long as possible but his productivity continues to decline.

THE SCENE

Mark has been very sick over the past few months. His many doctors visits have provided few answers, except to put him through more tests. After numerous doctor referrals and having specialists probing and prodding inside of him, they have finally diagnosed a very rare terminal cancer.

Because of his weakened health condition, Mark has not been able to maintain his full workload. Chemotherapy treatments cause him to miss several days each month. He frequently goes home around noon feeling tired and in pain. Because business dictates that customers are handled promptly, other staff members have pitched in and covered for him during those absences.

Mark has asked to continue to work as long as the company will let him. He has been very honest about his condition and has tried to manage his accounts as best he can. You already know that his condition will only get worse and his productivity will continue to decline. This has become more of a moral question for you as opposed to a financial consideration. Working provides Mark with a place where he is needed, where he can make contributions.

You would like to be able to train a new employee to handle his accounts, but you do not want Mark to feel that he is being pushed out. You're not even sure that personnel would approve another position.

POSSIBLE CAUSES

Communicating and managing are much more important than the cause.

The problem basically boils down to minimizing the discomfort and anxiety of one employee, even if this means that other staff members are inconvenienced for the short term. For the least amount of disruption, it is important that everyone works toward the same goals.

You must be willing to talk with all parties who will be affected by this decision. Open communication is essential. Discuss the situation with Mark, the remaining staff members, his customers, and senior management. By keeping surprises to a minimum, others will likely respond according to your lead.

This will be a difficult and trying time for everyone. Following your heart does not make you a weak leader. Reassure others that various emotions are only natural during such tense and uncertain times. This may be a time when you will learn to support each other the most. Mark may be your greatest strength.

CURES

Mark has come to you with a very personal request. He wants to continue working despite his weakening condition. While he may not be able to maintain his previous production levels, keeping him involved at a level he can handle is important to his emotional and physical well-being. Therefore, it is also important to you. Say yes to his request; find a way to make it work. Make sure that everyone is working together to make this happen. Communicate frequently with all parties involved so that you are aware of each person's feelings, and the effects of a constantly changing situation.

Have a conversation with Mark.

For Mark, his self-worth and identity may be directly connected to his contributions at work. Denying his continued employment would be tantamount to saying he wasn't worth anything anymore. While it may be an inconvenience for you, it seems a small sacrifice to give with a tremendous amount of rewards to be received.

Mark, I do want you to continue working as long as you can and as much as you are able. If you want to work part-time or flex-

ible hours, just let me know. Perhaps you can work on special assignments at home. I appreciate your honesty and ability to talk about this. I hope that you will continue to keep me informed. On those days that you might not feel as perky, don't worry; we can manage. In fact, if you'd like, we may want to consider combining your accounts with Ann (or whomever is a logical choice to cross-train) *so that if you are not available one afternoon, someone that is here will be familiar with your accounts. What do you think about working together with Ann?*

What is important here is that Mark feels his contributions are still important and meaningful. If he seems hesitant about sharing the accounts, then follow his lead. Perhaps you can be the one (for the short term) to fill in during his absences. Again, this will depend upon your schedule and the overall work distribution.

Ideally, everyone would make some concessions and help out so that no one person is overburdened. Realistically, this may not be possible. Instead, there may just be one or two individuals who feel the bulk of the sacrifices. Do the best you can to make the necessary adjustments. Find a way to make it work.

Have a conversation with the staff.

Assuming that the staff will voice resentment or reluctance is premature. Talk openly and honestly about the situation with them. Stay mindful of their feelings as well as the effects this decision will have on their workloads. The most important thing is to keep them informed of what is going on.

As you know, Mark has asked to continue working as long as he is able. I have agreed to that request. It seems to be very important to him, so we need to find a way to make it work. We already know that some days are a lot worse for him than others. Gradually, his health will continue to decline and we will see more and more bad days. Do any of you have suggestions on how we can make this work the least disruptively, so that the burden doesn't fall on just one or two people? I know this will be hard on all of us. It may be tough to stay strong, but we must try for Mark's sake.

Listen to their suggestions while guiding the conversation into areas you think are more feasible. You will never know the sacrifices others are willing to make if you don't ask. Remain open and flexible to a solution.

I would be remiss if I pretended that there are never any glitches, however. Some employees may be hesitant about accepting the additional workload and responsibilities without pay. Other employees may be reluctant about having a dying person around the office; this is more a statement of their own fears about death than about helping Mark to feel appreciated and needed. Try your best to work around these obstacles.

Establish boundaries to set the tone. For example:

> *I have already agreed to keep Mark on our payroll full time, even though he will not be able to work 40 hours. Personally, I feel that is the least we can do. We may consider having different sales representatives assigned to different customers, one person being the primary contact and everyone pitching in as they are able. Which of these suggestions seems to be the most workable?*

Have a conversation with his customers.

There may be cause for some of Mark's customers to know what is going on also. This should only be done, however, with Mark's approval. Otherwise, it might compromise his authority and professional image with his customers. If he does not want his customer to know about his condition, then honor that request.

On the other hand, if he provides some conditions or guidelines for engaging in a conversation, then stay within those boundaries. When talking with a customer, you want to make sure that everything is being handled efficiently. You may say something like the following:

> *As you are probably aware, Mark has started working part time because of his health. Other sales representatives are handling his accounts when he is not in. I do not believe you will see any difference in how your account is handled; if you do, please let me know personally. Your business is very important to us and we do not want to compromise this relationship at all. In fact, please call me directly if you see any way we can improve on the service we provide to you. Here is my business card with my direct number.*

This conversation mentions Mark's health without focusing on it. Some customers may feel a closeness to Mark and want to know more about his condition. If he has asked that you not give details, say that to the customer. *"Mark has asked that I not talk about the specifics of his illness. I am sure you will appreciate and respect his need for privacy."* Most customers will respect his request.

Have a conversation with senior management.

Senior management also needs to be aware of the situation and how you propose to handle it. Some companies will respond more compassionately than others, just as some individuals are more understanding and caring.

If compassion and concern is offered by senior management, it is still important that it be kept informed about his condition and the changes you are recommending. However, if senior management is primarily concerned about the bottom-line results, it may appear cold-hearted, inflexible, or indifferent. Finding the middle ground during these times can be more challenging. Never defy the employer, but having its support makes your job a lot easier.

> *One of my sales representatives, Mark, has been diagnosed with terminal cancer. His condition is gradually getting weaker. Currently, he is unable to work a 40-hour week. He has asked to continue working as long as we will let him, and I have agreed. I think that it is great that he still wants to work. Even though he is not able to maintain his previous production levels, other employees have shown a willingness to step in and help out whenever necessary. I realize that I cannot hire someone to replace him yet, and I want to find a way to make this work. It seems the least we can do for him.*

Hopefully management will agree and support your decision; it is unlikely that it would actually disallow it. Management may simply let you be, and not provide any support. Do the best you can with what you have, and be thankful management is not interfering with your plans.

Chapter Summary

A woman's need to be connected allows her to respond to these interruptions in a more positive manner. Women encourage working through personal problems no matter when they occur, whereas men prefer setting them aside during business hours. *Businessmen* often consider women's outward signs of concern at work as a weakness, and as professionally inappropriate.

Personal traumas can interrupt your office, cause added tension and panic, and create jealousy among the staff. On the other hand, these personal traumas can also bring staffs closer together, creating a cohesive, caring, and trusting department, and allowing employees to become stronger through the process. It is a matter of how you handle and communicate the situation that will dictate the response from other employees.

Accepting that personal problems may affect your work routine is very different from inviting them into the workplace. They are already there. Acknowledging feelings does not create more. Your role will be to make life the least disruptive while these outside occurrences run tangential to work. It will not be an easy task, but the long-term rewards will be worth the effort.

Many professionals consider it inappropriate to show emotion in the office. Emotions are a natural part of each of us, despite society's attempt to direct when we should show certain emotions and when we should not. By accepting emotions you are accepting the pain a person is feeling as well as valuing the individual. Showing emotions is not a weakness, but instead a strength, and women's style of leadership has been praised in many professional circles as one that elicits balance. Accepting that the employees have a personal life will win you their respect.

Working mothers experience a multitude of obstacles that are often not faced by working fathers. Fathers are not generally the ones taking children to dental appointments, staying home with sick babies, or finding available and affordable childcare. The majority of households still consider this as the role of a mother. Times are changing, but the balance has not been reached yet.

Many of these feelings leave working mothers filled with guilt for not being home with the child, for having to leave a child with a daycare provider, for having to work late some evenings. Guilt has many different guises and many different roots. What happens when the child hates a particular sitter? The mother must still go to work; whether or not she is forced to economically or chooses to, she still must leave the child. Often this leaves a working mother torn between wanting to pursue her personal career and trying to raise a family.

When you suspect guilt may be overtaking an employee's emotions, talk openly with her to see how she is dealing with this situation. Making a working mother feel that she must choose her career over her family is adding to the problem, not solving it. Family is—and should be—first in her heart and mind. Integrating the two may be impossible for some employees. Juggling is more apt the reality, not integrating. By helping the staff to juggle their priorities, you will gain their respect and appreciation.

Troubleshooting Your Own Personal Problems

Overview

Women experience different problems when they manage than men do. Few men (although the numbers are growing) are responsible for even half of the household duties, including childrearing, yet most women work full time outside the home as well as inside the home. Women are still limited by the glass ceiling, something men rarely experience, have childbirth issues, and are more susceptible to clinical depression.

Women have used these experiences to become stronger leaders. They have learned to juggle their roles as they wear many hats simultaneously, going from peacemaker, to chef, to banker, and disciplinarian within minutes. Prioritizing, organizing, and learning how and when to say no can reduce the stress, eliminate the guilt, and allow each woman to fulfill her dreams and ambitions. These are qualities that create strong leaders.

This chapter addresses the following problems, possible causes, and cures.

4.1 The Problem: The day-to-day pressures of the job are getting to you.

Possible Causes: Stress can originate from a variety of sources; minimize or eliminate stress factors; personal problems may be consuming your energy and focus; realize when there is not enough time for you.

Cures: Manage stressful lifestyles; identify stressors and improve organizational skills; have reasonable expectations; take care of yourself.

4.2   *The Problem: You want a career, but your family doesn't want you to work.*

Possible Causes: Competing careers may be an issue; don't try to be a modern-day superwoman; unresolved issues may lead to guilt.

Cures: Handle competing careers; understand the myth of the superwoman femme fatale; it would be nice to live guilt-free.

4.3   *The Problem: You are going through a bad divorce that is affecting your work schedule and job performance.*

Possible Causes: The causes are not what is at issue; instead how you handle the pressures and priorities can prove more meaningful.

Cure: Handle the pressures from divorce.

4.4   *The Problem: Your exhusband has gotten remarried and decided to file for custody of your children.*

Possible Cause: Focus on the response.

Cure: Don't penalize the working mother.

4.5   *The Problem: The school called you to pick up your sick child, today of all days!*

Possible Causes: Inflexible company policies penalize working mothers; children do get sick; you fear career limitations.

Cures: Work around policy obstacles; Anticipate common childhood illnesses; don't overreact.

4.6   *The Problem: You have a personal interest in the boss, and the feelings are mutual.*

Possible Causes: What might others think?; your goals and feelings may be in conflict; the company policy may implicitly or explicitly censor such personal conduct.

Cures: Know the image factor; what do you really want?; how much are you willing to risk?

4.7 **The Problem: A colleague made verbal attacks against you and the department, and you became very emotional in your response.**

Possible Causes: There are gender differences for how men and women play these games; others may not feel comfortable dealing with emotions at work; the lack of a support system can add to the frustration that you feel; your health and physical condition may be adding to the situation.

Cures: Know the gender rules, especially during conflict; understand acceptable emotions in the workplace; create a support system; monitor your health.

4.8 **The Problem: Your daughter calls you at work and asks that you come home early tonight, but you can't.**

Possible Causes: Children's demands can add guilt when you can't meet them; your priorities may be in conflict.

Cures: Juggle the mother/career roles; know your priorities and set boundaries.

4.9 **The Problem: Morning sickness is affecting your daily work routine. You are tired, nauseated, and very pregnant.**

Possible Cause: Separate those things you control from those you do not.

Cures: Manage your pregnancy carefully.

4.10 **The Problem: You are having a hot flash during a managers' meeting.**

Possible Causes: Know how to handle yourself; understand stereotypes that label women inferior; menopause is a reality of life.

Cures: Ease the awkward tension; break the stereotypes; know your medical and nonmedical options.

Whether you are going through a divorce, custody case, menopause, or a complicated pregnancy, your ability to respond to the situation will be watched and scrutinized by many. Women are faced with overextending themselves more than men. It is often a matter of knowing your priorities, knowing what you will and will not do, and creating boundaries within that zone. It is never an easy process; but it is one where you capture control of your own life.

4.1 The Problem: The day-to-day pressures of the job are getting to you.

THE SCENE

It's Friday morning, and the week has been a total disaster. Actually, you could say not a lot has gone right this past month; nothing has happened according to plan. Problems have been popping up where you least expected them. You feel yourself becoming very tense and frustrated with the smallest detail. Added to this pressure is the fact that you are operating short-staffed.

An employee who was working on a major report for you to present, called in sick today. The package is incomplete and copies need to be made by noon. You are not sure where all the information is so that you can even finish the report in time.

Anxiety is mounting. You feel absolutely drained. Are you the cause of this anxiety? Do you have a bad attitude? Are you a bad manager? Are you overworked? Underpaid? Short-staffed? Exhausted? Is it time for a vacation? Or perhaps you need a change of pace?

To ease tension that is caused by stress try:

1. physical activity;
2. talking to others about the situation;
3. scheduling time for yourself;
4. reducing your own personal expectations and goals;
5. finding some quiet place to relax.

Creating realistic expectations is another good solution for managing stress. You may be hardest on yourself, so learn to cut yourself some slack.

POSSIBLE CAUSES

Stress can originate from a variety of sources.

Work can be one cause; in fact, it is often a major cause of stress. Each person has a different level of stress that she can comfortably manage. Each person also shows signs of stress differently. Too much stress may produce symptoms such as being tired, irritable, overeating, lack of appetite, sleeplessness, crankiness, or short-temperedness. Getting away may not be such a bad idea, but only if the you are able to identify and control the stressors. Otherwise, when you return to work the cycle picks up where you left off.

Minimize or eliminate stress factors.

Before you can reduce the stress from certain situations, you must be able to identify those stressors that you control. If you cannot control something, you cannot change it. Your organizational skills, or lack of them, may also be contributing to the stress that you are feeling. If you wait until the last minute to complete projects, you may be disorganized, a procrastinator, or just not like what you're doing (or where you are working). By finding the sources of stress, you can identify your options more clearly.

Personal problems may be consuming your energy and focus.

Work may not be the most important thing in your life; frequently it isn't. You may be concerned with issues such as health, finances, or family which demands your attention and causes work to suffer. Do not feel like a failure because you find it difficult to concentrate during working hours; instead try to find out why you are distracted.

Realize when there is not enough time for you.

When is there ever enough time for you? Being in top physical and emotional health translates into a healthier work environment. If you are not taking care of yourself, everything else suffers. Work is not immune. If you are scheduled too thin with everyone wanting a piece of your time, you may be too overwhelmed to do anything well. Just being able to say *"no"* without feeling guilty is a start for some women. Pace yourself according to your own abilities, otherwise you'll find yourself lacking the energy to continue at any speed, much less a productive one.

CURES

Manage stressful lifestyles.

Stress is a fact of life. You cannot alleviate all stress, nor should you try. Stress is not the problem; how you handle it is. The ability to manage stress is individual; each person has his or her own comfort levels of stress. Beyond those limits, each person responds differently, depending on other contributing factors.

When stress is the underlying problem, it can lead to many other conditions (both physical and emotional) when left untreated. Individuals typically respond to excessive stress by one of three methods: alarm, resistance, or exhaustion. Watch for the early signs of these areas. If you see them coming on, be willing to respond immediately.

Caving into the pressures of stress is not a weakness! It is not a hormone fluctuation; it is not gender specific. Excessive stress is a by-product of our fast-paced culture. For women it often manifests from the many demands being placed on them between family and work.

Identifying how much stress you can comfortably manage is the first step. Know your own limitations, otherwise you will find yourself extended beyond your abilities—and do nothing well.

A vacation may or may not be a good solution. If this is a temporary situation, or you typically have a high level of stress, but have reached your limits, then you may want to get away for awhile. This can be a time to regroup, and come back rejuvenated. Realize though, that things may be the same when you return. While your stress threshold may be high, the situation may not have changed.

Identify stressors and improve organizational skills.

Identifying those things that cause you stress is the first step in managing it. Work to change those things that you can, and accept those things that you cannot change. For example, while you cannot change an event, you can change how you respond to the event. And finally, be sure that you are not adding to the problem by having poor organizational skills.

When you feel overwhelmed, create a list of things that cause you stress, frustration, or anxiety. This may include work, workers, interruptions, family, traffic, unrealistic demands, projects, personal problems, your health, financial hardships, children, aging parents, and so forth. Continue rewriting the list, becoming more and more specific about the stressful situation each time. What is it about your work that causes you stress? What is it about your aging parents that adds stress to your life? Individually each of these problems may be manageable; you may be overwhelmed by the cumulative effects.

Next, separate the list into those things that you have some level of control over and those that you do not. This process may take some time so keep the list handy and work through it for several days. Since this is the most important step, give yourself plenty of time. For example, if this is an unusually stressful week (or month), do you see things getting any better at some point? Or are these stresses the result of permanent adjustments you must make? If you feel the pressure because you are short-staffed, is someone on vacation or out sick, or are these the effects of a corporate downsizing to which you must permanently adapt? If you are frustrated by the many interruptions you have during the day, can you remove any of these interruptions and still get your work done?

Identifying items that are under your control is often difficult because many of the situations causing stress may be a combination of both. Continue to rewrite your list, being more detailed about specific events or situations. *Wherever possible, isolate those parts of a situation that you control and those portions that you are unable to control.*

For example, you cannot control when someone calls in sick, but you can control the basic flow of the department by having employees cross-trained. You cannot control how others will receive your presentation, but you can control how *you* feel about the presentation including how thoroughly you researched the information and the professional manner in which you present it. You cannot control the fact that your parents are aging, but you can control how much time you can give to them. Let's say your mother is in a nursing home because of failing health. She had picked a nursing home in her hometown where her friends are, but she does not have family there. The nursing home is an hour and a half drive away from you and you are the closest family member to her. You may consider moving her closer to you, even though it is more expensive. As you review this list, it may become more clear why you are so exhausted. Its size may be enough to overwhelm anyone.

Now that you have the list separated, look closely at those things that you are unable to control. Then tell yourself to *let them go*, to forget about them, to bury them somewhere else. The energy you exert on problems you cannot control is wasted energy, and right now you do not have any energy to waste! Don't expect things to change overnight; this takes time and a lot of practice.

Concentrate instead on the list that you *can* have some control over. Prioritize each item, and realize that not everything will be a top priority. Then start with the top three, and only the top three. Create a very specific plan about how you can tackle or begin improving these situations. Once these have been implemented, solved, and worked, then continue working your way down the list according to its priority. This is the beginning of building a framework that is realistic and within your control. Learn not to sweat the small stuff, but instead to exert your energy where it has the greatest need and impact.

Writing these lists will not make the problems go away. Those items beyond your control may continue to create turmoil in your life. When this happens, and you've reached your personal boiling point, then you need to find other outlets to release the pressures such as a vacation, a walk in the park, a hot bath, a massage, or physical activity.

The second step is to access your contributions to the total problem. Are you adding to a busy, hectic schedule by not being organized? Are you taking on more projects than you can handle? Do you add pressure to the situation by not allowing sufficient time to complete projects properly, and then find yourself panicked as the deadline approaches? If so, there are a lot of self-help programs available, depending on your specific needs.

As a manager, organizational skills also entail what it is you are doing versus what it is you are supposed to be doing. Women have a tendency to help out more with the details. Often they find themselves doing basically two jobs: one as manager, one as worker. Be careful to avoid this trap because it only adds pressure to an already full agenda.

To find more time for yourself, learn how to delegate. It is not enough to turn a project over to an employee if you are going to monitor his or her every move. Accept how someone else will do the job and know that it will be different from how you would have done it. It may be better or not as good, but it will never be the same as you would have done. Good managers are good delegators.

Have reasonable expectations.

Personal problems will affect your life just as they do other employees. Personal problems come into the office no matter how hard you try to keep them away. You may be unable to focus on work; instead your mind may be consumed with what is going on in your life.

Feeling bad because you cannot concentrate on work only adds to the problem. Instead, set reasonable expectations, goals, and boundaries. Even with these set, there needs to be room for flexibility and unusual circumstances. Allow some room for the unexpected, it always happens.

Try to pinpoint what is going on in your life that makes concentrating on work so difficult. Once you have identified it, you may find it helpful to talk to your supervisor about this situation. Sharing this information may allow some leeway, depending on the individual circumstances and your boss. Talking to superiors can also backfire; some companies expect 100% concentration from employees and have no tolerance toward personal problems coming into the office. When this happens, the risk to you includes that you may be penalized or looked upon as a weak manager for not being focused totally on your job. If the situation entails too much risk, do what you comfortably can do.

When you are unable to function properly at work, and the situation does not allow you to share your concerns, try to take some time off. Time away from work can help you rejuvenate yourself. If vacation time is not an option, do the best you can and hope that other problems get resolved soon so that you can focus your attention back toward work issues.

Take care of yourself.

Taking care of yourself may well be an underlying solution in all of the above causes. Its omission may be more of a casualty or symptom of the various situations that impact your life. Women (as caregivers and nurturers) often give to everyone else around them, and find themselves too exhausted to take time for their own needs. There are not 25 hours in a day or 8 days in each week—those are things you cannot change.

Make time for yourself. This is essential to your well-being (mental, emotional, and physical) as well as to those around you. If you are not strong, you will be the weakest link in your chain. When you become the weakest link, you can be the source of many problems that occur including getting sick, being short-tempered, irrational, and not thinking clearly or not putting things in their proper perspective.

The solution is actually rather simple. Schedule your time just like you do other appointments. This is not being selfish; it is preventive medicine. It is something that you cannot afford to do without. Whether you enjoy walks in the park, reading a good book, meditation, a massage, a hot bubble bath, or listening to a concert, make the time to do something special for yourself. Then honor that appointment like you do all other appointments. By honoring that appointment, you are saying how important your own well-being is to the equation. You are special. Now it is time to treat yourself like that special person you are.

4.2 The Problem: You want a career, but your family doesn't want you to work.

THE SCENE

Your husband recently got a promotion. Now his career demands are causing more problems; scheduling conflicts are being felt with greater frequency. His job is full of many last-minute changes and unexpected meetings. It is not easy for you to change your schedule at the last minute either. Doctors' appointments have been canceled because he had a last-minute business meeting he needed to attend. Children have been left waiting to be picked up after school because he forgot it was his day to drive. Everyone is beginning to feel the tension.

Your husband has asked you to stay home with the children. Even your children want you to stay home. You are not sold on the idea, and resent being asked.

You feel torn; you enjoy your career, but there is a part of you that would like to be at home with the children, to be like your mother was for you. However, you do not want to be the sole parent responsible for childrearing duties, and that is what is being asked of you. After your first child was born, you wanted to stay home for a few years but that choice was not financially available. It was less of an option after your second child was born. As your career began to gain momentum, work became emotionally satisfying and stimulating; it became an extension of who you are.

The financial constraints are no longer a consideration. Now it is a personal choice. You have worked very hard to achieve your current status; your professional future looks promising. Money isn't your primary objective; your career may not bring the financial successes that your husband's career provides.

It seems unfair that you are asked to make all the concessions. There is a part of you that wants to spend more time with the family, especially while the children are young. You are just not sure how to have both a family and career and be guilt-free.

POSSIBLE CAUSES

Competing careers may be an issue.

Your husband may feel threatened in his role as provider for the family. He may not want you to have a successful career that conflicts with his. He may expect you to be the primary caregiver and nurturer, as traditional roles have defined it. It is important that both you and your husband communicate effectively and agree on each other's roles and priorities.

Don't try to be a modern-day superwoman.

Career and family demands can often pull you in opposite directions. Add other people's expectations to these roles, and you quickly see why it is impossible to live up to everyone's image. It may be impossible to live up to your own expectations and images, leaving you instead feeling like a failure in both roles. When you look around, it appears that other women are managing these demands better than you do. Remember, though, that superwoman is just a myth.

Unresolved issues may lead to guilt.

When children feel neglected they can create mountains of guilt for women to climb over. Your desire to stay at home versus wanting to have a career may be a reaction from your personal feelings and insecurities. For example, you may equate your worth and success to career status and accomplishments. This may be a residual affect from a poor parent-child relationship that you had. You may feel guilty for not being home when your child gets off the school bus, and you may feel guilty for enjoying your career. For some women, the idea of staying at home full time raising a family is not enough. Staying at home does not fulfill their personal goals and, when forced to stay at home, these women are miserable. These women are not bad mothers for having these feelings; fathers are able to balance the two roles all the time.

CURES

Handle competing careers.

Some men feel threatened by the success of their mates. These successes may signify changes they do not want to accept. Changes in lifestyles, changes in time and attention, and changes in attitudes. You may no longer be willing to perform the domestic chores that you once did. You may no longer have dinner waiting on the table when he arrives home from work. You may expect him to share equally in duties and responsibilities around the home, including parenting.

Your husband may have a traditional concept of family roles or he may be threatened by your career development and the unknown changes that it entails. Communicating feelings, fears, and reservations is crucial to resolving this issue. There is no right or wrong answer to this problem. Each person must negotiate and decide on comfortable roles and boundaries, unique to him or herself and the situation.

Women have the right to choose. If they choose to stay at home, that is not less valued than if they choose to work outside of the home. It is important that both you and your husband agree on these roles, how to resolve scheduling conflicts, juggling career and family demands, and setting priorities.

A conversation with your husband might go something like:

> *I'd like to talk about what we are each willing to give to make this household work. I know you want me to stay at home with the kids. But right now I am not willing to give up my career. And I think it is unfair for you to ask that of me. I believe that if we both make compromises for our family, everyone can win.*

Compromises do not necessarily mean equal concessions. They simply mean that you both agree on certain rules and boundaries. For example, society continues to place the onus of childrearing responsibilities on mothers. Corporate philosophies and policies reinforce this stereotype by providing and encouraging maternity leave, while few offer equal paternity absences. However, you may reach a compromise that requires more shared childrearing duties (including taking the children to after-school functions, lessons, games, or appointments) while you continue to be primarily responsible for all meals.

Family should be first for both you and your husband. This is not always the case. Nor do all parents aspire to have these roles shared equally. Ultimately, both you and your spouse must reach an agreement about family issues. Whatever you both decide, the important thing is to create open and honest dialogue, and to agree mutually.

Talking may not solve all the issues. Third party mediation may be helpful when you are unable to reach a compromise: For instance, you believe in completely shared roles, and your husband believes that you alone should shoulder certain responsibilities. This could come in the form of a marriage counselor, a church minister, or a trained mediator. Share feelings honestly so that an understanding can be reached; if not, the resentment that continues to build inside could lead to even greater problems down the road.

Understand the myth of the superwoman femme fatale.

Being a mother is a full-time job. Working outside the home may have to be your second career. Feeling torn between these two demanding roles, and being exhausted is not at all uncommon for working mothers today.

The media continues to portray women successfully playing multiple roles without complications. The role of wife, mother, friend, lover, and manager seems to work in sync for these superwomen-type femme fatales. You feel like you are letting family and friends down because you aren't like these other superwomen that you see.

Instead, you are left juggling these demanding roles, trying desperately to keep your chin above the water just to survive. In order to achieve a more balanced lifestyle, focus on what you want to achieve. Determine your own set of priorities; don't let anyone else create them for you. You are the one who has to live with these decisions. Therefore, you are responsible for creating them, accepting them, and implementing them.

Finding balance means setting boundaries. Know exactly what you will and will not do given a particular set of circumstances. For example, you may set a boundary by knowing you will not work overtime because of your family demands. While your inability to work extended hours could be a hindrance for career advancements (in some industries), it is still your choice.

Sacrifices are not always easy. You may choose to pursue a career at home, that allows you to spend more time with your family while continuing to work. You may find a company that allows its employees to telecommute, and only come into the office one or two days a week. A pay cut may be an option for reduced work hours, or you may look at starting your own home-based business with the experience and talents you have already gained. Again, it is a matter of finding and reaching a comfortable place for you.

Look inside yourself to find what being a mother means to you. Your circumstances are unique to you. Your stamina is unique to you. Your expectations and personal ability to juggle will also play largely into this equation, as will the feelings of your family. Everything combined together will help you create the role and demands of what being a mother is for you and your family.

It would be nice to live guilt-free.

For many women, unresolved issues are deeply entrenched in their personas. These are buried under layers and layers of life's experiences and traumas, with guilt often the common thread.

Whether guilt comes from trying to win one or both parent's approval throughout your youth or from a childhood tragedy, or whether it comes from an abusive relationship, low self-esteem, or an abundance of self-doubt, guilt can eat away at the fabric of your being and can weaken your courage.

Uncovering these layers of unresolved issues does not happen overnight; nor did they occur overnight. There are probably years of practice and pain that encompass your current feelings. However, just because the process of recovery may be slow and the journey painful, does not mean that you should avoid it.

While it may be impossible to live life completely guilt-free, guilt should not overwhelm and smoother you. When it does, it is time to seek help.

Professional help can assist you through the layers of guilt and lead you to becoming a stronger person. Find someone you are comfortable with, someone recommended by a friend, clergy member, or doctor, then let the healing begin. Make sure that during this healing process, you are extra kind to yourself. Schedule some time to do something that you enjoy like a movie, shopping, a walk in the park, or bird watching. Have a great time; you deserve it!

4.3 | The Problem: You are going through a bad divorce that is affecting your work schedule and job performance.

THE SCENE

After sixteen years of marriage, your husband has filed for a divorce. Your marriage ended abruptly and with great bitterness; you still cannot believe this is happening. As manager, your current position puts additional demands on your time and energy, both of which are in limited supply right now.

Being a single parent is placing a great financial burden on you as well, not to mention the disruption to the lives of the children. You really do not want to sell the house, but you know you will be forced to. It is the only home they have known. The attorney fees are putting you in an immediate cash bind, even though in all likelihood he will have to reimburse you, that doesn't pay the bills today. It looks like it will be a long time before you reach a settlement.

This is the busiest time of the year at work. You are feeling torn between your own personal needs and giving of yourself to the staff and the company. Vacation time has already been used this year, so any time off would be without pay. You cannot afford to take time off without pay right now.

POSSIBLE CAUSES

The causes are not what is at issue in this situation; instead, how you handle the pressures and priorities can prove more meaningful.

Divorce can produce many other problems for you to address such as stress, financial hardships, self-doubt, or single-parenting. Having a plan and understanding these hardships will go a long way in providing you peace.

CURES

Handle the pressures from divorce.

Going through a divorce, especially when it becomes a bitter divorce, can be trying and exhausting for the most organized person. There are several steps you can take to get a better handle on the situation. If you do not already have an attorney, that will be your first step. Find an attorney who has a record of winning cases like yours. You may also want to see if the company will allow more flexible hours for you, maybe even working part time from your home, without docking your pay. This will be dependent upon the nature of your job, the number of employees you manage, and the company's policy for being flexible and telecommuting. It never hurts to ask.

Pace yourself during these stressful times. It may be impossible to maintain your previous standards because your mind is elsewhere. Do not expect too much from yourself. Being inwardly gentle and kind is not selfish; it is building strength and stamina for the long days ahead.

Avoid feelings of guilt. Guilt only adds additional anxiety to your full plate, and accomplishes nothing useful. Finding fault is often used as a defense mechanism, a distraction from the hurt you are feeling from the past. A much better and healthier approach is to concentrate on your present and future life. You cannot change the past; it is behind you now.

Throughout this process (either a bad marriage or an ugly divorce) the victims are often the children. Make sure that both parties agree to keep the best interest of the children as a top priority. This may be difficult, especially when neither party can agree on what is in the children's best interest. Unfortunately, the children are all too often used as pawns; it is a great tragedy when this happens.

Talk to your boss about your situation. This will allow the company to become aware of your preoccupation with issues besides work. At the very least they will know why you are unable to maintain your previous levels of output. Hopefully they will bend rules and provide the support and safety for you that your life currently lacks.

A conversation with your boss might go something like:

> *Things are really quite difficult for me right now. As you know, I'm going through a rather nasty divorce. I suspect it may drag out for awhile. I need for you to be aware of the situation, in case it does affect my job performance. There will be several meetings and*

appointments that I must attend, including with my attorney, and court. Since I've already used my vacation time, I was wondering if we could work something else out. Perhaps I could work from my house a few days a week? This would really help me out a lot, allow me to be home when the children get home, schedule the necessary appointments, and still maintain the same production level.

When you talk to your boss, it is better not to anticipate the response. Creating an expected response in your mind will only lead to disappointments and let downs. Instead, if you talk to senior management for your own benefit, sharing your ideas and being open to their suggestions, then everyone wins.

Seek the professional help that you need. A trained therapist or counselor can help you rebuild your strength and inner self. These are often shredded through the divorce process.

It is also good to stay busy. Too much free time will actually allow feelings of fear and emptiness to grow inside of you. By staying busy your mind is not constantly focusing on the current situation, much of which is comprised of things you cannot control. Even though staying busy is difficult, try. This may be especially true of weekends or times when you are not at work.

Your life has many changes going on right now. Look for something constant to provide the security you need.

4.4 | The Problem: Your exhusband has gotten remarried and decided to file for custody of your children.

THE SCENE

You were served with court papers last week from your exhusband requesting that he be given full custody of the children. He has recently remarried, and his new wife doesn't work outside the home. No outside childcare would be necessary. He is using the fact that you are a single mom with a successful career against you.

The thought of losing custody of your children is very frightening; you have always been active in their lives. Now you feel you are being penalized because of your career. It isn't fair!

POSSIBLE CAUSES

Focus your response.

The causes are not what is relevant. Instead, focus on your response. These types of personal problems can easily interfere with the job. Work may not be very high on your priority list between phone calls and attorney's meetings, and seeking support. It may be rather low because it seems that your career is being used against you right now.

CURES

Don't penalize the working mother.

You are a successful businesswoman. It seems like that would make you a great role model for your children, but some courts have said otherwise. Now you realize that you may actually be penalized because you work outside the home and have to put your children in after-school childcare programs. It is all so unfair.

Keep the children's best interest as your first priority. If you have temporary custody of the children, or shared custody rights, try to be positive and reaffirming in their presence. This may be extremely difficult, but no matter how much of an S.O.B. he is, he is still their father.

Be sure to hire a good attorney who has a record of winning custody cases. While in the past a mother had to be proven unfit to lose custody, today's courts are becoming liberated and are showing more of a willingness to grant fathers custody. A local attorney should know the likelihood of losing custody, given the particular judge you are scheduled to go before, and given the local judicial climate. Be willing to fight hard, play fair, and play to win!

It is important to discuss this situation with your boss. Together you may come up with a creative solution such as flex-hours, reduced work loads, working from home, and so on. that can provide you with more manageable time. This may either be a temporary arrangement or a permanent feature. The company may even be willing to create a new position for you, to accommodate your needs as well as their own. Good employees are hard to find: Do not underestimate your worth to an organization when you have a reputation and track-record. Most companies realize how difficult it is to find quality employees as well as the cost of training; a company may be open to more flexible solutions just to keep you as an employee. You never know unless you ask.

Even if these changes cannot be agreed upon, you still need to advise management of your situation and your potential time-off needs. Let them know early so that scheduling conflicts may be avoided. The more they know, the more they are able to support and accommodate your requests.

Try to be strong during this very difficult period. If you want to work, avoid the feelings of guilt. If you have to work, avoid the feelings of guilt.

This entire situation may make you mentally, physically, and emotionally exhausted. You are under an enormous amount of stress right now. Unfortunately, some times these situations can drag on for years. Section 4.1 offers some excellent advice for managing stress.

For your own well-being, focus on those things that you can control. Playing guessing games will only add stress and zap your energy, neither of which you can afford to lose at the present time. Take a deep breath, take control of the situation, and proceed aggressively to maintain custody. Simply because someone has filed for custody does not mean that he will be awarded custody. Don't concede the battle without a fight.

4.5 The Problem: The school called you to pick up your sick child, today of all days!

THE SCENE

The school just called you to pick up your kindergartener who is sick. She has an ear infection and a fever, on top of catching a cold. Your daycare facility only takes healthy children and there are no relatives that live nearby who can watch her. You must pick up your daughter and stay at home with her today.

It couldn't have come at a worse time. You are scheduled to make your first presentation before the Executive Committee this afternoon. The agenda has already been printed; your absence will be noted by some very influential people. It is a big honor to make a presentation, especially since you have not been in your position very long.

As the only female manager with young children, you anticipate your absence will be held as a mark against you and affect your career. Although not officially, you expect management will find excuses to hold you back. There are few women managers around anyway, and those who have broken through the barriers do not have childcare issues to interfere with their careers.

POSSIBLE CAUSES

Inflexible company policies penalize working mothers.

Changing business attitudes takes time; progress is slowly being seen. Corporate America is beginning to change to meet the needs of working parents (primarily mothers) when it comes to family issues. These problems should not be viewed as penalties or interruptions, yet most companies do not openly embrace them. Change is easier to achieve when you work within a system. Once you have gained experience and a track record, exceptions are more likely to be made. Because you are new, that doesn't mean change is impossible, only harder to create. You should still try.

Children do get sick.

While you cannot be expected to account for every event in your child's life, there are many common occurrences you can anticipate. It is common for children to have colds and other childhood diseases such as chicken pox or the measles. Your lack of planning may be part of the problem. Anticipating these situations would also entail finding back-up childcare provisions. It would be a different situation if the child were extremely sick; but colds, ear infections, or measles are just part of everyday growing up that you should anticipate.

You fear career limitations.

You sense that your future career may be cut short because of this situation, yet there is no such indication or proof to support that notion. Senior management, while not previously faced with these situations, may be open to and understanding of your needs. Your fear that others will look down on your ability to manage may never happen. Management may react according to how you frame the situation. Its response may be supportive if you are focused on your priorities, and communicate them in a positive manner.

Other Considerations: Your husband, the child's father, may not believe that it is his responsibility to stay at home with a sick child. Not all marriages are based on a 50/50 partnership agreement, especially when it comes to parenting or domestic duties. Nor do all couples want it. You may have some resentment about these expectations, especially if it affects your career potential. (If this is the case, see Section 4.2 for more information on competing careers.)

CURES

Work around policy obstacles.

You may find that society's allowances are not the same for working fathers as compared to working mothers. A working father may be praised when childcare issues affect his job duties, perhaps because it happens so infrequently. Yet a working mother continues to be looked down on as if she can't handle the pressures of work and family. For working mothers it becomes a choice; for working fathers it becomes a compliment.

You may be penalized for having to leave work and pick up a sick child. Some companies operate under old, out-dated philosophies that do not accept, respect, or integrate the pressures, reality, and practices of today's working families. Instead, these companies expect work to be the center of your life during working hours, and other "distractions" should be ignored.

If you work for a company that practices such a rigid policy, you may have few choices. But, even limited, you still do have choices. The best way to create change is not to demand it, but to show that it works better when the policy is reflective of the current lifestyle conditions. Fortunately there have been many surveys and papers written about the success of these newer models of managing which openly accept, respect, and integrate family as a priority into the workers' lives. Employees become more effective, productive, and happier, the company becomes more profitable, turnover rates are lower, and everyone wins.

To affect change, you will have to work harder, longer, and better than your colleagues, male and female. More leverage will be given to you once you have proven that you are a reliable, loyal, and conscientious employee. These characteristics take time to establish. Not only must you do a better job, but you also must call attention to the fact that you were the one who did it. The process of change is slow. Small steps add up; never give up a battle without a fight.

If you feel that the probability for change is unlikely, you may want to evaluate your future with this company. While reacting irrationally is not your answer, you must do what is in your best interest. Sometimes, it is best to move on, and not continue beating a dead horse. (See Section 9.7 for learning when and how to say goodbye.)

These are very personal decisions that you must evaluate and decide upon, based on your particular circumstances. Consideration may be given toward how the company views the role of the family. For example, if the company considers you less qualified because of childcare considerations, do you want to continue working there? Are there other career avenues for you to pursue? Is the money and benefits so good at your current position, that you do not mind being held back? How willing is the company to work with you to find a solution?

Chapter 9 also addresses numerous conflicts arising out of policy differences, and how they might be handled.

Anticipate common childhood illnesses.

Children get sick. This is common and to be expected. If you know that your childcare provider only accepts children when they are well, then anticipate this dilemma and find a back-up childcare provider for these situations. It is not a matter of if it will happen, but when it will happen.

Anticipating these illnesses is part of the planning process, and these interruptions require creating back-up resources. While having a back-up sitter should not completely eliminate the chances of a situation affecting your work routine, it should minimize the interruptions. A back-up resource may not be available on a particular day, for a variety of reasons.

Typically when someone is not organized in one area of life, he or she is not organized in others. Being disorganized can be the basis for a lot of stress and anxiety that could be avoided. Do not use the excuse that planning takes too much time; time you do not have. Planning saves time. It is a small investment today in minimizing tomorrow's interruptions. As a woman, mother, and manager, the more you plan, the more time you will have to do what you want to do.

The steps to begin planning are simple. But without consistent practice and follow through, these steps become meaningless. The initial planning stage is what takes the most time—beyond that it becomes a matter of updating various lists.

List writing is a critical factor in being organized. To start getting organized, take four sheets of notebook paper. On the top of each sheet write one of the following: *Projects Working On*, *To Do List*, *Priority To Do List*, and *Troubleshooting*. For the *Projects Working On* sheet, make a list of those projects you are working on (things to which you have already committed your time). Next, take the *To Do List* sheet, and write down those things you need to do (include both personal and business items). Some of the items on this list may not get done today, in fact they may not need to get done for a few days. Extend this list for things to do within the upcoming week.

Take these two lists and prioritize the items for the *Priority To Do List*. List approximate times needed to complete each project or item so that you do not overextend yourself or set unrealistic goals. If something absolutely must get done today, star it as urgent. Then get to it as soon as is possible. Marking off those items you have completed provides a sense of accomplishment. You may find it more helpful to rewrite the *Priority To Do List* each night before you go home. That way, when you arrive in the morning, it is already waiting. This allows you to start each day fresh, focused, and ready to go.

The *Troubleshooting* list is where you anticipate common problems. Start by writing down as many *what if* questions that you can think of. Continue adding to the list, updating and changing it as your needs change. For example: What if your child is sick? What if you got laid off from your job? What if you were sick for an extended period of time? What if you had car trouble? The solutions or plans may include the names of back-up childcare providers who accept sick children; having between three to six months of living expenses in your savings account; a good medical insurance plan (hopefully through work, but if not then you need to purchase one on your own) as well as neighbors or spouse to help with childcare issues; or knowing people with whom you could ride share.

While interruptions may not be eliminated, this list can provide solutions and ideas so that when a situation occurs you are able to respond quicker. This way, you would not lose a lot of energy during a crisis looking for possible solutions. Instead, this preplanning allows you to think through problems without the added pressure of a crisis.

Don't overreact.

Your fear of how management may respond to this interruption may be an overreaction. Management may not react in a negative fashion towards you, instead it may have a great deal of respect and admiration for you because of your personal commitment to your family. It may support your decision, not penalize you for it.

Do not make a mountain out of a molehill. In other words, wait until you are denied promotions before you start worrying about this. If you expect people to respond negatively you are likely to read more into their actions than was intended; you may create the negative response by your own actions. Neither of these situations produce healthy, good work environments. Both would be indicative of miscommunications. There is a difference between being prepared for a response and leading a response, and it is possible to cross the line without even knowing it.

Frequently, management reacts to how you set the stage for them to react. You are the one, in this situation, who can frame responses. In other words, if you feel that you have done something wrong, others may assume that it was a bad decision. Likewise, if you react as if your actions are perfectly acceptable, then the response is more apt to be positive.

4.6 | The Problem: You have a personal interest in your boss, and the feelings are mutual.

THE SCENE

Your position as a sales manager requires a great deal of traveling. Your boss, the regional manager, travels with sales managers to keep a pulse on the customers' needs, as well as to provide support in closing deals. During the past year, you have spent a lot of time traveling with him.

There appears to be a mutual attraction between you and your boss, and unless stopped abruptly by one of you, the relationship will only grow into something much more intimate. You are considering inviting him over for dinner; if you do, it will send a very clear message about your personal feelings.

You are not aware of any company policies against employees fraternizing, but you are worried about how it would look to others. You suspect that the other sales managers may think the relationship has something to do with your reviews, quotas, or raises. Your performance record may be forgotten, especially by those who think that you got the promotion by being on your back. You know this isn't true, but that will not stop those nasty rumors from circulating around the office.

> *Note:* It is natural that feelings may grow and become more than just professional when you spend so much time together, when you have mutual interests, friends, acquaintances, and a mutual respect for one another. Office romances are happening with more and more frequency. How you both handle the relationship is much more important than whether it is supported or encouraged by company policy. Before you begin, go into the relationship with your eyes open, and be aware of all the risks. It is important to establish and agree upon certain boundaries.

POSSIBLE CAUSES

What might others think?

Being involved with your boss may appear unprofessional to the other employees, especially managers. It may have absolutely nothing to do with the manner in which you respond to one another and everything to do with the way others interpret these actions. Unfortunately, this may place the focus away from business topics and on to areas of personal and hurtful gossip. Image can affect your career future; be aware of how others perceive it at all times.

Your goals and feelings may be in conflict.

You may want to have a successful career and a meaningful relationship. However, wanting it all may not be a possibility; instead you may need to make choices and sacrifices between your personal and professional lives. This particular relationship may hinder your career; are you willing to take a detour for the possibility of finding love? What will you do if (or when) the personal relationship ends? Will it be difficult to continue working for someone whom you have dated? Will he expect more from you to avoid appearing lenient? Are you willing to do more just to avoid these false perceptions? Will you consider transferring to another department to continue the relationship, or to distance yourself from personal feelings?

The company policy may implicitly or explicitly censor such personal conduct.

It may be that you are not aware of the company's policy or feelings because they haven't been tested. Even if the company is against this practice, it may not hamper your feelings. You still want to know the company's position on such practices, so that your choices and decisions are informed ones. The company may actually disapprove and reprimand such behavior through actual policy restrictions. Knowing that your actions have repercussions is important when deciding upon your next step. Section 9.2 deals with a similar situation from a policy conflict position.

CURES

Know the image factor.

Image sends many messages about you: positive, negative, professional, casual, conservative, personal. Image includes your words and actions, your tone and mannerisms, as well as your physical characteristics, including how you dress. It is your total packaging. Image is as much a perception as it is a reality; you contribute to it, but ultimately, it is what someone else perceives it to be that is important. The image you create can secure or nullify opportunities for you, both professionally as well as personally.

Your professional presence may be either improved or hurt by how you handle this situation. First determine how this relationship might be received by others, and how you will handle any fallout, should it occur. For example, your boss may be harder on you to avoid any illusion of preferential treatment; you may find you resent the fact that he expects more from you. You may think that it isn't fair, and you're right. Fairness isn't always the issue. The question then becomes: Are you willing to work harder for the same rewards, just to maintain a personal relationship with your boss?

Even though there are personal feelings and though you may be involved, it is better to keep your personal relationship out of the office. In this situation you must be willing to forego those momentary glances during business hours, not engage in sweet talk on the off-chance that it might be overheard, and not plan your personal getaways during work time. Keep your private life private. Plan ahead how you will react to each other at company social events like the Christmas Party or summer picnic. A transfer may be requested by either of you, to eliminate the perception of impropriety. It is advisable to let upper management know what is going on, to prevent any sudden surprises that are frequently not well received.

All these decisions contribute to your image. Decide on how to handle them *before* the relationship gets clouded by misinterpretations. You may decide that it is not worth the risk. If so, try to distance yourself but still remain professional. Avoid situations that may lead you down a path that you do not want to go.

Ultimately, the decision to continue or end the relationship is one between two consenting adults. There is no absolute best plan for everyone to follow. It is more a matter of knowing the risk, accepting the responsibility, establishing the boundaries, and communicating the feelings. The more you decide before you plunge forward, the easier the steps become.

What do you really want?

Sometimes goals and feelings collide, no matter how much you try to avoid the conflict. There may be little that you can do except respond to the situation, and minimize the effects.

To determine if goals and feelings are on a collision course, you must know what it is you want. First identify your goals, both personal and professional. Ask yourself questions like: Where do you want to be in three years? In five years? Do you want to continue pursuing your career? Are you happy at this particular company? Would you like to marry and have a family? What do you see as your role in parenting? If you have the option, do you still want to work once you have children?

Review your answers to get a sense of your goals. Then look at your feelings. Are they consistent with your goals? If not, try to identify those areas where they collide.

Feelings are often difficult if not impossible to control. You can try to avoid opportunities that allow these feelings to show or become more intense; although it may be impossible to escape all of them (especially if you must travel together).

Next, try to evaluate the consequences of what pursuing this relationship may be for you, your boss, both of your careers. Could this relationship interfere with your career goals? If so, are you willing to risk it? Deciding if the risk is worth the reward is a personal judgment call. You are either comfortable or not comfortable with the possible outcomes.

One of the hardest issues to resolve is when you perceive that a relationship is not in your professional best interest to pursue, but you still feel drawn to it. This may be a time when your heart and your head disagree. Your heart may show strong feelings that cannot easily be denied, while your head may say that it could be very damaging to your professional future. Are you willing to accept the sacrifices that may be associated with your choice? The decision is up to you.

How much are you willing to risk?

When people spend a lot of time together with so many connecting bonds, it stands to reason that personal feelings may intensify. The result has been more and more relationships emerging within the workplace.

Some companies support the development of personal work relationships among employees. Other companies prohibit employee fraternizing completely. Generally, smaller companies are more tolerant of office romances, although not always. Larger companies that are often trampled with too many rules and policy restrictions to start with, may formally address and restrict such behavior.

When company policies discourage or penalize these relationships, try to avoid pursuing them. It is never advised, suggested, or condoned to go against policy. The consequences could result in termination for one or both parties and make it difficult to continue on your career path.

Realizing that emotions are not easily turned on and off, you may not feel you have a lot of control over your feelings. This is a choice you must make. These are responsibilities you must own up to, and consequences you must accept. In this scenario a relationship has not officially started. It may be easier to avoid, and should never be encouraged.

Decide how much risk you are willing to take, along with the consequences and responsibility for your actions. Keep your eyes open as you proceed.

You may decide to look for employment elsewhere if the risk is too great. You may also decide to discuss this situation with your superiors, so that if they choose to make an exception they may. If an exception is to be made, it is their choice, not yours. Discussing this situation with senior management is showing that you are loyal to the company, that you respect its policy even though you may not agree with it, and that you want to remain straightforward and honest. The consequences may not change, but you can still maintain this posture.

What If: You are attracted to a subordinate? While it shouldn't change the basic scenario, it does present a peculiar problem. The perceptions are not the same, and it could more easily impede your career options. While the same may not be true for your male colleagues, your professional presence is more likely to be damaged. Look around, are there other couples who have broken this mold? If so, what were their consequences, if any? Are you willing to take that risk? How different was their situation? Try to avoid this situation if at all possible, but emotions are not easy to control. While it shouldn't be different, society still views this role as less acceptable.

What If: One or both of you are married (to other people)? Moral issues are often comingled in work lives. Companies handle these issues differently, from ignoring personal lifestyles so long as the work gets done to firing one or both employees for such actions. These actions are much more likely to damage your professional image, sending the message that your personal feelings are more important than anyone or anything else. Still it happens. And it happens with more and more frequency. Once again, feelings often develop, innocently and without warning. Proceed very cautiously, realizing that there are a lot of people who may get hurt, including you.

4.7 The Problem: A colleague made verbal attacks against you and the department, and you became very emotional in your response.

THE SCENE

Usually you manage to keep your composure, especially during managers' meetings. Even though the men become very combative in securing their turf, you have always stepped aside and let the boys play their verbal war games. You decided early on that you did not want to participate in their rude and childish behavior. However, that doesn't stop the mudslinging from being thrown in your direction.

At a recent managers' meeting, another manager made a comment about the department that was very brutal and offensive to you. Without realizing what was being said you entered the ring, defending your ground and becoming angrier by the second. You completely lost your composure.

Your actions stunned everyone in the room. They looked at you as if you had gone off the deep end, and were out of control. Someone even referred to you as a *madwoman*. The madder you got, the more you had to fight to hold back tears. As your eyes filled with tears, you quickly left the room. Were these appropriate actions and emotions to show in the office?

POSSIBLE CAUSES

There are gender differences for how men and women play these games.

Quite often the rules are not explained and are decided upon primarily by the men in charge, and you are expected to conform to specific behavior or else pay the consequences. There are some very real differences as to how men communicate with other men during conflict resolution and how men communicate with women, as well as how women communicate with men during these times. When a woman enters the arena, the rules change.

Others may not feel comfortable dealing with emotions at work.

When other people feel uncomfortable with emotions, especially at work, you may be expected to keep them under control. Many professionals still want work to be an emotionless environment; others concede that certain emotions are acceptable while others are not. Acceptable emotions are typically joy, happiness, frustration, and disappointment. Women crying, no matter what the reason, is typically placed into the category of an unacceptable emotional outburst. Emotions often leave the receiver powerless, and since business may be based on a structure of power, those who typically do not show emotion consider these outbursts as weaknesses.

The lack of a support system can add to the frustration that you feel.

Without receiving support you have no one with whom to share your anger or frustration, to lean on for strength, to bounce ideas or misunderstandings off, or from which to learn. The games are played differently, and your priorities may be different from your male colleagues, but that doesn't lessen your contributions. Sometimes you just need to be heard, and support groups are designed to listen. Support groups can be comprised of either your spouse, family, friends, other professionals, and specifically other women. These groups can provide a strong foundation for exploring these issues and help you to stay focused at the same time.

Your health and physical condition may be adding to the situation.

Depending on your age, you may be experiencing hormonal changes and feeling the effects. These are not conditions or weaknesses, but natural reactions the body commonly goes through. However, mood swings, fatigue, or irritability can affect your professional and personal life. Stress can also impact your physical condition and your ability to respond rationally at times.

CURES

Know the gender rules, especially during conflict.

Gender differences in communication continue to present us with challenges. While women prefer the private nature of conversing on more personal topics, men enjoy the public aspects and talking in generalities. These gender differences in communication are magnified when dealing with conflict.

Men and women respond differently when conflict arises. Women would rather avoid conflict than confront it, whereas men will try to control conflict. Part of this control is what leads men to become more aggressive, hostile, or combative during conflict. Neither of these styles are healthy to adapt. It is always better to confront conflict, get it out in the open, create open and honest dialogue, listen and work toward a compromise, or at least find a common ground where the conflict is minimized.

Realize that what goes on in these meetings, while it appears to be haphazard or perhaps malicious, does have some agreed-upon rules between the players. For instance, men may not welcome a female into their game. The rules may specifically exclude you from entering. In other words, their own ignorance or discomfort with acceptable gender roles may be a factor.

To be allowed to play requires skill, timing, fortitude, and luck. No matter how good, competent, or equal you are in other areas, when it comes to confrontational styles, you may not be permitted to play in the same manner as the male colleagues. And they may not be willing to play your way.

Finding neutral territory requires a willingness for all parties to be open to change. Try to talk senior management into offering conflict resolution seminars and training workshops to provide new tools for everyone to learn to manage conflict in a better way.

Understand acceptable emotions in the workplace.

Many professionals continue to believe that emotions have no place at work. This mentality is typically espoused by those who often show little emotion themselves. Since they do not allow their emotions to be a part of their professional presence, they expect the same response from you.

You may or may not agree with this theory; but emotions are at work everyday. It becomes a matter of how you handle these emotions at work, instead of whether you allow them into the workplace.

Some people qualify certain emotions as acceptable work emotions. For example, happiness and joy are acceptable, and even sadness and disappointment are acceptable, within certain limitations. You are allowed to show your disappointment in not getting a promotion, but you are not allowed to carry a grudge, be too vocal, or stay in this mood very long. If you show the acceptable emotions at the appropriate time, then your behavior is less likely to be questioned. Go outside of these confines and your actions may be criticized.

Crying is often excluded from what is considered acceptable emotions in business. It may be because men do not cry as easily, or because crying makes others feel powerless, or because some women (and men) feel it is a weak trait. Whatever the reason, there remains a negative shadow cast over certain emotions more commonly associated with females.

Most businesses continue to discourage certain emotional behavior. Showing such emotions could limit your career opportunities by weakening your professional image according to someone else's perception. While emotions are a normal part of life, and ideally society and business should embrace, accept, and not feel threatened by them, that does not happen in today's business climate. It is important to realize how others may interpret your actions, then proceed with a style that is comfortable to you.

Be willing to stand up for what you believe is unjust. Learn the limits women have placed on them in work environments. If you want to go beyond these boundaries, realize the inherent risk involved. Be strong. Sometimes being right makes for a lonely playing field. And don't forget that management will also reward you on your ability to get along with other managers. So it behooves you to learn the rules of the game for females.

Since each organization is slightly different, observe other women, and learn by their mistakes. Trial and error can be a costly approach, so use it only as a last resort.

Create a support system.

Sharing your feelings with other people can make dealing with these awkward moments much more tolerable. Yet not every woman has a strong foundation of support to share these concerns. Sometimes support systems emerge naturally, other times they must be formed intentionally. Support can come from a variety of sources.

Support often comes from family and friends. Your spouse may be a strong source of support, as well as other family members. Friends can also provide the acceptance and listening you need. However, when support does not exist, these relationships can lead to tension, conflict, confusion, and frustration for you. When it does exist, their support can be shown through acts of appreciation, respect, and admiration for what you do.

If you do not have these support systems already in place, then you can build them. One of the greatest sources of support comes from other women who are experiencing similar types of problems. Share these experiences, build an extensive network, and learn new ways to integrate, juggle, or communicate within business circles.

This solution may not fix the problem, but it does provide a way to express yourself, an opportunity to learn how to play the game, and a chance to be heard. Learning from other women can be an excellent, nonthreatening way to grow. Listen while other women share their experiences in handling confrontation, and the different approaches they have taken.

Monitor your health.

Your physical condition can have a direct correlation on your actions and temperament. Whether you are tired, under enormous stress, depressed, coming down with a cold, or faced with hormonal fluctuations, your body influences and affects your ability to respond.

Many of these physical conditions are more likely to occur in women than in men. Being tired, under enormous stress, and depressed are more representative of women's lifestyles than men's. Women are often tired because of working full time outside of the home as well as inside the home. Women are under more stress from trying to balance work with being a good mother, wife, daughter, and friend. According to the National Institute for Mental Health, approximately 17.4 million Americans (9.5%) suffer from depression in any given year. Women are twice as likely as men to show signs of depression. Hormonal changes are another factor women must consider; you may be overly sensitive or irritable due to normal hormonal imbalances. Whether it is menopause, PMS, pregnancy, or a prescribed drug reaction, these natural body changes happen primarily to females, not males. Therefore, the men who control the board rooms, who do not understand these responses, may consider them to be weaknesses.

Unfortunately, your reactions may be quickly dismissed by male colleagues. This may be their way of exerting power over you. If you believe you may have a hormonal imbalance, see a doctor. There are medications, dietary changes, and vitamin supplements now available that can help alleviate many of these symptoms.

Because physical conditions affect your actions, it is important to be in the best physical condition possible. Sometimes you can eliminate or minimize these conditions; other times they are contagious and must run their course. Take care of yourself. Rest, eat balanced meals, don't overextend yourself, and get plenty of exercise. It's not that you do not have the time to do these things, it is that you cannot afford to *not* do them.

4.8 | The Problem: Your daughter calls you at work and asks that you come home early tonight, but you can't.

THE SCENE

It's late in the afternoon, the phone rings, and it's your daughter. She wants to know what time you'll be home. When you say you'll be late, she is sad and adds guilt by saying "Please come home early tonight mommy. I miss you."

This year she has started staying at home by herself after school. Even though she is mature enough, you still worry. Every afternoon once she gets home, she calls. The thought that your daughter has become a latch-key kid has been difficult to accept. Financially, you have no choice but to continue to work.

You are in the middle of a major project that must be completed tonight, and cannot leave until it is finished. Still, your daughter wants her mom.

POSSIBLE CAUSES

Children's demands can add guilt when you can't meet them.

While the reason for saying *"no"* is legitimate, that may not lessen the amount of guilt you feel. You may fear being perceived as selfish. Because women enjoy nurturing others, the thought of a child wanting her mother can be very fulfilling. The inability to be there can leave you feeling sad, incomplete, or worse—a bad mother. There can be a great deal of anxiety between having to work, wanting to work, and wanting to be home with your child.

Your priorities may be in conflict.

The two major priorities in your life, family and work, may be in opposition to one another at different times in your life. How you manage or juggle these two roles is a very personal decision, often wrought with pain. When you want to stay at home but are forced to work because of financial obligations, then the forces tearing you apart can be felt more strongly. You want to take care of your family, and you want to be home when your child is home, but sometimes both are not possible.

CURES

Juggle the mother/career roles.

Children are vulnerable creatures. Few things can be as comforting as being needed by a child. When she asks that you come home, you want to fulfill her request and leave immediately but you have a career and responsibilities that will not allow that to happen. You have made previous commitments that cannot be ignored. Is it no wonder then that you feel torn and full of guilt?

Children have a way of knowing which buttons to push to complicate the simplest situation. When you cannot meet their requests, they may imply (or you may feel) that you are not being a good mother. This implication can be covert or direct, but either way the result is still guilt.

First, know why you are working. Is it because of financial obligations? Is it because you enjoy the challenge and opportunities of having a career? Is it a combination of both?

If your child is old enough to stay at home alone after school, he or she is old enough to understand about responsibilities and commitments. Your child, too, must learn about responsibilities in life. What a great opportunity to share this lesson.

> *I know that because I work, sometimes the schedule gets in the way of our time together. I hate when this happens as much as you do. But sometimes it cannot be avoided and I must stay late. I have made a commitment to this company that I would do the best job that I can. Sometimes, although not very often, I do have to work late because of special projects and deadlines. It is very important for me that I am thorough and complete in all of the details that my name is attached to. When you promise someone that you will do something, that is your word. It is important that you honor and keep your promise; otherwise, people will not trust you. Then your word becomes empty and meaningless. It is important that before you make a commitment, you know what it involves. Then, when you give your word, know that you will be willing to keep your end of the bargain.*

This conversation may not produce earth-shattering results overnight. But it is one that bears repeating time and time again, when these situations occur. Do not let these feelings turn into guilt. Even if you do not want to work but have to for financial reasons, you must accept the responsibility of these obligations.

Know your priorities and set boundaries.

If family is your primary consideration, develop your career accordingly. Family needs are important; no one denies that. When those needs conflict with work schedules, it is important to know just what you are willing to compromise. Establish boundaries early and communicate those choices to everyone involved.

Do you have a choice in working late? Is this work that could be completed at home, after your child has gone to bed? Or, could you do your project while he or she does homework?

Evaluate your options. Talk to your boss about how to accommodate the company's needs while still maintaining the family as your first priority. One does not have to eliminate the other; they can work together with compromise.

Because you must work late does not mean that family does not still come first in your life. Whether this is an unusual occurrence or becoming more and more routine, you are the one who establishes these boundaries, not someone else. And you are the one who lives within those confines.

Know your limits and your goals. Then realize that sometimes you may have to take a step backward to ultimately move toward your goal. This is not a defeat, nor should it be viewed as one. It is merely a step in the process.

4.9   The Problem: Morning sickness is affecting your daily work routine. You are tired, nauseated, and very pregnant.

THE SCENE

This is your first pregnancy and you are having a rough time. You are having difficulty keeping your previous pace. Not only are you very tired, but nausea seems an everyday occurrence as well. You have had to cancel some staff meetings because you were just too tired to sit and listen, let alone lead the discussion.

Your male colleagues have been less than supportive of your condition. Even some female managers have looked at your condition as a weakness because of these interruptions and adjustments. There has also been resentment because your work schedule has been reduced.

You want to continue working after your child is born and do not perceive a family as a limitation. During a recent manager's meeting, another manager actually said that if you were needing this much flexibility during your pregnancy, it was an indication that you could not handle career demands and family obligations. It was suggested that you should consider stepping down from a management position.

POSSIBLE CAUSES

Seperate those things you control from those you do not.

There are several things going on in this scene simultaneously, including some things you can control and others you cannot. Ultimately the outcome will depend on how you handle those areas you can control and how supportive the company is of family values and considerations.

CURES

Manage your pregnancy carefully.

You are pregnant and are having morning sickness, and must work around these conditions. Medication may help, but it may also impede your ability to concentrate and perform up to your previous levels. There may be times when you can control meetings by rescheduling a time when you feel better. For those meetings in which you are a participant, and are not scheduling the meeting time, you will have less flexibility.

If your pregnancy creates a need for special attention, then follow those needs. Your health is the most important issue; everything else revolves around this. If the fact that you are receiving special attention causes resentment, that is not your problem. You cannot change or control how others respond to a situation. Things are not always equal; that is a reality of life you must accept.

Your body chemistry is something you have little control over. Worrying about it does not help the situation. Focus on those things that you do have some control or influence over, and do not get lost worrying about things that you cannot control.

It is helpful if you can establish a routine for the staff, even if this routine is different from the old routine. For example, if the department meetings used to be held in the mornings, but those are your worst times, schedule meetings later in the day. Work around your body clock, at least while you are pregnant.

If you are flexible treating individuals individually, then there will be more acceptance for your need to change the meeting time. If you have been a hard and fast ruler, following policy procedures closely and allowing little flexibility and few exceptions, then resentment may develop from the staff. When this happens, learn from your experience and be open to a different management style in the future. Understand that exceptions may need to be made from time to time, for a variety of reasons or factors. Share these concerns and insights with the staff. They may welcome the change and support you during this difficult time. You do not have the ability to change the past; you can only learn from the present and work toward a different future.

In addition, your ability to delegate authority and responsibility will be tested during this time. If you have been one who delegates easily, then adapting to a reduced schedule will allow for others to step to the plate, assume more authority, and run the show in your absence. Make sure to give employees their proper rewards and appreciations.

Some women do not feel comfortable delegating. If you have trouble with this, you may feel boxed in trying to manage the department while having complications during your pregnancy. It is to your advantage now as well as in the future to learn how to delegate. Delegation shows other employees that you have faith in their abilities to complete their tasks. It shows your ability to trust someone else. To do this, you must learn to accept that others may do things differently than you might do them, yet still produce acceptable results.

Colleagues who are not going through a similar situation, either male or female, may consider your need for flexibility as a weakness. Stay focused on the department and your needs. Worrying about what others think will do little to change their opinions. Instead, as best you can, let your results speak for themselves. Trying to please everyone is a futile position to be in, a position that can produce confusion, inconsistency, and lack of direction.

4.10 | The Problem: You are having a hot flash during a managers' meeting.

THE SCENE

The meeting has been going on for about an hour, and all at once you feel your blood pressure rising, beads forming on your brow, and intense perspiration all over. You know why; it's those damn hormones. Hot flashes and meetings do not go together very well, as you are finding out.

Everyone looks at you as you take off your jacket. They are aware of what is going on. There are other women in the meeting, but since they are younger they have no idea how embarrassing this is for you. You hear a few snickers, but try to ignore them.

You hate to call attention to the situation but you need to get to the window and get some cool air—quickly.

POSSIBLE CAUSES

Know how to handle yourself.

Board rooms, meetings, and offices across the nation are having to accept the presence of menopausal women. Feeling comfortable about yourself will translate into other people feeling more comfortable about the situation. Taking control of your life and the situation means taking control of your body; it all begins with you.

Understand stereotypes that label women inferior.

The aging process affects the genders differently. Men are often oblivious to the fact that their actions and words can add to an already awkward moment. Feeling singled out, alienated, or misunderstood can add pressure to women when they need it least. Sometimes those with the power do not want to be open to change, for fear that it lessens their control and strips away their power. Therefore, they may choose to assert power over you when you are most vulnerable.

Menopause is a reality of life.

Both medical and nonmedical options are available to alleviate many of the symptoms associated with menopause. Hormone replacement therapy has grown in acceptance and popularity over the past decade. For many women this remains one of the most controversial decisions she will face. Although it is not recommended for every woman, there are some very significant benefits that cannot be ignored. In addition, other homeopathic and natural remedies are available. Information and knowledge translates into women empowering themselves through options, identifying choices, and making well-informed decisions.

CURES

Ease the awkward tension.

Menopause has long been one of those subjects not openly discussed in public, especially in the workplace. It is personal and it is female; therefore, it is generally not a topic for public discourse. In fact, women going through menopause have been considered dirty, ill-tempered, and even crazy according to some archaic stereotypes.

Because menopause also signals the end of childbearing years, many women feel less feminine. Their frustration with the aging process can create other signs of distress as well. Numerous feelings, emotions, and physical changes seem to be converging at once during this stage of life.

Today, menopause can be openly and honestly discussed in a number of different forums. While there are some who prefer to ignore its presence, others make light of it, almost treating a hot flash like a headache. It happens and soon it will go away; in the meantime, be patient with me.

Trying to ignore its presence does not mean no one notices. Quite the opposite is usually the case. During these awkward moments, others will likely take the lead from you. Whether you make light of the fact, or simply deal with it matter-of-factly, those around you will respond likewise.

If you are uncomfortable, they will probably respond in an uncomfortable manner. Some may stumble while trying to find an acceptable response when they feel such awkwardness. The snickers you hear may represent some people trying to break the tension when they do not really know what to say or do.

While there may be nothing to be ashamed about, you may still prefer not to discuss your personal life openly. It is your choice. If you do feel comfortable at least mentioning the situation, try making comments to ease the tension. These will be appreciated by everyone in the room.

Well it looks like I am having another hot flash. I'll be glad when my hormones settle down. But for now, please excuse me for a moment while I get some fresh air.

Understandably, this dialogue will not work in every situation. Again, it depends on how comfortable you are about the situation as well as the comfort level of those in the room. It may be just as appropriate to say, *"Please excuse me for a moment, I need to get some fresh air,"* and leave it at that. You will need to make the final decision on how much to say and whether it will be deemed appropriate in that particular setting. You do have the power to minimize the effects within the group, simply by how you handle the situation.

Break the stereotypes.

Women's bodies are different from men's. The aging process also affects genders differently. Not all women respond the same to menopause or aging; nor do all men respond the same to aging. Yet some men can feel so intimidated by the natural processes that women go through, that they react with control, trying to make a woman feel inferior and subordinate to him.

If you encounter these obstacles, take the high road. Turn what they perceive as a disadvantage to your advantage. Feel very good about yourself. Do not let their put-downs or inferences affect you.

Since you cannot change their opinions, it is important to accept that you may be watched and scrutinized more during this time. They will look for any indication that your actions prove their point. Be careful, thorough, and proud that you are a woman!

Know your medical and nonmedical options.

Today women have many options available to assist them through this next stage of life. Hormone replacement therapy (HRT) remains a major decision for most women. It is a personal choice, and one that should be made after much research, consultation, and consideration. Depending upon your medical history and other risk factors, it is not always a viable option. The benefits of HRT include minimizing or eliminating many of the symptoms you may be experiencing such as hot flashes and night sweats.

Because of the controversy surrounding the long-term use of drugs and their unknown effects on the body, as well as the lack of sufficient medical research supporting or denouncing these risks, many women remain skeptical about this choice. There continues to be a great deal of attention and research now, focusing on the many benefits and risks associated with its prolonged use. However, it is important for each woman to feel comfortable with her own choice.

Additionally, homeopathic remedies including herbal therapy and dietary changes are becoming more and more available and acceptable as forms of alternative treatments. Other nonmedical methods include increased exercise, vitamin supplements, and various relaxation techniques. During this time you should minimize the intake of substances that can aggravate menopausal symptoms such as alcohol, caffeine, sugar, and chocolate.

The more you know about what is going on, the different medical treatments available to minimize the symptoms, and typical signs of aging, the more normal the process will become for you. Each woman is unique and the decision of how she handles aging will be based on her own individual determinations.

Chapter Summary

You may find the role of managing one that leaves you feeling drained, that places your personal life in conflict with your professional career, and one that causes you to juggle the demands of raising a family and working. These are many of the same concerns faced by your employees as well, yet when they become your problem, how you handle them will be scrutinized much more carefully by many observers.

If you are a mother, you can draw strength from your background. Motherhood is an excellent training ground for being able to handle the multiple pressures faced as a manager. Motherhood teaches you how to prioritize, juggle, and wear many hats simultaneously. Each of these are qualities that are beneficial within the ranks of management. Women show a stronger sense of self and a better understanding of the needs of all workers because of their multitude of experiences. Women are more open to the everyday challenges faced between home and work and may offer more flexibility to their staffs, perhaps out of a necessity to survive.

If you are single, there are many feminine qualities that you have learned that are equally as beneficial to the working world. Women are looking at building and working together, and are often able to respond to changes and offer flexible solutions with greater ease. Women often try to manage within the ranks, as opposed to above the ranks—a style that is appreciated by other women but may produce resistance when managing males.

The demands for both mothers and single women can be exhausting. Women have a tendency to give to others before they give to themselves, whether this be family, children, parents, friends, or church. Is it any wonder that working women are so overstressed?

In order to gain control of your life you must identify and set boundaries. Know what you are willing to give, and just how far you will go to reach your goals. Sometimes establishing boundaries can limit your career potential. Those are the choices working women are making today. These are choices you must decide; no one can decide them for you. Only you know how far you are willing to go or what sacrifices you are willing to undertake in any given situation. As you pursue your career, these are choices you have to make and boundaries that you may set.

This section has addressed how different personal situations can present themselves to you. Whether you are going through a divorce, custody case, menopause, or a complicated pregnancy, your ability to respond to the situation will be watched by many. Remember, managing is never an easy process, but you can find solace in knowing that you are in control of your own life.

Troubleshooting for Teams with a Woman's Touch

Overview

Team building can be a great way to increase results, reach higher productivity, share ideas, offer more creative opportunities, and build morale in a department. The team concept is contrary to many of the primary principles businesses have operated under, such as power, hierarchy, autocratic leadership, and individual competition. Team building is frequently associated with women because of their willingness to forego individual glory for sharing the spotlight with others.

The more people you have in a team, the more opportunities there are for conflicts to arise. Working together can produce tension between the various players and even undermine the group concept as a whole. Some personalities do not work well together, no matter how hard you try. It is important to note that not all employees or departments adjust well to the team environment.

This chapter addresses the following problems, possible causes, and cures.

5.1 The Problem: How do you create a cohesive team?

Possible Causes: Deal with resistance to change; women are measured differently than male colleagues; poor communications may be a factor.

Cures: Conquer the fear of change; put your best foot forward; create open communication, especially during times of change.

5.2 The Problem: One employee is making it difficult for the team to get along.

Possible Causes: Personality conflicts can get in the way of effective teamwork; team spirit may be slowly waning; you have not responded to each person's needs; personal problems may be contributing to the tension.

Cures: Handle personality conflicts; build team spirit; manage individual personalities within the team; accept things outside your control.

5.3 The Problem: Sloppy work is being produced by the department.

Possible Causes: It could be a problem with another department; there may be underlying tension and frustration; employee attitudes can cause many problems, including a decline in productivity.

Cures: Work with other departments; identify and eliminate tension; change attitudes.

5.4 The Problem: The staff is suspicious of upper management.

Possible Causes: Senior management may not be trustworthy; you may be operating with your hands tied; profits drive decisions.

Cures: Should you trust management?; accept boundaries; create your rewards.

5.5 The Problem: No one in the department agrees on the best plan of action.

Possible Causes: Internal power struggles may be a factor; a compromise or consensus may be threatening to some employees; no one may understand their choices; you may fear losing a popularity contest.

Cures: Manage power struggles; learn to compromise; gain enough data to make a decision; earn respect.

5.6 ***The Problem: For health reasons one employee has asked to telecommute, and several employees resent the special consideration.***

Possible Causes: Is it the person or the exception that is being questioned?; no one may understand what the benefits are; jealousy and fear may be part of the problem.

Cures: Separate the person from the exception; sell the benefits; create a positive and pleasant work environment.

This chapter uses the term *team* both officially and unofficially. *Official teams* refer to those created to combine efforts and produce shared results. Individual competition would be completely factored out. The term *unofficial teams* applies to group behavior in general, the dynamics contained within a group, as well as various portions of official team systems that may be present.

5.1 | The Problem: How do you create a cohesive team?

THE SCENE

You were recently promoted to a busy and growing department. There is some reluctance from the staff regarding your ability to manage. While they are not really offering resistance to you, they are less supportive and enthusiastic than you would like.

After observing the department routines, getting to know the staff, and understanding the personalities, you've decided to implement some much needed changes. You want to create a more cohesive work environment for everyone. Currently, each person performs his or her task irrespective of what someone else is doing. For example, when one person is behind, no one comes to her rescue unless you intercede.

You had successfully introduced the team concept with another company. Now you want to implement some of those same concepts here. Senior management has given you its blessing; everyone is interested in results, not methods. Where do you begin?

Note: You can introduce the idea and create the opportunities, but you cannot make people work well together. The team concept has been introduced, modified, and improved upon in a number of settings. Do your research, know the players, be positive, and sell the benefits the *employees* will receive from working as a team. Sometimes teams do not work. Their failure may be attributed to many factors, some that you can control, but many that you have absolutely no control over. Timing is always a critical factor. If there are several other changes being implemented throughout the company at the present time, avoid introducing more than the employees are willing to accept.

POSSIBLE CAUSES

Deal with resistance to change.

This can appear in various guises: when someone feels threatened, when no one asks for an employee's input, the staff does not trust you or your judgment, or when employees are comfortable with the status quo. There is a popular saying that goes, "If it ain't broke, then don't fix it." You may see the problem as "broken" and want to offer solutions for improving or fixing it, but unless the staff is able to see that the problem is broken, change is slow if not impossible to implement. How you frame the benefits and the process can have a great deal of impact on how it is received by the employees.

Women are measured differently than male colleagues.

Different standards are placed on you than on men. The tests are different, the expectations are different, and the responses are different. Different does not necessarily mean worse, negative, less than, or bad. You have just as much of a chance to create a positive response as a negative response. In fact, women have many benefits and qualities that men do not have. Don't be overly sensitive about your gender; learn to use it to your advantage.

Poor communications may be a factor.

Communicating expectations, goals, and results can minimize many potential problems. If the staff does not know what is expected, it may fear the unknown. If the staff does not know what the goals are, it may not believe that change is for the better or in its best interest. If the staff does not know how results will be measured, it may be skeptical of the process and fear job security. The staff may also be afraid of losing its individual identity, especially if the members are overachievers who relish competition. Communicating these expectations, goals, and results can have a direct bearing on how the message is received.

Other Considerations: Does it matter whether you are new to a department or have been there for a few years? Introducing the team concept requires introducing change. Length of time does not change the possible causes; the primary difference comes in having an established foundation of trust and confidence that will allow you to move more quickly. Your job is made easier if you have been a good communicator, a fair judge, and a tireless listener. Otherwise, your old ways and bad habits could just as easily work against you when you introduce such a visible change.

CURES

Conquer the fear of change.

Fear of change is basically fear of the unknown. Even though the unknown may be an improvement over current conditions, people are naturally hesitant to embrace the notion of change. There are no guarantees that things will improve. It is this fear that can immobilize employees against the new ideas and challenges that the future might hold.

You represent change: as a new manager, as a woman, and as someone with fresh ideas. Everyone has made adjustments to your style, a style unique to you. Even though you did not introduce change, some things were changed simply with your presence. Changing routines, not adjusting to personalities, will become easier once the staff has confidence in your ability to manage.

Learning how to combat the fear of change is significant. Change, when presented as a new opportunity, has a greater chance for success. You must know and understand the staff so that when you are introducing a new idea, you know how to sell the benefits they want and can receive. Ideas, no matter how good, can fail miserably if you are unable to sell the benefits your audience will receive. Everything else becomes secondary or by-products of how these changes will make life and work easier.

Creating a team concept can be introduced on a very minimal level at first. For example, start by cross-training the staff to each other's positions, if that is not already happening. Convey your ideas during a staff meeting in a positive and caring manner.

> *For the past few months I have been observing everyone to see how the department operates. I have met with each of you to talk about your position and what improvements you would like to see. What I have found out is that each position works autonomously, without much interfacing with other positions in the department. Each job gets done, but sometimes one or two of you end up having to work late because you were faced with heavier workloads that particular day. Several of you have also voiced concern about this situation. As a solution, I would like to develop teams. Ultimately this will mean that we are all responsible for the department's operation. The first step will be to learn each other's jobs so that we can help out when needed and to have a better understanding of how the department operates. Everyone will need to be cross-trained to another position in the department. I have assigned work teams according to those positions that work together the most. After you and your buddy are cross-trained with each other's job, we will then cross-train one buddy team with another, until everyone is cross-trained. Obviously, this will not happen overnight; it is a slow process. No one should worry about their job being eliminated or merged into another position. We are not changing jobs, only sharing information. Later, I hope that we can find ways of streamlining the process to get more done, as well as to help out those who are getting a disproportionate amount of work on a particular day. There is another change I'd like to make at this time as well. When one person stays late, we will all stay late, unless it is an unusual circumstance. For this to work, everyone will need to communicate early in the day if your workload is unusually heavy, so that others will be able to make the necessary adjustments to their schedules. This is a learning process for all of us. In the meantime, I will remain open for new ideas and suggestions. However, I do ask that we give this plan enough time to evaluate it properly. There may be some initial*

bumpy roads as we integrate this plan. In six months we'll see how this system is working and what other changes you would like to suggest. I would like to thank each one of you for all your hard work, dedication, and commitment; I really appreciate it.

By anticipating resistance, you are ahead of the game. For example, what if one individual works at a considerably slower pace than the other employees? Is everyone getting penalized for his or her slow work pattern? No, in a team environment individual work habits are secondary to the total project. However, if some employees perceive that they are being penalized, then you must address that problem immediately. Their perception becomes their reality.

Put your best foot forward.

Your initial transition into management may be met with some resistance, especially by those employees who have not had a female manager before. Typically, men assume positions of authority, whereas women must go through many tests to prove their abilities. Employees, colleagues, and superiors will put women through a variety of tests requiring them to prove their capabilities and to make women earn the respect and trust of others. Men are judged independent of other men each time they are promoted, while women are still seen collectively, stereotyped by the positive and negative traits of the other women managers that have been promoted before them.

Knowing your audience as well as anticipating their responses and reservations will allow you to adapt and develop a style that is more likely to be well received. If the group prefers a strong, direct, confident leader, but your style is soft, caring, and inclusive, your message may be lost in your words and actions.

There are many advantages women have in leadership and building cohesive teams. The need to feel connected is at the very heart of team building and something the feminine style advocates. Paying attention to small details such as writing notes and providing words of encouragement and praise are more representative of women's styles of leadership. Women are more comfortable sharing the rewards and spotlight with others, especially the staff. Women are more likely to show physical signs of appreciation, while men, because of misconceptions and lawsuits, rarely touch or hug their employees. When employees feel valued and appreciated, their participation and results improve.

Women are comfortable in the role of nurturing, and nurturing within a group is important for team building. Respect, honor, trust, and compromise are essential for a team to become effective. The female style of leadership encourages these traits to be nurtured and developed.

Create open communication, especially during times of change.

Establishing strong communication channels is often a cure for problems found throughout management. This situation is magnified because of the possibility that miscommunications or poor communications may be a factor. Even if it is not the only problem, it is often a source of confusion which adds to other problems. Your role as manager will become easier by creating open, honest and trusting communication.

For you to be able to communicate succinctly the impact from the proposed changes, you must have a clear idea of what is going on yourself. What specifically do you want to accomplish? How long will it take to reach that level? How will you be able to measure the success of reaching those goals? What, if any will the penalty be for not reaching them? What are the benefits that the staff receives by participating in a team? Are the benefits that you see the same benefits that the staff wants?

When everyone understands the expectations and shares the same vision, your plan will have a greater chance of succeeding. Employees learn over time and through reviews what is accepted and expected of them. As you change the focus from individual performance and toward group results, it is important to state your expectations. Everyone needs to be clear about what it means to succeed or fail according to the team system. Employees will respond more positively if they know what it is you expect of them individually and collectively.

Another critical ingredient in communication is being a good listener. Ask the employees for feedback, suggestions, and ideas; then listen to what they say. Listening without action will only aggravate the situation, and no one wants to speak to deaf ears.

What If: There is a great deal of resistance and unwillingness to change? Do not read more into a situation than is there. Your lack of confidence because you are new to the position may cause you to overreact to the situation and misinterpret other people's actions. You may feel intimidated by the tests that you are being put through, and in fact you may even feel angry or resentful because your male colleagues do not have to go through this same criticism. Many things in life are not equal; managing is just one of them. All you can ask is to be treated fairly. In return, you should offer the benefit of the doubt when others respond to you.

5.2 The Problem: One employee is making it difficult for the team to get along.

THE SCENE

It is late in the afternoon and the office is winding down from a busy day. As you look up, Alice is standing at the door asking if she can talk. You invite her in.

Alice immediately begins complaining about everyone in the department. She is angry about her heavy workload and snipes, *"No one ever offers to help when I am overworked. No one cares about my work, or when I get it done. All they want to do is just go home. That's all that they're concerned with."*

As you listen, you realize that there is some truth in what Alice is saying. You, too, have noticed that the rest of the department doesn't get along very well with her. The situation has gotten worse in the past few weeks. Everyone else seems to get along just fine; there is a great deal of sharing and laughter among the other employees, while Alice is left out. It appears that Alice is difficult to get along with.

Alice is in her early 50s, married, and seems relatively content with her job and life. The rest of the staff is in their midtwenties to late thirties, either single or married with small children. There is not a lot in common between them. You are not sure where the problem started or exactly what needs to be done to fix it.

POSSIBLE CAUSES

Personality conflicts can get in the way of effective teamwork.

Personality conflicts are a natural side effect of life, and aggravated by situations in which people are forced into close working arrangements. When performance evaluations and expectations are done on a collective group basis, the tension may be magnified. Ignoring the personality conflict does not make it go away, nor does it become any easier to manage. Managing conflict means dealing with the situation head-on.

Team spirit may be slowly waning.

Dealing with Alice may be just the beginning of a long battle that you must undertake to rebuild the team's confidence and enthusiasm. Once work becomes routine, it is not uncommon for the excitement to decline. Once employees are no longer challenged, then they have a tendency to become dismayed. Their attitude may deteriorate naturally, unless you are constantly doing things to motivate and excite them. Some employees may show signs of neglect through their work output, others through their ability to get along. Something needs to change to get the spirit back into the team.

You have not responded to each person's needs.

Managing a team means managing the individual members within the group as well as the group itself. Sometimes within teams this can be tricky because you do not want to create competition where it is void. Since individuals have different needs, it is important to balance these two elements carefully.

Personal problems may be contributing to the tension.

If Alice is unhappy at home, for example, her anger and frustration could easily be targeted at whomever gets in the line of fire. Poor health, financial hardships, feeling unloved, overstressed, family problems, or physical abuse could be factors. In addition, you cannot rule out the aging process and its effects on different individuals at different times in their lives. This includes menopause and other hormonal fluctuations. Look for signs of irritability, depression, or mood swings for an indication that health may be a factor.

CURES

Handle personality conflicts.

When people work together, there will be times when personalities clash. There is nothing that you can do to avoid these situations. Instead, your leadership skills will be tested by how well you manage these clashes when they occur. Your objective should be to minimize disruption in the workplace.

If you have not already done so, observe the group dynamics carefully. See if you can identify where the conflicts are the most intense. Is there one person in charge, a self-appointed leader? If so, that person may be the primary clash for Alice, while others in the group may simply be supporting her.

Talk with Alice to hear what she has to say.

> *Alice, tell me what led up to this situation. It does not appear to be an isolated incident, but more like a trend. How long has it been building?*

It is more common to see fault in others and not in ourselves. Alice may quickly point a finger at someone else, not accepting any responsibility for the situation. You may need to establish some boundaries if Alice does not see herself as an active participant in these activities.

> *Alice, you are a hard worker. I know this situation must be very painful for you, but I would feel more comfortable if we didn't talk about others when they're not present to defend themselves. Instead, let's concentrate on your feelings and actions. Do you feel that you have done anything to contribute to this situation? Perhaps something wasn't done? We may consider having a department meeting so that everyone can share their concerns. My hesitation with this approach, though, is that it may not resolve anything, and only turn into a yelling match of who did what. From all indications, it seems that the rest of the department gets along fine. Why do you think that is?*

Depending on how Alice responds, you may need to have a similar discussion with the entire group. While members like bitching sessions, these produce few positive results and can actually be very harmful to those in the line of fire. Instead, establish ground rules for how everyone should contribute to the discussion, and then validate each person's feelings. This will keep the conversation on a more productive track.

Certain personalities get along better with one type while becoming antagonistic with another. When two personalities clash, talk to each party individually first. Then, bring them together and try to find a peaceful middle ground where everyone can work together. They do not have to become best friends; in fact, they do not even have to like one another, just so long as they can work together.

Sometimes, the only solution is to keep the personalities apart. Again, your objective is to find a solution that is the least disruptive to the office. Separating the personalities might be your best choice. Keeping these personalities separated does not mean you are a weak manager. It shows your strong leadership skills and ability to accept those things that you cannot change, and to minimize the negative effect on others. You may want to review Section 2.2 for more information on managing personality conflicts.

Build team spirit.

Teams that have been working together for a while often get tired of the job and tired of each other. Jobs become routine, co-workers become boring, and employees become complacent. Once the newness wears off, there may even be some resistance to helping each other out.

Team spirit must be constantly cultivated to continue to grow. While things may be fine in the beginning, time is the ultimate test for how well a team system really works. If you are not feeding the team with new ideas and challenges, it is only a matter of time before the players lose interest.

Talk with each employee individually. Start with Alice to find out what is going on with her, and what she thinks may be going on with the other team members. Listen to what everybody has to say. Make them feel safe and appreciated.

> *Alice, I appreciate that you are coming to me with this problem. This must be very frustrating to you. If you would, please tell me how we got here, and what solutions you propose.*

Alice may just be seeking a place to express her opinions. She may not have a solution. And she may not be expecting you to solve anything. Instead, what she may want initially, is simply to be heard. Make sure that you validate what she says. Make sure your body language is open and receptive and that you maintain strong eye contact with her, otherwise you may appear quiet but uninterested while she is speaking. Alice's body language will be an indication of how comfortable she feels with you as well.

Once you have determined that the problem lies with attitudes and boredom, you must decide if it is with just one person or more common in the group. Talk with several employees individually to get an idea of what is going on, what they are concerned about, and if they really enjoy what they are doing or not. If the problem is isolated to only a few employees, find ways to create new challenges and opportunities for them. Ask for their suggestions as well.

However, if the problem is more widespread, then talk to the entire staff. Frequent department meetings and planning sessions should keep you in touch with what is really going on. Make sure that your meetings are not simply a chance for you to talk and inform the staff. It is important that employees feel that they are part of the meeting, that they are not penalized for being honest (even if it has to do with one of your suggestions), and that they are valued and appreciated. By allowing and encouraging employee participation, they are able to share ideas and suggestions that are important to them. It is a courageous move to feel comfortable enough as manager to support the staff's ideas and suggestions. Fortunately, women are more comfortable than men admitting there is a problem and enlisting the help of others for solutions.

Recreating team spirit means that you are willing to work harder to improve what you had before, because it is not enough today. It will take time and energy to find those avenues that will challenge the staff for the future. In the meantime, keep communication open and remain flexible until you find what it is they need. Realize the process is neverending. To keep the team motivated requires constantly seeking new and innovative programs. Make sure that your spirit is not waning as well.

Manage individual personalities within the team.

There are two very different roles in managing teams. One requires you to be able to motivate all the individual players. The other asks that you take the concentration off of individual achievements and place it on the team collectively. Sometimes these two roles become a dichotomy, and the scales tip in one direction or the other. Balancing takes time and adjustment according to the specific needs.

Determining when an employee needs special attention to be motivated, or when special attention will cause disruption and jealousy, comes with practice. It requires that you listen to what is going on around you. Employees will indicate what they need in a variety of ways. For example, Alice may be wanting your attention and feel the best way of getting it is by disrupting the office or creating a scene. On the other hand, the remaining staff members could be alienating Alice because she is already getting (in their opinion) too much attention and praise. They may want to see her fail, and by not helping her out they are making work more difficult.

When these situations occur, evaluate your role in the balancing act. Perhaps you do not need to reduce Alice's praise, but instead can find ways to offer other team members praise as well.

You cannot make others get along. You cannot stop someone from becoming jealous, resentful, or angry. What you can do, though, is change how you respond and interact during these situations. This may require that you accept that you may not have communicated very well or supported the team members as much as they needed.

Be sure that you are not part of the problem by how you respond. Do not play favorites. When you identify problem areas, create a game plan for improving the situation.

Accept things outside your control.

Women are more comfortable then men in managing the personal aspects of employees' lives. These include managing things outside of your control that are affecting the workplace. This kinder, gentler, nurturing style can create a surrounding where people not only feel that their personal lives matter, but that you as a manager care enough about each person to ask.

When work routines are disrupted by personal circumstances, employees should know that they can comfortably talk to you about almost anything. Do not take this for granted. It bears repeating to employees with great frequency until they begin taking advantage of your offer. The employees must understand that they will not be penalized for bringing personal problems to work. Chapter 3 addresses how to handle a variety of personal problems from employees that may affect work life.

On the other hand, medical conditions such as menopause and aging should not be looked upon as disruptions. With an aging workforce, and an aging society, corporate America must welcome these changes honestly and openly; it must embrace the future as natural occurrences.

Talk privately to Alice to see what may be bothering her.

> *Alice, please come in and feel free to tell me what is going on. I want you to know this is a place where you can always share your concerns, where I will honor confidentiality, and where you will be heard.*

If you assume Alice is going through menopause, handle the situation carefully. If you have gone through menopause yourself, you have a distinct advantage by explaining firsthand your own experiences. However, if you have not gone through menopause, Alice may resent any suggestion that she is not handling her emotions well. See Section 4.10 for more information on menopause.

It is also important to realize that Alice may not want to discuss this personal condition with you. If she chooses not to discuss it, honor her wishes. It can be very embarrassing to assume someone is going through menopause, only to find out that at age 35 she had a complete hysterectomy. It could add to an uncomfortable and tense situation. Instead, follow her lead.

5.3 | The Problem: Sloppy work is being produced by the department.

THE SCENE

The quality and quantity of production from the department has significantly declined recently. Nothing has changed that you are aware of, except for the output. There have been no new employees, no changes in procedures, or major disruptions to the workplace.

Everything seemed to be operating smoothly until you received the monthly production report. The report showed production had been down slightly for the last month or two, but this month it dropped even more. When your boss asked you about these numbers, you did not have an answer. Now you have been asked to report to senior management about this situation and how it will be resolved. What's going on?

POSSIBLE CAUSES

It could be a problem with another department.

Oftentimes, departments work in conjunction with one another. The output from one area is required to complete the output from another department. While you should have been aware of these delays, unless it was brought to your attention, you may not know the total effect. It is important to notice how competitive one department is with another, and to determine if work is hindered or helped through these competitive channels.

There may be underlying tension and frustration.

When employees want to get your attention, they can cause internal problems, work slowdowns, or decreased production. It is their way of showing you that they have power. These tensions (whether they are personal, about management, work conditions, or clashing personalities) divert time and energy away from work and waste it on petty feuding or side issues.

Employee attitudes can cause many problems, including a decline in productivity.

Unless you keep a finger on the pulse of the employees' feelings, bad attitudes can erupt quickly. There are many warning signs, yet these often go unnoticed. One employee can hinder the whole team, as contagious attitudes contaminate the department. Productivity can become the casualty of such a war.

Other Considerations: Unless you communicate that production levels have declined, workers may think everything is fine and production is being maintained at its normal levels. Sharing information is key to resolving many issues. Don't assume that they know what is going on; it is essential that you keep them informed at all stages, not simply when a problem occurs.

CURES

Work with other departments.

It is not uncommon for one department to rely on the results from another department in order to do its job. This interdependence can easily create a domino affect of work-related problems. Finding the original source may be difficult since often it is the cumulative effect you are seeing. It may even be a continuous loop, one feeding on the information from another, who produces information for someone else to be used in making a product.

Identifying this problem will probably come from either observations, listening to the employees, or both. Be aware that your observations may produce only a limited understanding of the problem. Research a variety of perspectives to gain as complete an understanding as possible.

It is always helpful to listen and learn from the employees. For example, they may have a completely different handle on the situation than you have and therefore can provide insights you may have overlooked or considered to be less important.

Some departments display a competitive nature, whether or not senior management desires or encourages it. While some competition may be healthy and good, other times it can work against the individual systems. Unfortunately, some work environments actually produce competitive departments that intentionally try to sabotage each other to make someone else look bad. For example, when rewards (monetary or recognition) are given to the top department, that means there can only be one winner. However, when rewards are given for those departments that make quota, beat previous records, decrease returns, and so on, then departments are competing against themselves. Some employees may not find this kind of competition thrilling or motivating. Therefore, this healthier type of competitive atmosphere may not garner high enough spirits and results.

When you reward this extreme competitive behavior, there may be teams who want to win so badly that they will intentionally cause other teams to lose. While rare, this behavior can cause a great amount of internal damage.

If you determine that another department is causing you delays, you may either talk to senior management or go directly to that department's supervisor, depending on the dynamics of the organization. In either case, explain how the other department is impacting your production. Realize, though, that another department's supervisor may be just as competitive as its staff and may not want to provide any assistance to you.

Just as personality conflicts arise, there are also conflicts between groups. Not every team member or every team will respond to the same stimulation. Since you have measurable results that have been impacted, immediate action is needed.

Identify and eliminate tension.

There may be underlying problems within the department, between the department and management, with this and another department, or with you and the department. There could be any number of reasons for this tension, including: management ignoring the needs and wishes of employees, the staff not getting sufficient recognition, or employees not understanding what is expected of them. Perhaps recent changes have been implemented without the employees' participation. When employees feel left out of the loop, resentment can build easily.

Resentment often leads to a power struggle. Since the employees are the ones who actually hold power by their daily routines and productivity, they may be trying to get someone's attention by decreasing output. It is important to know what kind of attention they are trying to get.

They have gotten both your attention as well as the attention of senior management due to the decline in productivity. They hold the power; now you must listen and respond to their needs.

Finding the source of the problem may be more difficult, especially if it is *your* attention that they are after. You may be oblivious to their cries, instead feeling that you are doing an excellent job. Get the staff together for a meeting. Set ground rules and offer a safe environment to discuss whatever is on their minds. Allow enough time for this meeting to develop, without interruptions. Sometimes it takes a while for them to open up and share, depending on how comfortable the staff is with you.

This is not a time for you to argue or defend either yourself or management. This is the employees' time to share openly and freely what is on their minds. Interrupting their conversations will only confirm that no one is really listening to them. Sometimes the problem is as simple as the employees just wanting to be heard, where no other action is needed. Other times the problem may require actual changes to be implemented, or perhaps additional research into another area or concern.

Depending on the outcome of this meeting, you may actually decide to set up another time, perhaps in a week or a few days, to answer their concerns and let them know the progress of this first meeting. Remember, the employees *do* have power. And when they have gone to such extreme tactics to get noticed, you better pay close attention to what they are saying.

If you suspect the outcome has to do with some recent changes in the department or in the company, you may say something like:

It seems that production levels have decreased over the past month. Several of you have voiced concerns about the changes management has put in place. I realize that you feel these changes are making it more difficult for you to do your jobs. These changes directly affect you and you have not been included in the process. There is little I can do to change what has already happened. What I can do, however, is to listen to your concerns and together we can create solutions that help out this department. I am willing to take your concerns to management, but I need your support and trust to do so.

It is very important to use the *"we"* pronoun instead of *"you"* to let the employees see you as part of the team.

Change attitudes.

Bad attitudes can disrupt the most congenial of workplaces. It takes only one rotten apple to ruin the whole bushel. These rotten apples become highly contagious when left alone.

Bad attitudes can evolve for any number of reasons, including personal problems, poor health, fatigue, financial strains, or lack of career development. The reason, while important, is only half of the problem. Finding the original source is one step; regaining the respect and enthusiasm of the entire team, though, is equally as important. Sections 1.1 and 1.3 offer additional information on how to handle employee attitude problems and improve morale in the workplace.

What do you do when you are unable to get to the source of the problem? Or after you've identified and resolved the problem, how do you rebuild the department? For answers to both these questions, talk to the staff individually as well as in a group.

Individual discussions allow you to be in sync by talking and listening to those on the front line. You can do this by checking in with each employee to see how things are going, either casually throughout the day or a few times a week, depending on how serious the tension and disruption is. Some employees may still resent your coming around so frequently; they may assume you are watching over their work too closely. When this happens, talk directly with these employees and find other avenues for keeping close tabs on the situation. Hopefully, when employees know your objective they will not feel threatened by your presence. It is also important that your words and actions work together. In other words, do not say you are not watching over them when in fact that is exactly what you are doing. Most employees will enjoy the added concern and involvement you are offering, although a few will not.

Listen carefully, attentively, and respectfully to what the employees are saying. In general, they will be honest with you, unless you are a source of their resentment. While they still may be honest, it may be more difficult for you to actually hear what they are saying. Their honesty may be painful for you to accept.

> *Production output from our department drastically declined this past month. I have been asked to report to senior management about this situation, why it has decreased, and what we are doing to change it. Does anyone have any observations about this decline? Is there anything going on that I am not aware of?*

This dialogue would be used in a general format, to allow for comments and concerns to be shared openly and honestly. Assuming further that there are few comments generated from this conversation, which is often a response when negative attitudes are involved, then you need to create ideas and methods for improving attitudes.

> *Things seem to be pretty complacent around here. Let's talk this out. I am open for ideas to make this a fun place to work. Since we are together 40 hours a week, we might as well enjoy ourselves. I have a suggestion: If we can improve production by ____ amount for next month, then we'll have a pizza lunch on Friday, my treat. How does that sound?*

Admittedly there is a thin line between creating methods for improving attitudes and rewarding negative behavior; be careful not to cross it. By rewarding negative behavior, you may be instilling the notion that bad attitudes are good because they get results and changes not otherwise achieved. On the other hand, you may be responding to their needs, while before you had not known or heard them. Making concessions isn't the end solution, but can represent a fresh start.

Open communication is always important. By sharing information freely with the employees, you are including them in the decision-making process. Everyone becomes more concerned when they know what is going on and what is expected of them. Shared information is empowering to those with which it is shared, so give the staff the opportunity to respond.

5.4 | The Problem: The staff is suspicious of upper management.

THE SCENE

In a recent meeting, one of the staff members voiced doubt about how sincere the actions of upper management really were. Quickly, other employees joined in voicing apprehension and concern. Several employees echoed that *"management only cares about the bottom line, not about employees. Its loyalty is for the almighty dollar, not to us. Why should we care?"*

You were surprised by their harsh comments. While the employees noted that management may say words of encouragement, they also pointed out how management's actions reflected a very different position. Someone remarked that despite profits being up this past year, management continued to reduce its staff. Someone else commented on the reduction in several company benefits and the higher insurance rates employees were now having to pay. They are right about their observations. You feel caught in the middle, trying to pump up the staff while remaining loyal to the employer.

POSSIBLE CAUSES

Senior management may not be trustworthy.

You may agree that senior management mistreats the majority of its employees. You have a loyalty and obligation to the employees as well as to the employer. This obligation can sometimes put you in an uncomfortable position, feeling caught in the middle, and being forced to choose sides. This awkward tension is often felt stronger by women in their thrust to please everyone and avoid conflict. It can be one of the most challenging and frustrating positions for any manager.

You may be operating with your hands tied.

For men who are allowed to assume authority, this conflict is less likely to occur. Women experience this frustration much more frequently. Having responsibility without authority is still largely associated with women because women are tested more in the beginning, with male management assuming women are less qualified or that they will fail. While you sympathize and agree with the employees, there may be little if anything that you can do. It becomes a dangerous position to be in, unless protective measures are taken.

Profits drive decisions.

A company will have a goal, vision, or mission statement that reflects its ideals. In reality, a company actually operates under a philosophy that is representative of its actions not limited by its words. Profits may be the number one objective of the employer, despite what it says to the contrary. Neither you nor the employees can change this corporate directive. Denying its existence makes you look naive or gives cause to mistrust you as well.

CURES

Should you trust management?

For women, trust must be earned and is not given simply because of a hierarchical chain of command. Men are more comfortable adapting to this structured environment. Management may provide you with reasons to mistrust it. During these times your loyalty to the company and loyalty to the staff may be split. When this happens, deep soul-searching is in order. Disloyalty to the employer creates a situation in which no one can win. Instead, try to find ways to compromise and work within limited and structured boundaries. Create your own safe-zone.

First, identify those areas in which conflict or differences are the strongest between you and senior management. Are these morale concerns for you? Are these areas that greatly impact your ability to manage? Does it affect your pay or career future?

If not, then try to minimize the situation. Choose your battles carefully. In other words, don't sweat the small stuff and don't make matters worse by butting heads when you know you will lose.

Respect is an essential ingredient in any workplace. Without it, mistrust and disloyalty often erupt. Respecting the employer does not mean that you must always agree with its policies, but it does mean that you will never undermine its stature, especially among other employees. Look for things that do not threaten management but allow you to regain control and respect in the department. Never underestimate the power of listening.

Work with what you have, not what you don't have. A group meeting might include the following conversation:

I understand several of you do not feel like you can trust senior management. Let's talk this out, and I will try to explain as best I can what perhaps is going on that you may not know about. Not that it will change your opinions, but only show you the other side. Who would like to go first?

Then listen and allow each person who wants to speak the time to speak his or her mind. Try to keep the focus away from hostility and anger, while still being respectful of the person who is speaking.

I know this must be aggravating. Let's try to focus on those things that we can change. We are not setting the policy for this company, but we can set the routines in this department. I will make no false or empty promises; today's workforce does not have job security. It no longer exists, not just here but anywhere. If you are afraid of losing your job, that is something I cannot guarantee. Instead, by working together we can create a unit that is strong, results-oriented, and respectful of each member. What are some areas that we can change or improve on in which management will, we hope, not interfere with us? I am open for your suggestions. It will take a team effort. Everyone will have a say because everyone's contribution is important.

While senior management may continue to introduce obstacles for you to overcome, you can still create a positive and productive department. Despite these challenges and frustrations, the employees need to feel that they are safe in this department, or at least as safe as can be expected. Your job will be to constantly reassure them, to value their contributions, and to respond to their voices.

When all else fails, both you and the employees always have the choice of finding another employer. But before anybody leaves it is important to know exactly why and to devise methods for avoiding this situation in the future. There is no value in leaving this employer simply to work somewhere else, where the same philosophy, conditions, or mistrust exists.

Accept boundaries.

There will be times when management will make you responsible for certain results without providing you with the necessary authority to achieve them. This is a very frustrating position to be in, especially for women. Women continue to have more tests and challenges set before them than men do and therefore are constantly having to prove their abilities.

This position becomes worse when the staff senses that your hands are tied. It may impede your ability to motivate them in order to achieve the desired results. Section 9.1, while looking at interviewing and hiring, address-es the role of a manager when responsibility is expected without the neces-sary authority given.

When this occurs, it is important to identify what power you have and what power you are missing. It benefits no one to be consumed with what you do not have. Instead, your energy is better used investing in things that you can change. Do the best you can with what you've got. Accept that you will be tested several times before authority is slowly relinquished and be prepared. Do what you can do, what you have the ability to do, and what is in the best interest of the group.

Create your rewards.

A business cannot stay in business unless it continues to make money. No one denies that fact. Conflicts are likely to arise, however, when a busi-ness is consumed with making money and places little if any emphasis on the well-being of its employees.

This is the point where the employer has a different set of priorities than you would like. Depending upon what those differences actually are, some may be tolerable while others may not be. It is a value judgment that only you can make.

It is imperative that you support the employer. If not, then you should find another employer. Loyalty to the employer should never be compromised, no matter how frustrating the policy or philosophy. Chapter 9 discusses vari-ous situations where policy conflicts may impede your working conditions.

Look for ways to create rewards, nonmonetary ones, to show your appreciation for work done well. Complement employees frequently. Implement a suggestion box for nonmonetary rewards. Notes, lunches, comp time, balloons, and fun seminars may be explored. Other ideas include ways to reduce stress, organize closets, plan for college tuitions, prepare taxes, or swap coupon clippings. Make sure these are things the staff wants to do, oth-erwise they become wasted efforts.

What If: The tension is the result of downsizing or reorganizing within departments? Your job will be to regain the confidence of the staff.

It is never easy. Begin by listening to the staff; listen to what they say as well as what they don't say. Often the issues will be masked behind anger and fear. It will be up to you to move beyond these superficial attacks, and get at the heart of what is really bothering them.

What If: You are considered part of the problem? Because you are management you may be considered part of *them*, where the problems originate. No matter how much they respected you before, you are still a member of management. Try to distance yourself in their eyes, and work to regain their trust. Make the first move, and trust their judgment. Respect their feelings. Listen to their ideas. Do not make false promises; it will only keep the distances great between you.

5.5 The Problem: No one in the department agrees on the best plan of action.

THE SCENE

You are faced with introducing a new project in the department. How you achieve those results has been left up to you to decide. During a meeting, you asked the staff for suggestions and they were very forthcoming with them. After considerable discussion, the choices are narrowed down to two different plans that lacked any similarities or cogent features.

Without the support of the entire department you know neither plan will succeed. Currently the staff is split on which solution seems most feasible. At each offer of a compromise, the two sides seem absolutely unbendable. Neither side appears willing to concede the smallest of details. Now it is up to you to cast the tie-breaking vote. However, neither choice seems right to you, and both involve a great deal of risk. Where do you go from here?

POSSIBLE CAUSES

Internal power struggles may be a factor.

Within any group you will have some people who are stronger personality types, typically leaders, and others who are more comfortable in the role of followers. Problems occur when two or more individuals are vying for the leadership role, and do not want to share top honors. Even though you may discourage a leader from emerging, it is often a natural part of group dynamics and personality. These strong individuals may solicit followers in order to promote their own agendas. Reaching a compromise requires concessions; something no one is willing to do. As manager, understanding the group dynamics is critical to creating a cohesive unit. Without bringing the sides together, you are left managing separate divisions, who are supposed to be working together and doing one job as a team.

A compromise or consensus may be threatening to some employees.

It is important for employees to know that a compromise or consensus does not mean anyone has conceded or lost. When winning is at the forefront of someone's mind, anything less than winning could be viewed as a failure. Instead of looking out for the department or seeing the big picture, some employees may be caught in tunnel vision, seeking to win at all costs. Often competitive spirits are at the core of these problems.

No one may understand their choices.

It could be that no one understands what choices are available. Instead everyone may be trying to make decisions based on incomplete data which produces false or misleading conclusions. Your role as manager is to provide the necessary information for the group to be able to make well-informed decisions. You must also be able to communicate this information in a style that they understand.

You may fear losing a popularity contest.

Managing is not always easy. Managing involves tough choices, which sometimes make you unpopular. Asking for suggestions from employees is very different from letting them lead themselves and you. Democracies rarely work in management; someone must be in charge and have the vision, especially when it is lacking in others. And that someone is you.

CURES

Manage power struggles.

Strong personalities have a tendency to try to control everything around them. When you have two competing personalities who both want to be leaders, the remaining staff members may be followers of either one side or the other. How you handle this situation is critical. Mishandling it could produce a divided team that does not work well together. This type of friction can be deadly in the workplace by undermining your authority and eventually asserting power and control over you.

On the one hand you try to encourage employees to be independent and decisive, while at the same time these characteristics, when taken to the extreme, can be troubling to any manager.

Women have a tendency to avoid conflict, whereas men try to control it. Neither are healthy models for reaching positive conflict resolution. Instead, learn to identify when and where conflict is, and then to confront it. Confronting conflict does not mean that you are unbendable in your approach, but it says that you will open the door for meaningful dialogue to be employed.

It will be up to you to reestablish your control; if not, then these personalities will continue to create more and more hardships for you. Regaining control is imperative to resolving this conflict but that doesn't mean that you need to be a dictator. Your style can be both firm and caring, allowing for suggestions and the sharing of ideas while still taking charge. To do this, it is important that you create and communicate very specific boundaries. When people know what is permissible and what is not, they will typically stay within those boundaries. Problems are more likely to occur because the boundaries are not known, continually change, or have not been communicated clearly.

Create boundaries that everyone knows and can play by. For example, when you ask for suggestions make sure that everyone knows that you may not follow their advice, but that you are collecting a lot of data and will then put forth what you feel to be the best solution. If resentment does occur, be willing to confront it immediately. This source of dissention can spread to many other areas if left untended.

Learn to compromise.

Although compromising may sound easy and safe, for some people reaching a compromise involves a great deal of risk. These individuals feel uncomfortable compromising primarily because they have never learned how to reach a compromise or what benefits can be gained through it. To compromise means conceding in their minds, thereby lessening their power. It means they have lost, and winning is the very essence of their life.

It is these extremely competitive spirits that you must carefully manage. Handling competitive players takes tact and attention. You may be surprised to learn the company's stance on this: For example, when bonuses and rewards are based on individual production and achievements, working together may take second place.

Know exactly what it is you want to achieve. If you feel it is important for the group to make the suggestion and agree on its implementation in order to work, then gaining its support and consensus is absolutely essential. Remind everyone that compromise means everyone can win, and that you will base rewards on the successes and the results of the total plan as well as the ability to compromise.

As a group, evaluate both plans.

> *Let's talk about the benefits and the hazards of each of the two plans submitted. We want to be able to reach a compromise, which means each side needs to be open to give up something so that everybody wins. We can adapt the best of each plan and try to minimize any negative effects. Will the work loads be the same for either plan? Or will one require more time from certain positions? Also, how would each plan be measured for its success?*

The next step involves directing the conversation into positive feedback. Reassure each member that they are not losing ground or conceding. A competitive individual places a lot of emphasis on saving face, especially in front of peers. As the leader, you will need to reinforce safety zones so that compromising becomes analogous to winning.

Gain enough data to make a decision.

Without complete information it seems impossible to make well-informed decisions. Yet, that may be exactly what you are expecting of the employees without even realizing it. Some organizations protect knowledge as if it were power, and only let out small amounts on a need-to-know basis.

Whatever the reason, information may be insufficient to make a good decision. Incomplete information is just as damaging as inaccurate information; neither produce reliable results.

As manager, you have a great deal of control over communications within the department. That is, of course, assuming that you know what is going on yourself. The first step is to know what is necessary to make well-informed decisions, the next step is communicating that information so that the staff also understands it.

If you have identified any weak communications links, fix them at once. Open dialogue with the department is the best way of evaluating how well you communicate. It is not enough to know the information and to tell someone else; you must also make certain that others understand what you are saying. Ask for feedback, suggestions, and concerns frequently from staff members. This may be done in a group setting or randomly on an individual basis.

Create more and more opportunities for information to be shared openly. Sharing knowledge will not dilute your authority. It will provide better results because *everyone* will be working with a shared vision and with the same foundation. Someone must take that first step; why not let it be you?

Earn respect.

Managing is not always easy; nor does it always make you popular. However, as manager you are the one responsible for the department. Therefore, you are the one who must take control. Sometimes you must make some tough choices that are unpopular. This may be such a time. It doesn't mean that you should act like a dictator and bark out commands. Gaining the respect of the staff comes when you are viewed as strong, decisive, and in charge.

You are the one with experience, leadership qualities, and vision. Now you must become the motivator as well. As manager, you must know the strengths and the weaknesses within the team, and must know how to mold the players to perform at their optimum. You must also know how to persuade, listen, and lead the team.

Being strong doesn't mean losing friends. Your objective isn't to assert power *over* your subordinates. However, if you are forced into a corner, you must be able to stand up for what you believe is in the group's best interest. That is when your strength and leadership qualities will be tested the most.

As a manager learn when to be soft and when to be strong. Different situations require different approaches.

> *We seem to have reached an impasse as to which plan to adopt. I would like everyone to take two minutes each and sell me*

on the benefits of the plan they endorse. No negative comments will be made about any other suggestions at this time. Please understand that I am not siding with one plan or the other, but that I am looking at the total picture. I will evaluate everything tonight, and we will meet tomorrow at the same time, for unveiling the new project plan.

I realize that this may not be an easy solution. It will, in all probability, take time to develop, implement, and succeed. Because women seek the connectedness and bonds of others, going against someone can create internal tension and stress. Take a deep breath, review your options, and present the plan in a strong, positive light.

5.6 | The Problem: For health reasons one employee has asked to telecommute, and several employees resent the special consideration.

THE SCENE

While you've tried to keep the team spirit alive and strong, you have also tried to remain flexible to the individual problems that arise. Now, you are stuck in a no-win situation and are not sure what to do.

One of the employees, Jan, has been advised to reduce her work schedule at her doctor's urging. After discussing a variety of options, you agree to allow her to telecommute; working at home three days a week and in the office the other two days. Her home computer will link her to the company's mainframe and allow her to access her accounts. Because of the nature of her job duties, though, some adjustments in work assignments will be necessary.

Unfortunately, when this solution was introduced to the staff you had several employees stop by and tell you that they did not think it was workable. Throughout the day these disgruntled employees continued mumbling about this or that. No one, except you and Jan, seemed to think it might work. In fact, everyone complained about all the reasons why it wouldn't work. Their hostility and frustrations started you questioning your own decision. You began to wonder if it was such a good idea after all.

POSSIBLE CAUSES

Is it the person or the exception that is being questioned?

Sometimes people are less supportive of an exception because they do not like the individual who the exception is for, not that they do not like the exception. Separating the two can be very difficult. As manager, a person's popularity should not be a factor in deciding how to respond to a particular situation. Realistically though, you cannot deny that it impacts how readily an exception is accepted by the remaining staff members.

No one may understand what the benefits are.

Communication is a factor that must never be underestimated, and as manager it is one area in which you have strong influence and control. Employees respond according to your lead; when you sell the benefits, they will respond positively. If you present the information as a weak exception without any benefits, as if you had no other choice, they will respond similarly to those comments.

Jealousy and fear may be part of the problem.

At times employees will be resentful of exceptions, no matter how well you introduce them. Their resentment can be born out of jealousy or fear. For some, this resentment will pass quickly in time. For others, resentment will fester inside them until it ultimately interferes with work. Recognize that this resentment is another form of conflict, and respond accordingly.

CURES

Separate the person from the exception.

When employees do not like the person who is being granted an exception, they often try to derail the plan. When you identify that the animosity is personal, you may either confront it or leave it alone. Your choice will be dependent upon the obstacles that have been created by the group. Both are acceptable solutions, although both involve risk.

If you choose to ignore these infractions, they may disappear once others become accustomed to the change. Distance and space can make things less irritating. On the other hand, ignoring it can allow it to continue to grow, causing even more and greater problems.

Ultimately, the employees may respond to your decision based on the popularity of the individual, not on the decision itself. Anticipating this obstacle should not be a reason for choosing another option. It simply allows you to be prepared for this reaction. The decision is either a good or bad decision based on its own merits. However, not all good decisions work; you must be able to accept that the outcome, at some level, is out of your control.

More and more offices are finding ways to allow their staff to split time between home and work. Happy employees make for better employees. This could be introduced (with management's blessings, of course) as an experiment that may be offered to other employees if it works. See Section 2.8 for more details concerning introducing telecommuting in the workplace.

Sell the benefits.

Communicating this exception is something that you control. Think through how you will tell the department, when you will say it, and exactly what you will say. Depending on the various factors affecting the situation, Jan may ask that the reasons be limited or she may allow that they be shared openly.

As manager you will need to weigh these choices and try to find balance. Balance doesn't necessarily mean equality, nor does it mean you will win any popularity contests. In fact, you can expect to lose a few while maintaining your vision and objectivity. Balance, however, does mean that you have evaluated all your options and feel that this is the least disruptive and best solution.

Look for the win-win proposition, then sell the benefits to everyone. There is greater risk in finding a replacement worker than working around a few obstacles for an employee you know, and who has a proven track record. Interviewing, hiring, and training are all costs that should be factored into your final decision. Do not penalize Jan for something she cannot control, even though it means an inconvenience for the rest of the department.

As you assess each of these factors, timing is another critical element of the equation. Make sure that you haven't placed an enormously high burden on one or two employees to make up for Jan's absence from the office. Also, employees will want to have some level of assurance that Jan is working at home and not napping all the time. If her job is one that can be quantified, this will be to everyone's benefit. If it cannot be quantified, do the best you can to explain the situation and how each person will be affected.

Create a positive and pleasant work environment.

Sometimes resentment cannot be avoided. It may be a passing feeling, or it may be the result of much deeper animosity. As manager, you will need to assess the situation and decide if it is better to confront feelings or give them time to settle down.

Allow a week or two to pass, and the shock to wear down. You may find after the initial conflict that everyone has settled down and accepted the changes. If so, then you can continue about your daily routine. A pleasant work environment may emerge on its own.

If the resentment continues or quickly builds and becomes more of an agitator, then step in immediately. It is time to take charge. Avoiding conflict only leads to greater problems down the road.

Determine if the problem is with one or two employees primarily, or if it is shared among many. If you see that it is centralized, talk specifically to those individuals involved. If the problems do appear more widespread, then a departmental meeting would be necessary.

> *It appears that several of you have been complaining about my decision to allow Jan to work from her home. I am surprised by the comments because I felt that I had considered all the consequences before I made my decision. However, I had not anticipated the lack of support I am receiving here. So, what I'd like to do is talk this out and see what your feelings or concerns are about my decision.*

Then listen to the responses. Address each concern separately and try to reassure each person that this is the best solution. Whether their comments are vented out of jealousy or fear, answer each one directly. Others may like the opportunity to work from home; this is the time to consider if it is something that the company wants to explore for the future. Telecommuting has improved many workplaces and increased productivity, but it is not for everyone or for every situation. Consider the consequences carefully before moving forward with this plan.

Don't forget to find other methods of rewarding those employees who are coming into the office every day. This could include having office parties when Jan is present and or perhaps even when she is working at home. Special recognition and appreciation is another tool that produces excellent results.

Chapter Summary

For a woman, the need to build and unify is often best expressed through her desire to create and utilize teams. Teams can be a great way to increase results, reach higher productivity, share ideas, offer more creative opportunities, and build morale in a department. What has been natural for women is finally finding its acceptance throughout corporate America: Within the last decade businesses have begun placing greater emphasis on building teams within units, sharing power and authority, and sharing responsibility as well.

The team concept is contrary to many of the primary principles businesses have operated under—the power, hierarchy, autocratic leadership, and individual competition. Instead teams allow for a true sense of togetherness and connectedness to develop. Working together eliminates or minimizes individual competition and allows everyone to share in the successes and the failures of the team. For a team concept to work, however, everyone must be willing to forego individual accomplishments and allow the team to completely share in these achievements. You will be no stronger than your weakest link.

The most common cause associated with team failure is with the lack of authentic and convincing support from senior management. When shared responsibility is given lip-service, and staff members are not involved in the decision-making process, they may create numerous impossible roadblocks to overcome.

Having a voice and being heard is a critical aspect of team-building success. The more involved the employees become in various processes, the more they will feel an ownership and commitment to each project.

Empowerment is an overused phrase often associated with teamwork. You cannot empower anyone; you can give them the opportunity and tools, but ultimately individuals must empower themselves. Empowerment comes from within. Your role as a leader is in encouraging, supporting, and honoring someone's ability to empower him- or herself. You can provide the foundation that encourages the employees to become empowered, but ultimately it is theirs to do, not yours to give.

Not all departments or all employees adjust well to the team environment. First, it takes a leader who is willing to relinquish power and control, a leader who is willing to concentrate her efforts on motivating the players and listening to their concerns. Then it takes the individual players' belief that the loss of individual identity is not a negative. And finally, it takes the support and flexibility of senior management to add the glue that makes it all work. At any step along the way, obstacles can be present.

If the total team concept does not work within your environment, you can still benefit by using various aspects within your group. The team concept has been devised, revised, and rewritten to fit numerous working relationships. Find something that works for you.

𝒯roubleshooting Problems Involving Peers

Overview

As women enter various ranks of management, they are likely to feel pressures from those who were their friends as well as from their peers and fellow colleagues. Promotions may mark friendships with an awkward tension and uneasy feelings, whereas peers or colleagues may resent your promotion and not welcome you as an equal.

Not all friends will abandon you, nor are all peers problem makers. It is not even the majority who cause these waves. However, it is important to be able to identify and handle these situations quickly. This remains a significant part of conflict resolution.

This chapter addresses the following problems, possible causes, and cures.

6.1   The Problem: Other women in the company are not supporting your promotion.

Possible Causes: You may be expecting too much; you are viewed as an outsider; others may have been happier with the way things were before.

Cures: Have realistic expectations; work to be accepted; do not threaten the status quo.

6.2 *The Problem: You are intentionally left out of conversations and decisions by male colleagues.*

Possible Causes: Gender differences in conversation may be an issue; your actions, lack of participation, or expectations may add to the frustration; group dynamics may alienate new members.

Cures: Understand gender dialogue; Take responsibility for what you do; be part of the group.

6.3 *The Problem: You are being criticized by other managers because you manage differently.*

Possible Causes: There may be jealousy; your style of managing may be causing friction; you may have broken an unwritten rule.

Cures: Adapt a nonthreatening approach; change your style to match the audience; know the rules of the game.

6.4 *The Problem: After you were promoted, your closest female friend at work has disappeared from your life.*

Possible Causes: Competition is not always healthy; she may feel uncomfortable with the hierarchical gap; your qualifications may be an issue.

Cures: Ease the jealousy gap; flatten the hierarchical structures; believe in yourself.

6.5 *The Problem: As the only female present at a meeting, you have been asked to take the minutes—again.*

Possible Causes: Yes, there is gender bias in America; you may be overreacting to the situation; you may be the most qualified person to take minutes.

Cures: Minimize gender biases in the workplace; place things in their proper perspective; accept your strengths.

6.6 *The Problem: You received dishonest feedback from a colleague, which made you look bad during a presentation.*

Possible Causes: Surprise attacks can blind-side you; you may not know how to play the game; this may be a test of your willpower and management abilities; your style may add to the confusion.

Cures: Anticipate surprise attacks; know the rules of the game; defend your position; find a style that is accepted.

6.7   *The Problem: The male colleagues are gloating about their various memberships and club participations, knowing that you are excluded.*

Possible Causes: The playing fields are not always equal; these exclusions may be representative of the corporate philosophy.

Cures: Play fair; deal with sexism in the company.

6.8   *The Problem: Inappropriate sexual comments about an employee are made in your presence by male colleagues.*

Possible Causes: They may not know any better; some people enjoy the shock value of their comments; they may think they are being funny.

Cures: Ignorance is not an excuse; do not react with shock; humor can be gender-specific.

6.9   *The Problem: Work conversations frequently contain sexual innuendos and other suggestive comments that you find inappropriate.*

Possible Causes: Determine what is appropriate talk at work; some people may be crude, while others just have poor manners; humor takes many forms, including suggestive styles.

Cures: Determine acceptable business talk; know your boundaries within a particular group; understand feminine humor.

When clashes occur, it becomes time to manage the conflict. As we've discussed, when confronted with conflict, men are more likely to try to control, while women will try to avoid the situation. Neither are healthy approaches to managing conflict. This chapter will provide a healthier method to adapt.

6.1 | The Problem: Other women in the company are not supporting your promotion.

THE SCENE

Within the company you see that women have been promoted into various levels of management. Your recent arrival into a management position has not been met with the open arms you were hoping for. There have been several occasions where you've tried to create a sense of solidarity and unity with female colleagues, but instead have received the cold shoulder.

At a recent lunch break you sat at a table with several other women managers and tried to introduce conversation topics but were ignored or brushed off. You mentioned an upcoming meeting of a local chapter for professional women executives and managers and received the harsh reply, *"No thanks, that's not for me. I like my job just fine the way it is."* Then the conversation quickly changed to areas that excluded you. You felt this change had been done intentionally, with malice and spite. Their actions had hurt your feelings. Where was the sisterhood you were looking for?

POSSIBLE CAUSES

You may be expecting too much.

It takes more than gender to create unity within a group. You may be expecting more than is possible or feasible from the other women, thereby setting yourself up to be disappointed. People bond together for a variety of reasons; predicting these bonds is impossible. Some people feel close because of gender, race, or family similarities, or perhaps hobbies, outside interests, education, or religion. Until you identify bonds that can draw you together, not just similarities, you will be fighting a losing battle.

You are viewed as an outsider.

Whether defined as a clique or as close friends, you are currently sitting outside of the circle. It is not uncommon for people who spend a lot of time together to become very close. These bonds can also alienate new members. Before you can penetrate that wall, you must know why it is there and what you win by breaking through it.

Others may have been happier with the ways things were before.

You may represent change. This is especially true if you are up against individuals who are content with the status quo. Your presence on a new playing field may be enough to signify a threat. Change is often met with resistance and denied easy acceptance. Given that women have a tendency to ignore conflict (including when it arises out of fear and change) instead of confronting it, these women may find it easier to practice distancing and alienating you. They may even be jealous of the opportunities that you now have that they were denied. While it's not your fault, you are feeling the brunt of their frustration.

CURES

Have realistic expectations.

You may be expecting a bigger reception from your co-workers than they are capable of, or than they care about giving. Without realizing it, you may be expecting them to respond to you how you would respond to them if the situation were reversed. Yet the situation is not reversed, and you cannot predict how they will accept or respond to you. When you create expectations, you are setting yourself up to be disappointed. Human nature is unpredictable. Expecting other women to accept you simply because you are a woman is naive.

People are drawn together for a variety of reasons. For some, gender may be a major factor; for others it could be education, lifestyles, common interests, family similarities, length of time with a company, and so on. Whatever bonds draw people together is outside of your control.

If gender solidarity is important to you, then seek other women that it is equally important to. Accept that your views may not be shared by the other women in the organization. That does not mean your views are wrong; nor does it imply that the views of the other women are wrong. Instead, it reflects individual priorities and the importance of certain issues at that particular point in life.

Try to connect with either gender, depending upon the particular situation and need. There are several reasons why you will want to widen your circle of friends and be open to acceptance and appreciation by your colleagues. First, the office grapevine moves on several levels, including management, and if you are outside the circle you will be excluded from a primary method of sharing news within an organization. In addition, getting along with your colleagues will provide opportunities for exchanging new ideas, for troubleshooting problems within departments, sharing management concerns, and developing a sense of comradery. By alienating yourself, you are making work more difficult than it needs to be. Part of being a good manager is your ability to get along with others.

Work to be accepted.

When you feel alienated, and not part of the group, step back and see what binds the group together. Who are the group members? What are their interests? It may be length of service to the company, something you may not have. It may be coming up the ranks slowly, something you did not do. Or it may be shared stories and memories, something you have not experienced.

Feeling left out can be frustrating, especially when you are new. By judging yourself against other women, you may believe that you are a failure, not good enough for their company. All those insecurities you harbor may begin to emerge.

Start by trying to talk with women on a one-to-one basis. This will put you outside the power of the group and equalizes the playing fields.

Learn about your colleagues by listening to them, then look for interests you both share. Listen for topics they enjoy talking about, styles they emulate, and things they like to do. This process takes time. Be patient; stay with it until you can see movement in a direction you enjoy. You do not need any enemies, especially when you are new. They can wreak havoc on your young career and cause irreparable harm. Win your enemies over to your side one at a time.

Do not threaten the status quo.

Change is often met with resistance. There is nothing personal about it. We are all creatures of habit; if we can avoid change, we will go to great lengths to maintain the status quo. Even when change represents a better situation, we may find ourselves resisting it.

Your very presence may represent and threaten change. There may be little that you can do to extinguish that flame except to be patient. The future will show whether or not you are the true agent of change.

Other women may have perceived your presence and conversation as changing what they currently have, and they may resist you personally in the process. Try to find neutral territory to open dialogue. Perhaps talking with women individually is less threatening to all concerned. Show interest in their lives, their routines, and accomplishments. Look for opportunities to show that you are not to be feared, and you do not want to destroy their comfortable surroundings. Try neutral and nonthreatening conversation styles.

Joan, do you have some tips you might be willing to share with someone new to the game? It sounds like it might be risky for me to get involved with the women's group. Can you give me some insight into that?

If you can accomplish the same goals without turning over the apple cart, then by all means do so. The path of least resistance will be the best one for you to follow. While the other women managers in the company may not support networking among women, that does not mean that you cannot participate.

6.2 | The Problem: You are intentionally left out of conversations and decisions by male colleagues.

THE SCENE

The monthly managers' meetings continue to be awkward and unsettling for you. There are very few women present, and the men tend to congregate and alienate you from their conversations. At yesterday's meeting, you approached three male managers. Quickly they changed the topic to subjects about which you were not able to participate. You suspected their action was intentional, but you have no way of proving it. It has happened several times before; you try starting a conversation on topics about which you can participate, but no one responds. Instead they continue talking about college sports, something you know little about and for which you have no interest.

Isolation and loneliness are overshadowing your ability and your attitude. Recently your boss commented that some of the other managers find it difficult to talk to you. He suggested that you try to *"fit in more."* Your attempts at fitting in appear to have failed; you still feel left out.

POSSIBLE CAUSES

Gender differences in conversation may be an issue.

Men and women converse differently. Whether in public situations, private conversation, giving suggestions, asking questions, making small talk, or telling jokes—these differences may explain why there appears to be a communication barrier. Feeling alienated and left out is simply the result of this barrier. If you want to participate in conversations with men, you may need to meet them on topics they prefer. What is their incentive to change? Understanding these differences is the first step in deciding *if* you want to play and *how willing* you are to change to a style more acceptable to your male audience.

Your actions, lack of participation, or expectations may add to the frustration.

Conversations with your boss suggest that you are partly responsible for being excluded. Whether this is correct or not is another matter, but it should be assessed. You may be expecting people to react to you in a certain manner, meet you on your turf, and participate in conversation that *you* find interesting. These topics may be as uncomfortable for the men as their topics are for you.

Group dynamics may alienate new members.

Groups can be either open or closed. Those groups that are open tend to welcome newcomers; whereas those that are more closed operate like cliques. Groups are created for a variety of reasons, including common interests, personality cohesiveness, age, or any number of other variables. Some groups are formed out of convenience, others are carefully put together. Being accepted into a group takes time. Excluding yourself from a group could be damaging to your future career.

CURES

Understand gender dialogue.

Men and women speak differently, hear differently, and interpret differently. The tremendous success of books such as *Men Are from Mars, Women Are from Venus* by John Gray, Ph.D. and *Talking from 9 to 5* by Deborah Tannen, Ph.D. continue to support this notion. Your actions, words, and subtle gestures are often misinterpreted by the opposite gender because of this barrier.

While there are many factors that comprise your pattern of communications, including social, economic, education, region, and race, gender remains one of the most divisive categories. You are not the only person who needs to understand this influence, but *you* are responsible for your participation.

To break through this barrier means making unequal concessions, at least initially. You will need to move past the halfway mark to meet your colleagues. Since men still dominate management positions, their style of communicating has been assumed appropriate. You are in the minority; therefore, the onus of change will be on you, not them.

Listen to the men in conversation with one another. Are they discussing sports? Are they joking around with each other? Are they trying to one-up each other? Also, realize that their style, while accepted by men of men, may not be accepted by men of *women*. There continues to exist stereotypes and expectations of the roles and styles considered appropriate for each gender. When you attempt to change or broaden those role definitions, it can produce confusion as well as resistance.

Men are more likely to focus on general topics, not personal issues when making small talk. Often they will spice up the conversation with humor and a little playful competition. On the other hand, women prefer engaging the individual on a more personal level.*What did you do this week-end? How are your children? What are their ages? Where do they go to school?"* In this level of conversation, women still feel the need to validate the other person, to let them know they understand what is going on in their life. When including humor, women often make themselves the butt of the joke, not someone else. Yet this style is seen as self-deprecating by some men, making men feel uncomfortable when around it.

You must find a comfort zone for yourself that is also acceptable to these male colleagues. Test the water—to see how far you are willing to go, and how far the men expect you to go—to find a style that is inside their definition of acceptable and within your own boundaries and comfort zone.

Take responsibility for what you do.

Your thoughts, words, and deeds may all play a part in this situation. You may be approaching a group and trying to force their conversation around topics you want. You may not have learned how to participate in small talk or how to gracefully enter a conversation. And you may be expecting others to respond to you in a particular manner.

These managers are not you. By establishing expectations, you are setting yourself up to be disappointed. Anticipating responses will lead to misunderstandings and confusion. Avoid reading more into a situation than is actually said or done. Sometimes this will be a very challenging request.

When you are part of the problem, the solution becomes easier to see (although it may not be easier to do). You can change your own actions, behavior, and style. You cannot change someone else. Understanding the problem is the first step. Then you must be willing to take responsibility, at least for that portion that you control. And finally, you must be willing to try new styles and modify your behavior to be less intrusive.

While this may be easy to say, it is one of the most difficult aspects of managing that women face. Not being accepted for who you are does not mean you are a bad person. It takes time and practice. Observe both men and women to see which styles work and don't work in that particular organization. Make small changes and allow enough time before you evaluate the results. Then continue until the process is complete.

Be part of the group.

Without realizing it, everyone participates in groups. Even if you do not like the idea of being part of a group, you are a member of several groups already. Groups may consist of friends, family, co-workers, or simply folks whom you find easy to talk to or with which you have shared interests.

Why all the hassle about groups? There are two main reasons. First, groups are a natural part of any organization. To succeed within the organization depends on how well you learn to maneuver within the boundaries of certain groups. And secondly, groups are a very common way of sharing information. If you are not part of a group, you may be missing out on information that could help your career future.

It may be easier to find acceptance with a group by meeting one member at a time. Try to find one person you feel comfortable around and intentionally work on creating a meaningful dialogue. Find mutual topics, whether it is children, sports, alma maters, or social events. Talk about things *they* are interested in, and listen for areas that may also interest you. Women in management who have succeeded in being accepted by men often are able to converse on numerous topics, including sports. These women accept that certain topics such as this are considered safe conversational areas with most men. It is a great place to begin.

Groups are nothing more than a lot of individuals lumped together by some common bond. From a group emerges a sense of both power and safety in numbers. But whether a group is open or closed depends on many variables. While one member may be more outgoing or accepting of new members, the group itself may still be closed. By observing the group, you will likely be able to assess its strengths and bonds. Once these have been identified, then work to be part of the group. Start by working on areas that interest the group as a whole, if this is possible. For example, what if the primary bond of the group is college football? Add to that the fact that the two primary state rivals are the basis of group membership. You may have difficulty gaining acceptance if you did not go to one of those two schools. This may be compounded by the fact that you dislike football, thinking of it as a brutal, foolish game.

All is not lost. Typically groups have more than one common denominator. When one avenue is eliminated, begin working on other areas. Continue in your research and observations until you find that bond. Part of your concession may be keeping up with college football. At least you will know what everyone is talking about on Monday mornings.

Never underestimate the importance of groups within any organization. Information can be shared, knowledge learned, support given, and cooperation offered. But often these are only extended to group members. When you are outside the group walls looking in, you are missing many opportunities. Try to fit in. It is in your professional interest.

6.3 The Problem: You are being criticized by other managers because you manage differently.

THE SCENE

You were asked by an employee if he could start coming in late two days a week because of his childcare situation. He agreed to work late on those days when he started late, so his schedule could be adjusted while his workload remained the same. After careful consideration and research, you agreed. The company had previously not offered flexible work schedules, but you felt it was justified in this case and you were ready to defend your decision. Each manager has been given the ability to set his or her own work schedules according to department needs.

You hadn't expected such an uproar to come from your fellow managers. Several of the managers have been less than supportive of your decision. In fact, David (who was promoted at the same time as you) came into your office this morning, closed the door, and shared his regrets about the way you were handling the department. Much of what he had to say was unfounded, still, you were forced to listen and defend your actions. David is someone you respect, which made his statement all the more difficult to accept.

David said that several of the other managers had been talking and had agreed that you had made a bad decision. They wanted you to change your decision and maintain standard hours for all employees. You suspect these managers are all male.

The other managers seem to resent your successes and are continually trying to hold you back. Despite the tremendous improvement of morale, you recognize that these changes have not been implemented without glitches. At every stumble there have been several men pointing fingers, gloating, *"I told you so, but you wouldn't listen.*

POSSIBLE CAUSES

There may be jealousy.

Unfortunately, jealousy is often difficult to pinpoint. These managers may resent the respect that you have gained from the employees, that they had not offered flexible scheduling first, or that they "lost" to a woman. Yes, their egos may be bruised.

Your style of managing may be causing friction.

It is no easy task to find a management style that is both reflective of you and that is accepted by the majority of the employees within the confines of the company's models. Each person must discover or create his or her own unique management style. The kinder, gentler approach many women prefer to follow may be met with resistance by males who are more comfortable with a hierarchical, rigid, or autocratic approach. Finding a comfortable balance may be a challenge.

You may have broken an unwritten rule.

Since some rules may be "unwritten," this is often difficult for women to perceive. And even if the rule *is* unwritten, the consequences may be just as severe. It is not that rules should never be broken, only that it is important that you accept responsibility when you do break the rules. Breaking rules not only threatens those who observe them, but also threatens those who implement them. Rules represent order.

CURES

Adapt a nonthreatening approach.

Jealousy can be hard to identify as the root of the problem because the signs may be similar to many other problems. Few individuals ever admit they are jealous. However, jealousy can be very disruptive to your routine and your career. Proceed carefully if you suspect jealousy is a factor.

If you assume the problem stems from jealousy, then you have three avenues to follow: confront the individual, win them over to your style, or adapt a style they accept. The first solution, confrontation, can easily backfire and should be used judiciously. Trying to win others over to your style assumes that your style is better and one they are comfortable adopting. And finally, adapting to their style suggests that you agree with their style and that you are willing to change. All of these solutions have some risk.

Try to determine where the jealousy is coming from. For example, David may be the only jealous person. The other managers may simply be side issues he has created to support his claims against you, your style, and your successes. If you determine this to be the case, talk privately with David.

> *David, I've been thinking about what you said to me concerning my management style, and I'd like your input. First, I do not believe that I can change my position because I gave my word to my employee. I will not go back on my word; trust is very important to me. It appears you would have responded differently. How might you have handled that situation? What factors do you consider important?*

This dialogue uses portions of all three choices, integrated into one. It confronts the individual without attacking him or her. It states your firm position and why you cannot or will not change. It also asks for input from him, respecting the differences, and listening openly. This approach is designed to defuse some of the anger and tension that may exist between you and David.

Neither of you may be willing to change your styles. When that happens, review your position and why you are so determined to defend it. If you still believe it is the best solution, do not waste your time trying to change someone else. Your role is simply to communicate your position. If the person chooses to disagree, that is his or her choice. Do not feel weakened because someone disagrees. Remember, managing is not a popularity contest; stay true to your convictions.

Getting along with other managers is an important tool in management. If making some concessions or changes means fitting in better, maybe it is not such a bad option.

Change your style to match the audience.

While no two management styles are identical, there are some acceptable models and guidelines that managers are expected to follow. These models change from organization to organization, depending on the particular corporate climate.

Deciding when a style is gender specific or exclusive, as opposed to when it just doesn't fit, is a slow and tiresome process. There are some models patterned after men that are not as acceptable or natural for women to practice. For example, when women adapt autocratic leadership styles they are perceived as bossy while men become powerful and assertive for the same actions. When using a straightforward, no-nonsense language women are considered abrupt whereas men are viewed as direct. In fact, numerous research observations indicate that when a woman speaks approximately one-fourth of the time during a conversation where a man is present, she is considered speaking an equal amount by both male and female participants. But when she speaks as much as the male participants in that group, she is perceived as being too talkative, controlling, or as dominating the conversation. These findings have been reported and written about by such notables as Dale Spender in *Man Made Language*, Carole Edelsky in *Who's Got the Floor?*, Deborah Tannen in *You Just Don't Understand*, and Myra and David Sadker in *Sexism in the Schoolroom of the '80s*. Obviously, the expectations and understandings are not the same by either men or women when gender is a factor.

Winning the support of those who manage differently than you will be an uphill battle. Women must accept that these stereotypes did not happen overnight, nor can they be changed quickly. In fact, there are many stereotypes that women also employ.

Girls are taught at young ages to *not* be the center of attention. This conceded trait is considered unladylike. Instead, a girl learns early in life how to share the spotlight with others, calling attention away from her own accomplishments and focusing on the group. Women are more comfortable using the pronoun *"we"* instead of *"I"* when speaking. Men are much more comfortable claiming ownership of their accomplishments even when they haven't actually done anything. The style patterned after men has become acceptable in business circles while women's modesty and selflessness is used against them.

You do have more than one style though. And perhaps when with certain managers your style should be more reflective of what they expect. This is not to say that you should become a chameleon, but that conversations and styles should reflect particular audiences.

Know the rules of the game.

Organizations operate with many rules, which are necessary to provide order. Rules reflect a semblance of how things should be done. Some of the rules may be written and observed through various company policy provisions, while others may be observed by the players but not be written down. Both written and unwritten rules play an equally important role in the orderly operation of a company.

To challenge the organization and its order can be pivotal in your career. It is risky if you fail. Before you break any rules try to understand how the rules evolved, and who put them into play.

Since David has approached you about the subject, find out what he knows first.

> *David, I know there has been a lot of talk and frustration about my decision to allow flexible work hours. Why do you feel there has been such a backlash? Do you think it is my style? I understood managers could set their own schedules, was I wrong?*

Be prepared for the fact that David may not know all the rules or whether one has actually been broken. He may not be privileged to this knowledge any more than you are.

Researching rules that are not written is more difficult. It requires finding someone who knows the answers, whom you can trust. Your boss may be able to provide some guidance and insight into this phenomena if you are willing to ask.

This is one place where a mentor can be very helpful to your career success. If you choose a mentor within the company who knows and plays by the rules, try to talk frankly about the history of these rules and the consequences for breaking them. Some companies have official mentoring programs; others do not. In either case, find the support and guidance of someone you trust, who will share knowledge with you.

6.4 | The Problem: After you were promoted, your closest female friend at work has disappeared from your life.

THE SCENE

Over the past several years Joyce and you have worked for the same company and become very good friends. You even socialized after work and on weekends together. Since your promotion last month, though, Joyce has been conspicuously absent from your vicinity.

While almost everyone in the company has come by to congratulate you on your promotion, Joyce has stayed away. Your feelings were hurt by her obvious lack of support. Now, your friendship seems to be lost because of this advancement.

You've asked Joyce to lunch several times, but each time she has made lame excuses like *"I'm too busy."* Before your promotion, there was always time for lunch. You know she's taking lunch breaks; they're just not with you. Now you wonder if the promotion was worth it. You feel that you have lost your friend.

POSSIBLE CAUSES

Competition is not always healthy.

In fact, competition can disrupt a workplace and lead to jealousy among the players. Women compete against other women on a different level than men do. Men learn through a variety of sporting events how to win and lose and continue playing the game. Few women have learned this healthy style of competition, although the numbers are increasing. Instead women learned to be much more covert in their competitive spirit, and rarely learned to accept loss. Joyce may be jealous because she did not get the promotion. Whether or not she was qualified is less important than the fact that *she believed* she should have been promoted. This may be compounded by the fact that she feels your promotion denied her the ability to move up, almost as if it were an either/or situation.

She may feel uncomfortable with the hierarchical gap.

Joyce may need some distance and time to sort through this transition. Her awkwardness may be the result of not knowing what to say or do around you now that you are *on the other side*, as part of management. Joyce may need some time and space to find a comfortable way of handling this new situation.

Your qualifications may be an issue.

It is not uncommon for friends to judge friends against a different standard than they do others. Perhaps Joyce feels you were not qualified for the position or that she is more qualified. Joyce may feel that almost anyone else in the company is more qualified, for that matter, than you. Friends often see your weaknesses before your strengths. While you mask your weaknesses around other people, your friends provide the safety net where you can let down that shield and be yourself. Sometimes friends may forget that you do have strengths.

CURES

Ease the jealousy gap.

When jealousy surfaces between friends, it can be difficult to salvage the friendship. It takes two to make a friendship work, and you cannot resolve this problem alone. Depending on how much Joyce is willing to work on the problem, it may not be one that can even be fixed.

Before you completely write the friendship off, try to get some time alone with her. If lunch worked before, ask her to pick a time when she might be available to go out for lunch with you. Be open, flexible, and sensitive to her schedule.

> *Joyce, I was hoping we could go to lunch sometime. How does your schedule look? I'll let you pick the date. I really miss our times together, it seems like we've both been so busy it's hard to get our schedules to cross.*

At lunch, focus on Joyce and her feelings. Share with her the fact that you miss not going to lunch together, and that you hope you can continue to be friends. She may or may not be willing to open up at this point. If she does, listen to her response.

Joyce may respond with something like, *"You have changed so much since your promotion. You're not the same person I knew."* If she does, ask her to give examples or to explain her perceptions. Don't feel that you must defend yourself; this is a time for you to validate Joyce and her feelings. Try to work on a way that you are able to meet her needs.

However, if Joyce denies that anything is different, but instead says that she has been really busy lately, believe in her time constraints. Ask about her projects without appearing too judgmental or too inquisitive. You do not want her to have the impression that you doubt she is telling you the truth. She may be busy, or she may feel uncomfortable around you now; those are her decisions and choices. If Joyce is not willing to work on the friendship, there is not a lot that you can do alone.

Ultimately, you must be willing to accept the fact that some friendships may be lost for a variety of reasons as you ascend your career path. Your own personal time constraints may impede their growth as well as the fact that some friends may feel uncomfortable with your promotion. Losing a friend because of a promotion is tough to accept. But that may be your only choice, to accept that a friendship has been lost, and then move on.

Flatten the hierarchical structures.

Organizations vary in how they regard management and subordinate staff alliances. Some companies frown on the two groups mixing, implying that it is somewhat unprofessional for them to become close. Others treat all employees as equals, regardless of their job descriptions or titles. The situation may also be complicated by individual comfort levels and perceptions, which may not necessarily mirror corporate philosophy.

If an employee feels threatened or uncomfortable because you are now on a different hierarchical level than she is, your options may be limited. Understand that you've changed. You are now responsible for the output of a department, and must motivate other employees to perform at their optimal levels. You now may have access to information that you didn't have before.

The real questions become *how* have you changed and *how much*? Talking to Joyce may provide an excellent opportunity to see how you have changed, assuming the strength of your friendship is built on honesty.

> *Joyce, I know your schedule is very busy. I was wondering if you had five minutes so that we may be able to talk?* (Assuming she says yes, then continue.) *How have you been lately? You know, I hope that our friendship will continue. I have always appreciated your candor and honesty. I admit that I am nervous about this promotion. And I hope I can rely on you to keep me centered, to tell me if I have changed. Have I?*

You must be willing to accept that at some level it is Joyce's responsibility to share her concerns. You can open the door and invite the conversation, but you cannot force it. There is only so much that you can do. Don't feel selfish because your career is taking off.

This is not meant to make light of a very difficult situation. In fact, women have a strong need to be accepted. Joyce's alienation can be interpreted as rejection. What was it about Joyce that drew you together before? Are those bonds still there? Or have they been lost over time?

Believe in yourself.

Not everyone who deserves a promotion gets one, nor is every person promoted deserving of their promotion. Unfortunately, this is something you have little control over.

As a woman you can expect and anticipate that your qualifications will be questioned. It is rare that a woman is promoted without someone, somewhere questioning her qualifications and abilities. Your greatest admirers and friends are just as likely as anyone else to put you through these tests. Winning Joyce's approval may only be achieved in time.

Each decision you render will represent a separate test. You may never know what actions you can or should do to win the approval of your adversaries. Instead, it is their game, rules, and scorecard. You become only a pawn in their game, never aware of the score or when the game is over.

During this transition time, self-doubt can leave you feeling unqualified and unprepared. Someone obviously believed you were qualified enough to promote you. Review your previous accomplishments and feel good about yourself. Do not let the tests and challenges get in the way of your confidence; it will only bring you down. When you are bombarded by tests, seek the support and guidance of those who give you encouragement. Surround yourself with positive people, not critical ones.

You will better serve yourself by concentrating on the department, yourself, and your future. Friendships may be lost either temporarily or perhaps permanently through time. It is unfortunate, especially for women who feel the need to be connected with others above their individual needs and desires. But it can happen.

6.5 The Problem: As the only female present at a meeting, you have been asked to take minutes.——again.

THE SCENE

You were asked to take the minutes at the managers' meeting again. This is the third meeting in which you have been relegated to the role of playing secretary. It makes you feel inferior to the other managers, almost subservient. You are the only female present, which to you suggests that being a secretary is a female task.

You feel that it diminishes your authority and minimizes your position as a manager. Taking the minutes also limits your ability to participate freely in the discussions. No one took the minutes before you came, reiterating to you that gender is a major factor.

When you confront your boss about this gender bias, he says not to worry. He quickly adds that everyone thinks you are doing a good job and that you should feel honored. You don't feel honored; instead, you feel that his response is adding to the patronizing atmosphere.

POSSIBLE CAUSES

Yes, there is gender bias in America.

The business community is not immune from its presence. Some biases are more blatant than others; subtle biases can be more damaging because they are harder to detect. Bias (including gender bias) is based on stereotypes and role expectations, and is everywhere in our society. It takes more than simple tolerance to change these reactions, it takes a willingness to be open to people who are different. To change biases starts with the realization that each person, yourself included, has some propensity to stereotype people and roles.

You may be overreacting to the situation.

Not everything that happens to you is the result of your gender. Your sensitivity to gender issues may be causing a distorted reality to occur. When you highlight the difference as gender-related, you may be manufacturing the cause to fit your own hidden agenda without even realizing it. Review your motives carefully before you start stirring up trouble where there is none.

You may be the most qualified person to take minutes.

Whether your qualifications are based on previous work experience or your penchant for details and organization, you may be the most qualified person of that group to take minutes. Your sensitivity to gender relations may be causing you to overlook that fact.

Other Considerations: Are you more frustrated in how you were asked or told, instead of that you were asked? Sometimes the underlying issue isn't that you were asked to do a specific job, but that it was expected of you. You may resent feeling like you do not have a choice, which is another way of saying that you have no voice in the matter. Women are likely to fight causes based more on principle than on substance. Winning isn't as much the issue for women as is making a difference, gaining respect, and being heard. Women are comfortable reaching a compromise or conceding when they feel that their voices have been heard.

What If: You had a female boss? Would you consider her response as patronizing or demeaning to you? The same statement by a female boss would likely be interpreted as validating to you or construed as words of encouragement. When you feel the words and actions are targeted a certain way because of gender, change the gender and see what you think. Does it change your reaction? If so, how? and why? Are you interpreting the words differently than they were intended? Or was your boss making such a comment intentionally? These are the questions you must ask.

CURES

Minimize gender biases in the workplace.

Biases represent stereotypes. By predisposing of a person because of race, religion, or gender you are limiting his or her options. On the other hand, generalizations are a reflection of the majority. The line between generalization and bias is often gray and crossed frequently. The workplace is a microcosm of society; when society has biases, you can expect to find them in the workplace as well.

Everyone is guilty of some type of bias or stereotype, including you. These can exist without your even realizing them. For example, the profession of nursing probably conjures up images of females. Yet men continue to enter the field of nursing. If you think of a nurse and see a female in your mind, or refer to nurses with the pronoun "she," you are stereotyping. When you are talking about a man in the nursing profession, you may refer to him as a "male nurse," as an exception to the norm. This is a common stereotype. Of course, your image is based upon history: in the past men rarely entered the field of nursing. And still today, the majority of nurses are females. Even though there is a basis for such a generalization, it can unintentionally exclude or alienate men who are nurses. The same generalizations are true of women entering management levels.

Talk to your boss and try to get some clarity or direction on the situation:

> *You know that it frustrates me to take the minutes at the meetings, especially since I am the only female present, and no one took the minutes before I came. Is it possible to rotate the job between different managers so that no one person gets the brunt of the work? There is a great deal of work that goes into taking the minutes during the meeting and afterward; it limits my ability to participate freely in the discussions because I am writing down comments. Rotating the job would allow everyone to participate in the process and help everyone appreciate the job more. Please understand that I don't feel like it is a compliment, even though you say it is. I feel like it takes a lot of my time away from managing.*

Ignorance would be the easiest situation to defuse. Education is your best armor against comments made toward gender stereotypes. Someone may actually not think that they are being demeaning to you by asking that you take the minutes. Becoming too defensive or sensitive about this assignment will work against you, so proceed cautiously.

When the company philosophy is founded on gender biases, then your best option is to find employment elsewhere. Corporate attitudes are set from the top. You would be taking on too many warriors at one time.

Place things in their proper perspective.

Everything that happens around you is not a personal attack on your gender. You may be reading more into this situation than is healthy, and more than is actually there. This is not said to lessen the responsibility of others, minimize the situation, or devalue your own feelings.

Deciding when an issue is gender-related and when it isn't is an arduous task and one that may never be decided upon with complete certainty. You may find answers by looking inside yourself for your motives and sensitivity levels. For example, you may be too defensive, making it impossible for anything not to be gender-related.

Ask yourself some very basic questions: Why does this appear to be a gender issue to you? How would you respond if a male had been asked to take the minutes? Does taking minutes impede your ability to participate actively in the meeting? While these questions may not provide the answers you were looking for quickly, they will cause you to think about your own attitudes.

Accept your strengths.

You may be the most logical person for the position of secretary in the meeting. Its importance or lack thereof may only be troubling to you. Other managers may perceive this as a task that needs to be done, with you as the person most qualified to do it.

Look inside yourself and outline your strengths objectively. Do you have qualities that make you a perfect candidate for taking the minutes? If so, be proud of your strengths. Learn how to promote yourself and use them to your advantage.

There are many benefits to this position, if you are willing to look for them. For instance, a great deal of information is contained in the minutes, information that you will have at your fingertips. You can use this information to your advantage by how you disseminate it, process it, and share it. In order to have consistent minutes taken it is better to assign the task to one person. Also, you may be able to elevate the position to one of greater importance and prestige by the results you achieve.

If you feel you are unable to participate equally in the discussion if you are taking the minutes, you may consider taping the meeting. This creates more work afterward in transcribing and organizing the information, but it allows you to participate more freely.

Attitude, something you control, can change your whole outlook. And attitude can cloud your judgment if you let it. Keep your attitude positive and always look for the benefits of a situation.

6.6 The Problem: You received dishonest feedback from a colleague, which made you look bad during a presentation.

THE SCENE

After a lot of research and preparation, you have just presented a controversial project to a major corporate division. The results were not what was expected. The resistance you anticipated from another department had been resolved before the meeting. At least that was what you thought when you had met with Scott, the plant manager. Now you feel that you had intentionally been set-up to look bad at this meeting.

Scott had raised some concerns and made some suggestions when you met with him. After making some adjustments and answering his questions, Scott seemed to agree with your conclusions and supported the project. He even complimented you on your thoroughness.

Then, during your formal presentation Scott had the audacity to lambast you in front of the other department managers. It was as if he had intentionally misled you, only to attack your presentation during the meeting and to look good in front of his peers. Not only did you look bad in front of these managers, you also looked unprepared, as if you hadn't done sufficient research, which wasn't the case at all.

POSSIBLE CAUSES

Surprise attacks can blind-side you.

Sometimes no amount of preparation is enough to defend these intentional assaults. By their very nature, these come from the individuals who play unfair, waiting for the moment to gain any tactical advantage at your expense. Part of the success of managing becomes anticipating these attacks and maintaining a defensive posture of readiness.

You may not know how to play the game.

When playing the game of management, you must accept that other members may be playing a different game. They may not only want to win, but they may also want to see you lose. When you do not assume that same mindset, you are at a disadvantage. The idea of sharing may be foreign to how these men have played. Competition throughout life teaches boys that there can be only one winner while girls games often show them how to play so that everyone can win. If you have a style that is inclusive, a style that works best by consensus, open and honest dialogue, and by agreements being reached, you may be the rough edge rubbing against their skin. It is important for you to know what the rules of the game are, otherwise you may find yourself in an awkward position that could have been avoided with some planning.

This may be a test of your willpower and management abilities.

Other managers may be testing you to see how much you know and how good a defender you are. Women are tested more often than men on their ability to manage. Each presentation, project, and comment must be carefully thought out before spoken. This may be one of many tests you must undergo. You will have to be smarter, tougher, and more prepared than your male colleagues just to be considered their equal.

Your style may add to the confusion.

You may have a management style that antagonizes certain individuals. It could be a style that is not generally practiced within the environment, for whatever reasons. Whether these individuals feel threatened, superior, or simply uncomfortable around you, your style may not work well here. All styles may not fit comfortably in every situation; to be successful in any environment means finding one that works for you as well as for that environment.

CURES

Anticipate surprise attacks.

Some individuals like to withhold information and spring attacks on vulnerable prospects. These individuals are definitely in the minority, but when you are matched against them there is little that you can do other than survive and be better prepared the next go around.

In the meeting with Scott you may say something like:

Scott, I went over these findings with you yesterday and you were very comfortable with my conclusions. What has happened since yesterday to create such hostility toward this project?

However, realize that there is risk in this conversation. It can be made to sound like you are a sore loser or that you are part of the problem. Scott could then respond with a barrage of ammunition he held back, waiting for such an opportunity.

At some point it may be necessary to simply let this battle go. This will depend on the nature of the project and its long-term effects on your career, but it is worth consideration. You may need to accept that you lost this battle to the surprise attack by someone waiting in the wings; work harder the next time, be better prepared, and be ready to stay for the duration.

Know the rules of the game.

Sports metaphors continue to be common in the business world because men use the corporate structure akin to playing sports. They play hard and they play to win. Women may have trouble adapting to this style. It is more aggressive and combative then women are comfortable with.

Most of these games continue to reward individual performances, even when they are played as a team sport. For example, awards are given to the most valuable player of a particular game, someone who stood out from the team. Corporate America may do the same thing, subconsciously finding ways to reward those players who go above and beyond the call of duty.

Although you are supposed to be playing for the same team, Scott may create situations where he has a distinct advantage, so that he gets the rewards and goes home with the MVP trophy, even if these are won at your expense.

Talk to Scott to understand his feeling on this situation. Because of the complex nature of these attitudes, though, you should proceed cautiously.

Scott, I'd like to work with you to resolve this problem. I hope that we can both create a strong and workable solution together. How does your schedule look next week?

Be willing to compromise if it gets you the results you want. Scott may want to take credit for your accomplishments, and you may let him. Choose your battles carefully; the war may be a long one and you don't want to wear yourself out too soon. Compromising doesn't mean you lost, it can mean that you both won. Short-term inequities balance out in the long run.

Defend your position.

Time and again women find themselves being tested more by their co-workers, staff, and upper management then their male colleagues. Instead of assuming that a person promoted to a position knows what she is doing, women are faced with proving that they deserve the promotion, are qualified, and know what they are talking about. This may not be equal, or even fair, but it happens with great regularity.

Your best defenses against these attacks are confidence and preparation. Without these virtues, you easily become prey to the many vultures waiting to see your demise. With confidence and preparation you are better able to defend yourself. Although you may not always win, without them you become a weak leader.

Find a style that is accepted.

Management styles are influenced by a variety of factors. Gender plays a significant role in interpreting these variances, but it is not the only source. Finding the middle ground may be difficult. Women's style is often considered weak by males, while other women admire and respond to it. However, when women find a style "acceptable" to men, it is often viewed as harsh, aggressive, or pushy by other women.

Style is neither right nor wrong. There are many different styles. Look at the various players within the organization and determine how much change, and what type of change is acceptable. If there are other women in management who have come before you, how have they been viewed? When they are highly regarded by their colleagues, watch their styles closely. Not that you should mimic someone else, but be flexible and resilient in finding what works best for you.

Be patient. It may be a matter of other people learning about your style. Time may prove to be your best ally, if you will only use it wisely.

6.7 | The Problem: The male colleagues are gloating about their various memberships and club participations, knowing that you are excluded.

THE SCENE

Sitting around the conference table, the men are chatting about who is going golfing Friday afternoon with which customer. They intentionally go around the room asking who has played at the different local golf courses. Since you do not golf, and since women are not welcome in some of these clubs, you are left out of the conversation. They flaunt their various country club memberships for which the company pays.

You have seen their routines over and over again. They take a customer to lunch at an elite country club, charging it to the company account; instead of returning back to the office that afternoon, they play a round of golf with the customer. You remain in the office working and helping their customers while they are out of the office. Even though they close a lot of deals, you feel alienated and left out.

POSSIBLE CAUSES

The playing fields are not always equal.

In fact, the playing fields are seldom equal. Sometimes people do not even play fair. When this happens, there is little that you can do other than accept this reality and learn to play where you are more comfortable and where you may actually have the advantage.

These exclusions may be representative of the corporate philosophy.

In business cultures, many attitudes are bred from the top down. When sexism and elitism is common at the top, it is often practiced throughout the company. Men may like their special treatment; they may not be willing to share these opportunities with women. Some men may say, *"If you can't play how we play, you shouldn't be playing at all."* Beware of such overt sexism and inequality.

CURES

Play fair.

The playing fields in business, as in life, are often unequal. This does not necessarily mean things are bad. Women also have advantages that are taken for granted that men seldom have. Likewise, a man may take his opportunities for granted not realizing that women do not have the same choices or paths available.

Ask yourself: *What can you change? And why do you want to change it?* Change needs to come from within. Forced change is often met with animosity and resistance. Instead, look inside yourself and around you to find opportunities where a win-win situation can result.

Should the men in the organization be penalized because they are taking advantage of an opportunity afforded them because of their gender? If so, the losers would be the customers and the company, not to mention the employees. Creating a game in which no one wins doesn't seem to be the right choice. Better yet, accept that differences do, have, and always will exist on certain levels. Spend your time and energy exploring areas where your feminine style may work to your advantage. Whether or not your male colleagues have those same advantages is beside the point.

Feminine advantages include many mannerisms and styles. For example, the ability to nurture and care for the employees is a female characteristic, to be able to ask about their personal lives without being considered nosy or patronizing. Other advantages include being able to hug an employee, to show you care without fear of sexual harassment charges being filed against you. You can celebrate special occasions by bringing food to the office to share with the staff, and find different ways to show your appreciation including rewards, recognition, and thank-you notes. The list is endless.

None of these advantages are exclusive to one gender or another, and are only more representative of the female style. In other words, some women go golfing with customers and are very comfortable and effective around country club atmospheres. On the other hand, some men have successfully found balance in being strong leaders while remaining sensitive to the needs of the staff.

Learn to accentuate your own positives; work within a system where you are comfortable, and find the rewards you deserve. It can be a win-win proposition when everyone works toward their best interest and remains collectively working for the good of the company.

Deal with sexism in the company.

When sexism is rampant within the company, chances are that it is supported and encouraged by senior management. There may be little that you can do to change a system that has been operating this way for years.

If you sense that sexist attitudes are representative of senior management and corporate philosophy, leave it alone. There is nothing that you can do to change someone else, and by stirring the pot it will only boil over. You risk losing a great deal of longevity with this company by bulldozing your way through and demanding change.

All is not lost; you do have choices. You may choose to stay and do the best you can within this system. You may choose to stay while trying to change a system to offer more advantages for females. Or you may choose to leave, to find another employer that is more representative of your style and appreciative of what you have to offer. As always, the choice is yours, given your particular circumstances and style. You may want to review Section 9.6 for information on how to handle a similar situation from a policy perspective.

6.8 The Problem: Inappropriate sexual comments about an employee are made in your presence by male colleagues.

THE SCENE

You walk into the room and notice clusters of people gathered around, talking, waiting for the meeting to start. You approach a group of colleagues. This group happens to be all men, but you have never felt excluded by them in the past. You have felt as though you'd been treated equally by colleagues from both genders.

Everyone swaps morning cordialities with you, but they continue their conversation. It takes you a moment to figure out what they are talking about. You realize that it is the new employee: female, single, young, pretty, and rather shapely. The men are making jokes and comments about the *"lucky manager she reports to,"* and how envious they are of him. Their comments are very suggestive, leaving little room for imagination.

You have never heard these men make such crude comments, or act in such a sexist fashion. It takes you by surprise. You don't know what to do. If you object, they may or may not stop in your presence, but that doesn't change how they truly feel. They may try to trivialize your objection by saying *"Don't be so serious, we're only joking,"* implying that you don't know how to take a joke. But if you don't speak up, nothing will change. They may not even be aware that their behavior is offensive to you.

Is their conversation purely harmless? Are you overreacting to these comments? Should you risk their disapproval, and share your feeling about how their words offend you?

POSSIBLE CAUSES

They may not know any better.

Ignorance may not be an excuse when it comes to laws, but ignorance is often a reality of the world in which we live. People frequently make inappropriate comments without meaning harm. They respond by how they were taught. Whether a person is speaking truthfully or they are just naive, some people are not aware that their behavior may be interpreted as inappropriate, rude, suggestive, or wrong. This does not make their comments appropriate by any means, and only goes to explain the condition, not support it.

Some people enjoy the shock value of their comments.

There may be some situations where individuals are aware that their comments will have a negative impact on you, but they say them anyway. In fact, that is exactly why they say them: to make you feel uncomfortable. Some people may intentionally try to aggravate a situation by provoking you; they want to see how far they can take it before you speak up. In other situations, these actions are used to assert power over you. A few men may be trying to remind you that power still comes with gender tags; they may be reminding you that you are still not a member of their club. While they make these comments, they may be observing your response, ready to defend their egos.

They may think they are being funny.

Men and women do respond differently to humor. Women are more apt to place themselves central to a joke, laughing at their own mistakes while men look outward to find humor. Men are more comfortable telling jokes; women prefer telling stories. Even locker-room trash talk is considered by some men as light and humorous in nature, harmless by their standards. The confusion may be based on how you speak and what you speak about, and not be meant in a personal or degrading fashion.

CURES

Ignorance is not an excuse.

Unfortunately, some people just do not know any better. Even if individuals are ignorant about how their words are heard, or how their actions are felt, that does not lessen their responsibilities. While ignorance may explain behavior, it doesn't excuse it.

If you felt the comments were offensive to you, then you must say so despite someone else's understanding of the event. To ignore your inner self is to quietly support these continued offenses. Honoring yourself is the cornerstone to having others honor and respect you.

Your options include speaking up immediately, saying nothing, or speaking to the individuals at a later time, when they are alone. Speaking up immediately has the greatest risk of alienation. Much depends on how and what you say, as well as the respect others in the group have for you. Risking the male bravado in front of other males generally turns into a competition. A contest you will surely lose because you are outnumbered, and because you are female.

To say nothing is tantamount to supporting these comments. While you are not actually adding to the conversation, by your silence you are not objecting.

It is important to find a style that is not threatening or alienating to these colleagues. Making yourself sound superior will backfire. Instead of making a scene, try talking with colleagues individually and on neutral territory. Sharing how their comments were offensive to you educates them without threatening the hierarchy or status of the group.

Here is one way to approach a colleague:

Frank, earlier today you were making some comments about the new employee, Suzie. I know that you meant nothing by those comments, but I felt uncomfortable. Women are judged more by appearance than men; women feel beauty and success are only skin deep according to men's perceptions. In the workplace, women continue to fight these stereotypes and until we are seen as employees, where gender is not the issue, there remains an invisible barrier separating us. Those comments reminded me that the barrier is still there. I hope that you understand why I left.

For a person to change, they have to want to change. If Frank or the other colleagues involved are perfectly comfortable in asserting their manhood, and feel that their comments were completely innocent and that no harm was done, then change will be met with resistance and is unlikely to occur.

Do not react with shock.

Sometimes people say things for their shock value, hoping to get a comment, reaction, or rise from you. They know their comments are offensive, especially to you, but they make them anyway—with blatant disregard for your feelings.

Their personal lack of consideration could be from jealousy or a perceived threat. Women seek the connection of the group and the equal involvement of everyone, whereas men seek status and hierarchy. Your presence may threaten either or both these structures. Your style may be awkward for men. While on one level they may accept you into their ranks, they may view you as the exception and have a total disregard for other women in the company; or they may inwardly resent you encroaching on their territory. In fact, their rude comments made about other women may well be spoken about you when you are not present. This may be their way of putting you on notice.

How you respond is tricky. Unfortunately, these men may be creating a playing field that is not equal, and not fair. Your approach is to neutralize the hostility as much as is possible, avoid playing their game, and be willing to share your concerns openly.

When you are confronted with a group setting, your voice is immediately minimized. To assert yourself in their presence can sound childish, as if you are defending yourself. You would be falling right into their trap by taking their bait. Do not take this step.

Instead, you should leave when the comments are being made because staying would only anger you, and produce nothing beneficial. You can either discuss this matter individually or just forget about it. Since the comments were made intentionally, any response by you would indicate that they had been successful in bothering you.

If you do choose to confront them, expect their response to be belittling. If this is intentional, they have no regard for your feelings. However, your objective should be to honor yourself and not win their approval. Speak up whenever you feel it is necessary.

Humor can be gender-specific.

Humor is one of the most misunderstood qualities, especially in the workplace. It becomes even more complex when looked at through gender biases. There are some very stark differences between what men and women consider humorous.

While men may be making light conversation and consider these comments both harmless and funny, you may interpret them quite differently. They may come across as alienating and hostile to you. In fact, you may not see anything humorous about their comments concerning women's physical appearances.

Men prefer teasing someone else while women place themselves central to their jokes. Neither gender understands the other's style of humor very well.

If this is unsettling for you, then you should speak up. Make certain that your comments continually reiterate and are focused on *your* feelings and *your* personal interpretations.

The only lasting results will probably be achieved through educating them on what you consider humorous and what offends you. By the same token, they may have a similar dialogue with you. The bottom line may be that you agree to disagree. You may need to be more sensitive when the other gender is present and they may need to be more sensitive to their own understandings of these comments when you are present. Learn not to take everything so personally.

What If: This same conversation occurs as part of a meeting? Your options remain the same, but the recommendation changes. When this behavior is introduced into a situation where you cannot leave, it should *not* be tolerated, accepted, or allowed. Even at the risk of being ostracized and alienated by your peers, ask that the conversation change in substance and explain why. Attacking their style will prove counterproductive; instead be willing to elaborate about your feelings and sensitivities about certain topics. While it may not change their feelings, hopefully they will respect you enough to honor your request.

6.9 | The Problem: Work conversations frequently contain sexual innuendos and other suggestive comments that you find inappropriate.

THE SCENE

Everywhere around the office, including the cafeteria, you are confronted with men and women making sexual innuendos and insinuating comments. You know that some people consider these to be funny, but they seem awkward, unsettling, and even inappropriate to you. At the very least they should be looked upon as unprofessional comments.

You have noticed that the women who have been accepted by these men, however, are those women who can hold their own in conversations of such a crass nature. These women do not get embarrassed easily. You have witnessed some women who could dish it out as well as they could take it.

Still, it doesn't seem right. Why can't businesspeople talk more professionally? Why must so many topics be centered around various body parts, functions, or activities? Sometimes you feel like a prude, even old-fashioned in your beliefs, but you still feel it is wrong.

Note: Simply because you think it is inappropriate does not mean it is wrong. Often rightness and wrongness are decided by the group, not by individuals. Therefore, if it is accepted by the group, it may be perfectly "right" according to their standards. That doesn't mean, though, that you should participate in something that you feel is inappropriate.

POSSIBLE CAUSES

Determine what is appropriate talk at work.

Business talk is more than just acquiring a professional dialogue, it also means understanding how the conversations are created and accepted within these particular confines. Each group will decide for itself what is appropriate dialogue within its own environment. There may be some conversations between certain individuals that hold one tone, while these same conversations may be deemed inappropriate between other participants in the company.

Some people may be crude, while others just have poor manners.

Even though certain behavior is accepted within a particular setting doesn't make it right. Nor does it mean that you should adapt such an offensive style. Words can be a very effective tool for asserting power over another individual, if someone chooses. Bad manners do not make a person less responsible for their actions; they explain the situation, not justify it.

Humor takes many forms, including suggestive styles.

These are the times when nothing dirty or sexual is actually spoken but only implied, leaving your mind to wander down those suggestive paths. Men have found this form of dialogue both humorous, as well as gender-inclusive. It is almost as if they are speaking in third person, and allowing you to participate in the same tone. According to your own observations, some women within the company have had great success in being accepted by adopting a similar style. You should embrace a style that is natural and comfortable for you. If this type of humor does not feel right, then by all means do not try to make it work for you; it won't.

CURES

Determine acceptable business talk.

There are a variety of styles and forms of business talk that are used around offices. Sometimes these are negotiated according to personal preferences, and other times these are indicative of industry standards and acceptable practices. Whatever the case, there will already be some guide-lines and styles that have become acceptable in this particular environ-ment.

This is not meant to imply that one style is right while another is wrong, nor to determine what is appropriate or inappropriate dialogue within a par-ticular setting. Those are items negotiated within a specific organization. Value judgments will only confuse the issue. What is accepted within the organization is just that, the accepted business talk at that time, in that place.

You may or may not choose to participate. What is not appropriate, however, is to condemn someone else simply because they have chosen a style with which you do not agree.

If you want to be accepted, you must learn that the game began long before you arrived at the scene. Your arrival does not signify that a new game must be started, or that a new game will even begin now. Instead, you must accept that you are a new player entering an existing match.

Know your boundaries within a particular group.

Sometimes people do cross the line. When this happens, the first thing to do is step back and see who drew the line and where it was drawn. It might be that you drew the line so far that no matter what was said, some-one was bound to cross over it.

You will create boundaries that you are comfortable operating within, at the same time the company already has created boundaries that have worked for a variety of players. It is important that you know both your boundaries as well as the company's boundaries for conversations.

If you determine, according to generally accepted standards in society, that certain topics or behavior are not appropriate in the business setting, then remaining quiet is tantamount to accepting and supporting such con-duct. At the same time, you do not want to alienate anyone else, just like you do not want to be alienated from conversations. Instead, strive to create a safe dialogue that hopefully will allow everyone to understand each other better.

Talk to your boss first, to find out what his or her suggestions are for handling this situation. Be prepared to explain why you feel such conduct is reprehensible. You will probably be asked to defend your position, since it appears to be in the minority. Avoid name calling and personal attacks, even though you may be tempted. Focus on your feelings and your con-cerns.

Next, talk to those individuals who are participating in what you deem is inappropriate behavior. Explain your concerns and ask that they change, at least in your presence. Admittedly, this may have little impact on them, and only agitate the situation more. Nothing will change unless you speak up though.

If the situation does not improve and you feel it is inappropriate, remove yourself from it. Ultimately that may mean finding another employer. Remember to focus on those things that you *can* change. You cannot make someone else do what you wish; you can only change yourself.

Understand feminine humor.

Women tell funny stories, while men tell jokes. The styles of humor are completely different. It remains one of the greatest communication barriers between the genders, yet it often goes unnoticed. While each person considers his or her style appropriate, the other may seem completely foreign.

Men enjoy standing up while telling jokes. They like laughing at someone else's misfortunes. Even in casual conversations men have learned the art of joke telling and timing.

Women are more comfortable telling stories from their personal life experiences. Women are often central to the stories. It is their way to ease tension and to put themselves on a level with which anyone present can readily identify. They use this same style when speaking informally in small groups as well.

One style is not right while the other is wrong; instead, this is a matter of comfort and preference. How you choose to respond to this situation is your personal decision. Knowing humor is often gender-based may not make you feel more comfortable around this dialogue. Unfortunately, there may not be a middle ground for each party to reach. The lesson may be simply to understand the differences and use this knowledge however you see fit.

Chapter Summary

Women seek a connectedness with other people and to threaten that connectedness may present difficulties for women entering the management arena. That threat may come from friends, colleagues, or co-workers.

Men may be fighting to protect their egos, maintain their power, resist change, or to create a sense of control for the future. By not welcoming women into their club, men may be sending territorial messages, while at the same time protecting their turf.

As for the friction that occurs between other women, the underlying factors are likely to be jealousy or competition. While on the one hand women rely on other women for support and validation, there continues to exist a level of competition between women that is different than it is between men. Whereas men measure themselves against their own level of achievement, women measure themselves against other women. The competition is much more covert in nature, and can be difficult to manage because it is frequently denied.

Within any group it is necessary to find a style that is not threatening to the group's position, one that allows you to be heard, promotes your abilities, and presents a strong image. To find that style, women must be willing to adapt styles similar to those currently being accepted within a particular setting. The style must be natural for a woman, or it will not work, and gender does play a very strong factor in communication styles, although it is not the only factor.

Learning how to play the game, to promote yourself, and to accept criticism without taking it personally are all excellent lessons for anyone entering management. For women, these lessons have often not been learned through team sports, an advantage many men have had. A mentor, if available, can help you learn these tools. Try to find someone who knows how to maneuver through this environment, and learn from the master.

The problems addressed in this chapter include not getting the support from other women that you were expecting, feeling like you have lost a best friend because of your promotion, feeling left out of the conversation intentionally, being criticized for managing differently, and how to respond to sexual innuendos and comments in conversations. This section focuses on identifying those things that you can change within yourself, and examines why a particular situation may be bothersome to you.

Troubleshooting Tensions from Superiors

Overview

Tension generally occurs when you do not agree with someone else, for a variety of reasons. It could include differences in styles, approaches, perceptions, values, or it may be seen in differences such as pay, status, title, or promotions.

Corporate America produces power structures and hierarchies that place you under another manager's supervision. When tension is a direct source between you and this superior, you may feel trapped or unable to perform at your best. There is a gender slant on this hierarchy, because women are more likely to report to male superiors since they are still stopped by the glass ceiling.

This chapter addresses the following problems, possible causes, and cures.

7.1 ***The Problem: During your first review, the boss stated that you were not assertive enough with the staff and gave you unfavorable marks.***

Possible Causes: You are faced with indecisiveness about your role, authority, and responsibility; you may not be performing up to acceptable standards; there are still chauvinistic attitudes in the workplace; there may be a clash between the two styles.

Cures: Communicate role expectations; improve your performance; manage while dealing with a chauvinist; adapt a different style.

7.2   ***The Problem: You have been offered less money for a new position than a male colleague had been offered for the same job.***

Possible Causes: Salary discrimination remains a problem; there may
be a difference in qualifications; you may have asked for less.

Cures: Understand salary discrimination and the law; determine when
discrepancies are justified; learn how to negotiate for more.

7.3   ***The Problem: As a woman, you feel promotions and career
opportunities are limited.***

Possible Causes: You may be bumping against the glass ceiling; you
may be lacking the professional image of a leader; you may not be ready for
a promotion; your boss may be holding you back.

Cures: Break through the glass ceiling; create a positive and professional image; know your limitations; work around obstacles.

7.4   ***The Problem: Your boss has made an unwelcome pass at you.***

Possible Cause: The cause is less important than how you handle
yourself.

Cures: Handle sexual harassment by: notifying human resources, confronting the boss, removing yourself from the scene, ignoring the situation,
or filing an EEOC complaint.

7.5   ***The Problem: Your suggestions during a meeting are ignored.
It is as if you are not even in the room.***

Possible Causes: You are not being heard; you are fighting an invisible microphone; identify and understand politics and fear.

Cures: Learn to speak up and be heard; gain access to invisible micro-
phones; play the game to win during territorial wars.

7.6   ***The Problem: You have been offered a promotion that you do
not want to accept.***

Possible Causes: Politics makes strange bedfellows; declining this offer
may limit your career; you may be doubting your own abilities.

Cures: Accept politics in the workplace; learn to deal with missed opportunities; gain confidence.

7.7   *The Problem: There is an internal promotion that you applied for, and you blew the interview.*

Possible Causes: You may not know how to promote yourself; your style may be in question, not your abilities; you were not prepared for the interview.

Cures: Learn to promote yourself; find a style that works; do your homework.

7.8   *The Problem: You are getting into a loud, heated, verbal discussion with a senior executive.*

Possible Causes: This may be another of your many tests as a manager; do you have the reputation and experience to back up your claims?; no one may be willing to concede.

Cures: Learn how to defend your position; build a strong reputation; reach a compromise and save face.

You will always have options and choices. It is in your best interest to carefully evaluate all your options before you decide on a solution. Some of the solutions may include legal remedies; at other times events may be unjust, but if no laws are broken, you may have to chalk this up to a situation that is, in this instance, out of your hands.

7.1   The Problem: During your first review, the boss stated that you were not assertive enough with the staff and gave you unfavorable marks.

THE SCENE

You dreaded this first review as a manager because you have received very little encouragement or guidance. You had heard that James, your boss, was difficult for women to work for. Although there had been no specific problems, you felt uneasy with the situation. James has a reputation for not liking smart, successful, strong women.

Your apprehensions were correct. James began by stating that he is concerned that you are not handling the position well. His comments are vague but all negative. He states that: *"I do not believe you fit in. You are not managing well. You are too nice with the employees, and do not show them who is boss."* He suggests how you should change, but does not provide details to show what you had actually done wrong.

You feel as if the wind has been let out of your sails. You are devastated. At the end of the review, James places you on a 30-day probation period. His closing remarks state that your future with the company will be decided at that time.

POSSIBLE CAUSES

You are faced with indecisiveness about your role, authority, and responsibility.

Perhaps these roles have not been defined clearly between you and James. You may believe your role is being measured on certain criteria while management (or at least James) is anticipating very different results. It is important to agree on what your role is and how it will be measured; otherwise, there remains a great deal of subjectivity that cannot be disputed or justified easily. Vague information works to no one's benefit.

You may not be performing up to acceptable standards.

Your ability to manage may not be as good as you think it is. The role of manager may seem natural and easy to you, but leave the company's expectations unfulfilled. Managing takes a lot of time, energy, and for most people some training. If your substandard performance is the result of not understanding what is expected of you, see the cure on role expectations.

There are still chauvinistic attitudes in the workplace.

James may be a sexist manager who believes consciously or otherwise that men make better managers and leaders. Whether he personally feels threatened by your presence or whether he believes that management is a man's game, your gender still excludes you. Your successes may be of little consequence to him.

There may be a clash between the two styles.

Your style may be one that James does not believe is representative of a leader, while the style he advocates may seem equally as inappropriate to you. Each person's style is slightly different from another, but there are some general characteristics that can be categorized. James may be looking for a style similar to what he practices, one that is more authoritative, direct, and firm than you are comfortable adapting. James may believe that your style is too soft, inclusive, and open because he is not comfortable with that style.

CURES

Communicate role expectations.

James' expectations of the role of manager may be entirely different from yours. You will never know unless you are both willing to discuss this subject openly. Many problems have been solved simply by improving communication.

Your approach needs to be as nonthreatening as possible. The following questions are offered as suggestions for a dialogue between you and James. Hopefully, these questions will provide answers and direction for your role as manager.

1. *"What specific steps should I take to get the results you want?"* This allows James to feel in control and less threatened. While your reaction may be of a defensive posture, it is important to understand what management expects of you. It holds the cards, and you must play by its rules.

2. *"What measurable results should I be striving for?"* The key word here is "measurable." Since many of James' comments sound subjective and personal, you want to move the conversation to quantifiable methods. This approach allows both you and James to measure your achievements on an equal footing.

3. *"How would you specifically like me to change?"* This question may even be modified to incorporate specific comments James made about you. For example, *"If you perceive that I do not fit in, what specifically can I do to change that image?"* Then continue to get him to elaborate on each comment or suggestion he makes.

None of your questions state that you agree with James' observations. Instead they ask for his opinion. Arguing with James, or any manager for that matter, will win nothing. While your reflex may be to defend yourself, know that you cannot gain any ground by that action. Fighting fire with fire only causes more fire. It may not be easy, but staying on the high road is the better path to take.

The nicest part about these questions is that you do not have to accept their answers. It is very important, though, to listen. How else will you know what is expected of you, and whether or not you want to work toward those goals?

Remember that you do have options. If James offers specific patterns for change, you must decide if you are willing to adopt those changes to win his approval. Do you suspect there will always be more asked of you? Are these expectations in sync with your own personal goals? Are you willing to make concessions? Review your choices, make decisions you are comfortable with and can adhere to, and then move forward with your plan of action.

Improve your performance.

Criticism may be hard for you to accept. Before you discount James' comments as his problem, make sure that you are not guilty of those things that he states. Even though his style and delivery may leave a lot to be desired, he may have some valid points about your work habits.

Goals are an essential part of reaching a plan. Have you defined specific goals for yourself? Without creating goals you will never know if you are on target, or how far off the target you really are.

As Corporate America continues to downsize, the expectations of managers increases and the time provided to learn these techniques becomes shorter. If you thought this was your honeymoon period—that you just needed to find out the routine, personalities, and procedures before taking action —you may be gravely mistaken. There may be some validity in James' comments about your job performance.

Another dilemma can occur when your perception of the department is that everything is running smoothly, while senior management sees many things that need to be changed. It is up to *you* to be sure that you understand these expectations, and what results management is looking for within a particular time frame.

Accepting responsibility for not performing up to a certain level is difficult, but it does show your maturity and willingness to grow with the job. If the company doesn't offer the necessary training programs, look to outside resources such as seminars, continuing education classes, and night-school programs to get the training that you need.

Manage while dealing with a chauvinist.

There is chauvinism in today's workplace, unfortunately. Attitudes have to be open to change, in order to be changed. If James does not want to change, you cannot change him simply because you want to.

Fortunately, all is not lost. Feeling like a victim benefits no one, least of all you. Instead, isolate those things that you can change and concentrate your energy and effort on them. You can change your attitude, your perception, and your employer. You cannot change the boss' attitude. You may or may not be able to transfer to another department depending on opportunities available, your qualifications, and the company policy.

James' problems are just that: James' problems. Yes, they do affect your review. That is one of many obstacles you will face as a manager. Your gender disqualifies you from being one of the boys. This is not to suggest that you must sit there being weak and submissive, or buy into his degrading comments, only that you accept your limitations and the reality of the situation.

There are some steps that you can do before the review which will allow you to maintain some control over the situation. First, be prepared with facts, figures, and accomplishments before you meet. Since you anticipate problems, be prepared with the ammunition to defend yourself prior to the meeting. It is also important to know exactly what James expects you to accomplish in your position. If his goals and your goals are not the same, then you need to work to create goals on which you can both agree.

Often women feel uncomfortable tooting their own horn because it sounds egotistical. Instead, women like to share their accomplishments with everyone who has contributed. Women may try to avoid being in the limelight. If no one else is patting you on the back and singing your praises, you must do it yourself. In male-dominant companies, it will be expected of you; modesty will work against you. Be ready to present your results factually and succinctly, and to sell yourself and your accomplishments.

Results need to be quantified whenever possible. Subjective statements are more easily disputed and contradicted, especially in an area where styles and personalities are already at odds.

If you feel that your review is totally biased and unfair, all is not lost. Identify each option as well as the risks associated with it. To gain something usually means to sacrifice something along the way. Sometimes these are small sacrifices; other times they are not worth the risk.

For example, talking to James will, in all probability, not produce a change. You may consider talking to someone in personnel, another supervisor, or maybe even James' boss, if possible. The downside risk is that nothing changes and you become marked as a troublemaker. The upside risk is that the situation improves. Only you know how much risk you are willing to undertake in any given situation.

Adapt a different style.

James may be looking for a style much like his own. He may be a "man's man" kind of manager. Your feminine touch may seem wrong or even inappropriate to him. Accept that no matter how much you change, you can never be a man's man, nor do you want to be.

This becomes an unequal playing field. There is little that you can do to change his perceptions or to gain an advantage. Adapting another gender's style is easier for men to do than women. Men can adapt feminine leadership qualities and still maintain their strong masculine images. When women adapt a more autocratic, masculine style they are called aggressive, harsh, or bossy.

Your options in reaching a compromise on styles may be limited. People expect women to nurture and be caregivers, and to be compassionate and understanding. Those same people look to men for guidance, leadership, and direction. Men assume that other men are qualified for a position, unless they prove themselves otherwise. However, women must pass through numerous tests to prove themselves competent.

Men have learned to adapt a variety of styles for different situations, a lesson women should learn. For example, when you are around James you may need to be more forceful and in-charge, but while around the staff, you may find the results are better achieved when you continue in a compassionate and inclusive style. Look toward other women for finding styles that may be easier for you to adapt. To be successful, though, the style must be natural for you.

Ultimately though, unequal playing fields may mean you have to work harder just to be noticed. It is a method women have been utilizing for many years, and have found beneficial. If it works, and provides the long-term results you are aiming for, it remains another option.

7.2

The Problem: You have been offered less money for a new position than a male colleague had been offered for the same job.

THE SCENE

You were just offered a new position, but there is some question about the salary. You know the salary offered recently to a man was more than is being offered to you for the same job. The company claims not to discriminate, but you do not know how else to interpret this information.

Salaries are supposed to be confidential, so you cannot mention this discrepancy. Many employees openly discuss their pay, even against company policy. Besides, if it is kept quiet, it seems easier for discriminations to go unnoticed and unchallenged.

Personnel knows your current salary, and this would be a substantial increase. They expect you to jump on it quickly. You feel they are confusing the issues.

If you speak up you may lose the offer. You are not sure what you should do: legally, morally, or professionally.

> *Note:* Sometimes the legal answer may be in conflict with the moral answer. And sometimes the professional answer is not in sync with either of the others. You must decide how to proceed, given your own code of ethics and values, not one imposed by someone else. You must determine which factors weigh more importantly with you, and which do not.

POSSIBLE CAUSES

Salary discrimination remains a problem.

Recent studies show the gap is closing, but is still there. According to the U.S. Department of Labor, women now earn $0.75 for every dollar a man earns, up from $0.69 the previous decade. While Federal laws have been written to protect women against wage discrimination, it is often difficult to prove. It is important for all women and men to work to close this gap, and hopefully eliminate salary discriminations completely.

There may be a difference in qualifications.

Whether or not you agree, you may not be as qualified as the male employee. Individual situations require individual attention. Not every discrepancy is discrimination. Before you get upset about the difference, make sure that, gender aside, everything else is equal.

You may have asked for less.

Women typically ask for less money, or expect less than men do. Women, afraid of or naive about the negotiating process, often sell themselves short. Businesses, being fiscally conservative by nature, are always looking for places to lower expenses. In order to achieve progress, women need to learn how to assert and sell themselves during the interviewing and negotiating process. The negotiating process takes acquired skills that women need to polish, practice, and present.

CURES

Understand salary discrimination and the law.

The Equal Pay Act of 1963 prohibits pay discrimination based on gender. It requires the employer to pay equal wages within the establishment to men and women doing equal work on jobs requiring equal skill, effort, and responsibility, performed under similar working conditions. Pay differences based on a seniority or merit system or on a system that measures earnings by quantity or quality of production are permitted.

A number of court cases have established that jobs need be only substantially equal, not identical, in order to be compared for purposes of this act. Job descriptions or classifications are irrelevant in showing that work is unequal, unless they accurately reflect actual job content, and mental as well as physical effort must be considered.

Your legal options include filing an Equal Employment Opportunity Commission (EEOC) complaint. This can be a slow process, with discrimination difficult to prove. If a violation is found, remedies are negotiated, often including back pay.

Also, under the Equal Pay Act, you are able to sue privately for injunctive relief, back pay, interest, damages, attorney's fees, and court costs. You must file a suit within two years of the violation, except in the case of deliberate violations, in which case there is a three-year limit.

Now that you know your legal rights you can proceed with evaluating your other options. Realize that the moral and professional answers may cloud your decision to seek legal remedies. All three factors should be carefully evaluated before proceeding.

Moral evaluations are often the most obscure and hardest to identify. Besides reviewing your own moral codes, this review includes the subjective attitudes of the company that may be represented in policy guidelines as well as how the company handles certain events. Answering the following questions can give you an indication of moral conflicts. Is this company one that you want to work for, given that you believe it is discriminating against you? Is there a pattern of discrimination practiced by senior managers? Do some of the senior male managers have little respect for women in the workforce? What affect would accepting this position have on you personally? Do you feel that you are selling yourself short if you do accept it?

Morality is a difficult subject to evaluate because there is not an universal acceptance for what is morally right or wrong. Many items are factored into it; there is not one standard by which everyone agrees to the same moral code or how much weight should be given each issue. Instead create your own measuring device and system based on your individual life experiences and your system of beliefs.

Even though moral codes are not universally right or wrong answers, this is the one area that may have the greatest influence because it is truly an issue "of the heart."

Finally, evaluate the professional repercussions of your actions. Even if an EEOC complaint is filed confidentially, many companies can readily assume who the filer is. Companies must respond to these complaints. If your identity is known or assumed, in all likelihood, the ties of loyalty and trust would be severed between you and the company. The atmosphere surrounding discrimination complaints varies within organizations, but often is hostile and isolating.

As you evaluate what is the most you could win, and what you could lose, your decision will become clearer. You must make an informed decision that is in your best interest. The only way to do that is to evaluate the legal, moral, and professional repercussions of your actions. Then proceed according to your own best interest, not according to someone else's agenda.

Determine when discrepancies are justified.

Under the Equal Pay Act there are certain conditions that must be met before a situation qualifies as discrimination. Companies often skirt the discrimination issue by basing salaries on qualifications, and assuming that the more qualified an individual is the higher quantity or quality of work he or she will produce; therefore the higher the salary offered. More qualifications may or may not produce greater results, but it is hard to argue against this theory.

To determine the qualifications factor, you need to look at yourself objectively as well as the other individual in question. Qualifications come in a variety of packages including education, work experiences, specific training programs, and achievements. These qualifications are not limited to what is written in a resume or on an application form, but can also include information received during the interview process.

There must be a pattern to classify as discrimination; otherwise you have individuals negotiating individual salaries. If you have been offered an entry level management position and you know that all men start at $21,000 annually, and that all women start at $15,000, then discrimination exists. But if you are looking at one individual who was offered more than you have been offered, discrimination may be harder to prove.

What If: That individual happened to be a female instead of a male? Gender could not be the excuse, but the discrepancy would still be there.

Unless the differences are staggering and a pattern can be found, you may find a better use of your energy is spent on improving and selling your own special attributes and talents. Ask management what seminars or special classes it would like you to participate in, and then follow its advice.

Learn how to negotiate for more.

The negotiating game is one many women fear. To avoid defeat and humiliation, women often respond by conceding, all too quickly, to whatever is offered.

There is an art in knowing how to play the salary negotiation game. In order to gain the advantage, you must have something they want. It is better not to discuss any salary ranges until a job offer has been made. At the point that a job offer has been made, then you have become a commodity they wish to purchase; you have an advantage.

During the negotiating process, they will ask your salary expectations. Try responding with something like *"My compensation package is based on several factors,"* and elaborate on those things that are important to you. Monetary and nonmonetary compensation may include health insurance (especially deductible amounts), tuition reimbursement, on-site childcare facilities, comp time for special projects, flexible hours, generous maternity and/or paternity leave, number of days for paid vacation and holidays, or whatever else is important to you (free parking, professional sports discounts, health club memberships, and so on). Long-term career potential is often a major consideration.

During the interviewing or negotiating process, the employer may insist that you give a specific dollar amount or range for your salary. Don't play coy; it could backfire and leave you without any offer. You want to know that what they can offer and what you need are in the same ball park. Hopefully your earlier research would have produced that information. When pushed for an amount, answer honestly. You can still keep your salary figure in a range rather than mention a specific dollar amount, to provide you with some leverage for later negotiations.

Assuming, for the sake of this example, that you have already been offered the job. They have made you an offer of $23,500, which is a salary increase for you. But, it is still less than what has been recently offered to another entry-level manager, who is male. First, look at the relevant information to begin negotiations. *Offers to other individuals are not relevant to your discussions.* They are important to you only because you now know what the company is willing to pay for this position. Also, *your previous salary is not an issue.* You will be assuming greater responsibilities, and you want to be paid according to these increased expectations.

Concentrate instead on selling yourself and your attributes. Reiterate your accomplishments, knowledge, and expertise, and how they specifically fit into this position and the employer's long-range plans.

Before making your decision, make sure that you know all the details about the total compensation package. It is not uncommon to ask for a chance to review this information, to take some time to consider the offer, and let them know the next day. This would be a good time to indicate that the salary offered is lower than you expected. It puts them on notice that you want to negotiate for more without declining the offer or threatening the power structure.

First, let them see your enthusiasm and interest. Then tag on something about the salary offered. You may want to respond with:

> *I am really interested in this position. I can see so much potential for using my sales talents and organizational skills. This is exactly what I am looking for. It's a perfect match. But, $23,500 is less than I was expecting for this position. There is a lot of responsibility with the job.*

It sounds risky, but you have put them on notice that the salary did come in low. With this response, you did not reject the offer, you only indicated that it was low. Sometimes the amount offered is a firm offer. Usually the employer will say if that is the case. If they immediately say so, you can always ask about nonmonetary compensation (additional days off, working from home, flexible hours, and so on).

When you negotiate, expect the person making the offer to need approval from someone else. The response may be something like, *"I will have to see if that is possible, but I'm not really sure we can do it."* This gives everyone time to review the information. It is part of the game.

The game of negotiating may involve bluffing. There is great risk in knowing when it is a bluff and when it is not. If you decide to call someone on what you assume is a bluff, the downside is that it may not be a bluff, and you may lose the job offer completely. The upside is that you call the bluff and get what you want.

Negotiating means knowing what you want. It means establishing a minimum that you will accept and then creating a wish list of other benefits. It means placing value on your own contributions and taking credit for what you have done.

Now is the time to begin valuing each of your accomplishments as just that—your accomplishments. You are worthy of the praise, the recognition, and worth every dollar you are asking for!

7.3   The Problem: As a woman, you feel promotions and career opportunities are limited.

THE SCENE

There are few women in the upper levels of management; opportunties for advancement seem limited for women. Women have made their way into entry-level and middle-management positions, while men comprise the inner circle, making policy and vision decisions.

Last month you applied for a position that would have made you the highest ranking female in the company. You met all the requirements posted; your reviews have been very positive. This would be a logical promotion, given your experience. You knew you were the most qualified applicant for that position, but you were passed over for a less-qualified male.

When you questioned your boss, Jeff, about this, he just shrugged it off saying, *"You're great where you are, why move?"* Few women have broken through this barrier, despite qualifications. You are not really sure what your options are or how you should proceed.

POSSIBLE CAUSES

You may be bumping against the glass ceiling.

Corporate America has not responded to the challenges of integrating women and minorities beyond the glass ceiling. Stereotypes about women continue to cast a doubt about their abilities to manage in the highest ranks. Men continue to choose other men to be their predecessors. Some men believe that women are too easily diverted from their careers by family considerations; that women are not able to function effectively in such a tough environment; that somehow women's leadership styles are too soft and gentle for these high stress, competitive environments. But the number one obstacle that women must overcome to break through the glass ceiling is that the men at the top feel uncomfortable with women beside them.

You may be lacking the professional image of a leader.

Qualifications include both achievements as well as perceptions. Image is always an important factor. It is important to see if you are perceived as a leader, and by whom. While your results may be high within the department, it could be that your image needs some additional work.

You may not be ready for a promotion.

Being good at one thing does not automatically mean that you are ready for the next step. Jeff may be correct in saying that you are at the best place for your talents. It is important for you to know your limitations as well as your strengths. It is also important for others not to limit your potential because they lack vision.

Your boss may be holding you back.

You may be doing such a great job where you are that your boss does not want to lose you. You may be hard to replace. There are some people who do not consider themselves successful when their subordinates rise around them. Look closely at why Jeff wants you to remain in your current position; he may be creating a major roadblock by not supporting your career advancements.

CURES

Break through the glass ceiling.

The *glass ceiling* refers to invisible, artificial barriers that prevent qualified individuals from advancing within their organization and reaching their full potential. These barriers result from institutional and psychological practices, and limit the advancement and mobility opportunities of both women and minorities. The criteria for breaking these barriers has changed as each obstacle has been met. First was inexperience, than came lack of education. Women and minorities are gaining the experience and the educational prerequisites, but still are making little progress.

After a decade of evaluating corporate movement, only a 3% difference was recorded according to The Glass Ceiling Commission of the U.S. Department of Labor Report. There is still much work to be done to break through this barrier.

A recent U.S. Department of Labor survey done by *Working Women Count!* shows that women place a high priority on needing pay and benefits that provide economic security, a workplace culture that supports and respects families, and opportunities that reflect the value of women's work. Women are distressed that their work both at home and on the job continues to be devalued, and they are frustrated with the visible and invisible signs of this inequality.

Further findings show that:

- 65% of women place a high priority on improving pay scales
- 49% say they do not get paid what they think their job is worth
- 61% of those surveyed say they have little or no ability to advance, (this increased to 69% for blue-collar workers and 70% for technical workers)
- 63% of mothers with young children (under age 5) and 61% of single mothers give high priority to getting paid leave to care for children or relatives
- 56% of women with children age 5 or under state that finding affordable childcare remains a serious problem
- Stress ranks as working women's number-one problem and is particularly acute for women in their forties who hold professional and managerial jobs, and for single mothers
- Health and pension benefits are a critical concern for all women, and the number-one priority for change

We agree that the glass ceiling exists. We agree that opportunities are often denied women based on gender. And we agree that Corporate America needs to make changes to meet the growing needs of its workforce. Where do we go from here?

The solution is not simple nor is it fast. Change is often met with resistance in any situation, but especially when change may represent additional costs up front (albeit long-term investments with excellent returns). Management must believe in those benefits before they will make these investments.

While much needs to be changed within the confines of the corporate structure, there are some decisions you can control. It is important that you know what you want, its priority in your life, and how hard you are willing to fight for it. This information provides a foundation for whether or not you even want to fight this battle.

If you find the work environment currently discourages the advancement of women, you may want to look around for another employer who appreciates and values your contributions. Finding one may not be that easy, but you always have the option.

Create a positive and professional image.

Everyone has an image. Sometimes these images are influenced by stereotypes and expectations. Women are constantly fighting to break the mold of what others expect their images to be, and find these stereotypes too limiting. Men fit the image of "manager" because men have successfully filled that role for years.

Women who have reached the upper ranks of management often find themselves judged against the styles and presence of their male counterparts. To break that mold requires more and more diversity to be accepted into management ranks.

Images are both created and perceived, and men are simply given more leeway for their professional image than women are. The range is wider for men and the judgment less harsh. On the other hand, everything about a woman contributes to her image, and nothing is taken for granted. Her clothes, shoes, hairstyle, and make-up all impact how she is perceived. In addition to her appearance she is judged by her tone, actions, and mannerisms. The package is scrutinized and reviewed countless times, every day. A woman's ability to fit the acceptable mold allows for very little individual expression. Section 4.6 also provides advice on creating and maintaining your image.

Women spend less time on marketing their image than do men. Women are more apt to simply do the job than tell others how much they've accomplished, while men learned the importance of marketing their image early on. It is a lesson women need to learn in order to advance in these ranks.

Let senior management know that you are serious about wanting a promotion and that you want to be a leader in its eyes. By asking what it is looking for in these positions you will be able to see if this really is within your reach or worth the sacrifices management is asking of you.

If your strong leadership qualities translate into weaknesses according to company interpretation, then you can decide: (a) if you want to change to their standards; (b) if you want to find other employment that values your qualities; (c) if you want to continue where you are, knowing the limitations.

Know your limitations.

Each person has strengths and weaknesses. Sometimes it is hard for you to evaluate yourself objectively, and sometimes it is hard for others to see how you have grown. Both can be limiting to your career—one you can control, and the other you cannot.

You may not be as ready as you think you are for this promotion. Moving too soon could have devastating effects on your career potential, including negative reviews, and unhappiness, setting you up to fail eventually. How do you know when you are ready for the next move? Both luck and an educated guess continue to be the best answers; there are no absolutes or guarantees. Knowing about yourself and your personal limitations will go a long way in assessing these factors.

Talk to Jeff to find out more about why he feels the job isn't a match for you. He may know more about the position than he first indicated.

> *Jeff, you know that I had applied for that promotion recently and was not chosen. You said that I should be happy where I am. What exactly did you mean by that? Do you think that I need additional training or experience before I would be qualified for such a position?*

Everyone has weaknesses, which can be a double-edged sword. There is danger in ignoring them or advertising them. By identifying your own limitations you are already ahead of many who are playing the management game. Once you have identified your weaknesses, and learned how to minimize them, the next step is gaining the confidence, experience, and knowledge to move beyond them. A mentor can play a big role in helping you through this maze.

Work around obstacles.

There are some people in positions of power who want to hold back good employees and not promote them when they deserve the promotion. Their motives may be selfish, claiming it is difficult to replace a good worker. The true losers of these actions are the employees who are held back, unable to reach their full potential. Your options will be significantly limited if this occurs. Do not expect Jeff to admit that his decision is personally motivated. Confronting him about these findings will resolve nothing.

Jeff has presented you with an obstacle. Not an insurmountable obstacle, nor the only one you will face. Work within the system, not outside of it. It is not enough to do a great job; usually it takes a lot more to get noticed and promoted. For example, Jeff may need assurances that you are training the employees to handle the department and create a smooth transition.

A better solution would be to get Jeff to list the qualifications and experiences he sees as necessary to get a promotion. For most companies, a recommendation from your superior is essential to getting a promotion. Jeff could create the roadblock simply by stating that he does not recommend you for this position.

You may either be content where you are knowing your professional future is limited, or look for employment opportunities elsewhere that provide greater potential for advancement.

7.4 | The Problem: Your boss has made an unwelcome pass at you.

THE SCENE

Richard, your boss, is known for his romantic escapades around the office. Your relationship with him has always been professional. It was Richard who recommended you for your current position and it was Richard who taught you the ropes.

In the past, you had always worked well together. However, during your last review Richard made some rather sexually insinuating comments to you. They seemed harmless enough at the time, and by ignoring them nothing happened. You are not sure that it was the best way to handle the situation since the comments are starting again. You feel uneasy around him and try to avoid times when you are alone. To complicate the situation, Richard has been making more and more arrangements for the two of you to work closely together. He frequently calls you into his office for closed-door meetings, and even suggested a business trip that the two of you should take.

You love your job, and you love the company. Everything seemed to be going great. Now, things are coming apart at the seams, and the situation is out of your control.

You do not want to overreact, but you are not comfortable when you are alone with Richard. You do not want to jeopardize your career, if it can be avoided. Richard has a lot of influence within the company, but you are not sure what that means to you. What should you do to make him understand, to protect yourself, and to continue to do what you love?

POSSIBLE CAUSES

The cause is less important than how you handle yourself.

In this situation the cause is much less important an issue than how you handle yourself. Whether this is considered a situation of sexual harassment, will be an issue for you and others to resolve, should you pursue outside remedies. There appears to be some indications that sexual harassment exists. Sexual harassment is about power, and Richard does have power over you. Section 2.2 also addresses concerns and information on sexual harassment.

Regardless of the cause, however, you need to take certain steps to empower yourself. While you have done nothing to initiate or create the situation, your future may be at risk. Without taking control of the situation, you have even more to lose.

Empowerment means putting into action the power that you have inside. No one gives you that power and no one can take it away. You must use your innate power to regain direction of your future, otherwise your life and career will continue to spin on its own, out of control.

CURES

Handle sexual harassment.

You may be asking yourself, *"Why do I have to change, I didn't do anything wrong!"* No, you didn't do anything wrong, but still there are some precautions that you should take to protect yourself. While you did not create the situation, your response is integral to its outcome.

When you are faced with resolving a situation it is important to identify and analyze all of your options. This situation is no different. Your options include the following:

1. Notify human resources. The first suggestion involves notifying human resources about the situation. Human resources may or may not be supportive or sympathetic to your claim. Whether the claim is sexual harassment or a matter of poor judgment on Richard's part, the department often tries not to take sides until everyone has had an opportunity to present their side of the story. However, sometimes company policy and procedures will favor the person with the most power.

If you make sexual harassment claims, companies often become very nervous. The legal ramifications of these charges have made companies more accountable for these actions. It is important to note that when you seek guidance from human resources, you may also be putting the company on notice.

Many companies have created formal sexual harassment policies or procedures to follow. When you approach the human resources department, you need to know what it is you expect from them: guidance, support, to be made aware of the situation, or intervention. That way, human resources can respond to your specific needs, and you can assess its ability or inability to meet those needs more specifically.

2. Confront the boss. The second solution, confronting the boss, is very risky. It has the potential to be an excellent solution or produce devastating results. Chances are that none of these encounters have been witnessed by a third party. Without witnesses, it becomes one person's word against another person's word, and nothing is proven. Innocence is more apt to be presumed for the person with the most power, which would be Richard.

While you have some areas that you can control (how and where you confront him) you cannot anticipate his response or ultimately his motives. If he takes rejection personally, then it may be a very difficult situation for you to continue to work in the company. If he seeks power, he may try to sabotage your career.

Even with this risk, do not rule out this option too quickly. If you choose to talk with Richard directly, there are some steps you can take to protect yourself. First, keep the conversation centered on you, not him. Saying something like *"I do not approve of your behavior"* may be interpreted that there is something wrong with him and his behavior. Instead when you respond with, *"I have a great deal of respect for you, but I do not feel comfortable taking this relationship to another level,"* it keeps the focal point on you.

Safe and comfortable surroundings will work to your advantage. Keep professional dialogue in professional settings. In other words, having after-work drinks would not be appropriate for such a conversation. If you want to keep the relationship professional, then focus on the work aspects. Meetings held in private, such as in an office, could eliminate the possibility of embarrassing either of you. Or, meetings held in public, such as having coffee or lunch together, provide potential witnesses as well as allow the tone to remain more calm.

3. Remove yourself from the scene. The next solution includes removing yourself from a potentially uncomfortable situation, if at all possible. Admittedly, this is not always feasible. If the business trip is a legitimate trip that you should take, establish boundaries and guidelines before you go. If you can avoid certain situations such as dining alone together, do so. Otherwise, you may find yourself in a situation which is even more awkward and uncomfortable for both of you.

4. Ignore the situation. Ignoring the situation, or hoping that it will get better on its own, is probably the worst solution and yet the one most often used. By stopping the situation before it goes too far, everyone can be spared future hardships. Ignoring the situation only increases its obscurity. Misunderstandings remain.

It will not just go away. Realize that lack of action is a choice; it is action. This is a solution that does *not* empower the individual. Instead, it allows for everyone else to maintain power and control over you.

5. File an EEOC complaint. If you suspect sexual harassment, you have the option of filing an EEOC complaint. The Equal Employment Opportunity Commission defines sexual harassment as *"unwelcome sexual advances, requests for sexual favors, and other verbal or physical conduct of a sexual nature"* when consent is a condition of getting or keeping a job, promotion, or a pay increase. Hostile work environments are also considered under this law because sexual language or gestures can interfere with an employee's ability to perform his or her job.

The EEOC recognizes that sexual conduct may be private and have no other eyewitnesses. Therefore, in appropriate cases, it may make a finding of harassment based solely on the credibility of the victim's allegation.

Contact the Equal Employment Opportunity Commission, a federal agency, for information and assistance in filing a complaint at 1-800-699-

EEOC. Maintain a record of incidents of harassment, including date, time, who was present and exactly what was said or done. Having written notes can be very useful in refreshing memories and establishing a pattern of misconduct.

In addition, a victim may look into filing a claim under state regulations. If the claim involves physical contact, it could also be a violation of criminal laws.

Empowerment comes through knowledge. Know your legal rights and company policy and procedures. Then resolve this issue as you see fit. The only way to make the world a safer place for all women is by putting a stop to these situations! Save other women from the pain and suffering that you have already endured.

7.5 | The Problem: Your suggestions during a meeting are ignored. It is as if you are not even in the room.

THE SCENE

Various department managers are seated around the conference table discussing how to increase market shares and lower costs. Department cutbacks continue to be mentioned, although everyone has been spared to this point. Tension remains in the room; no one is immune.

The meeting is not very structured. People are offering ideas, interrupting speakers, and jumping from topic to topic. The Vice President of Sales, whom you report to, is leading the meeting, and writing down various suggestions as they are offered.

You make two strong points but no one responds. It is as if you didn't even open your mouth, but you know you've been heard. The Vice President does not include your ideas on the board, and the conversation continues as if you had said nothing.

Then Mike, who happens to be seated next to you, makes the same two suggestions you had just offered. They are immediately the topic of discussion and everyone seems interested. Mike is getting the credit and not sharing the spotlight with you.

This is not the first time this has happened. It is happening with more frequency these days and adding to your insecurity about your career future with this company.

POSSIBLE CAUSES

You are not being heard.

It is not enough to speak up if you are not heard. Women feel this conflict more than men because the expectations are different. Being assertive in meetings takes practice. Being assertive, however, will not guarantee that you are heard. Depending on what is accepted by the group members, one style may work better while another style works in a different setting. Finding a style that works within a particular setting takes time, patience, and a judgment call.

You are fighting an invisible microphone.

In hierarchical groups such as businesses it is not uncommon for one or more members to be given access to an invisible microphone to allow messages to be heard. This microphone may provide credibility to whatever ideas that particular individual presents. You may be denied access to this invisible microphone for any number of reasons, including your gender. The consequences of not being heard may be that your ideas are dismissed quickly no matter how good or creative they are, while those with access to the invisible microphone can sell the most obscure ideas or simply steal yours.

Identify and understand politics and fear.

Politics refers to your ability to persuade others and to be heard, especially in hierarchical environments. Fear may be in the room because of possible company cutbacks. Mike may be protecting his own territory by simply stealing your ideas, although he may consider them "borrowed." The Vice President may be oblivious to the competitive, cutthroat nature of the meetings. Some people want to win at all costs. This attitude is difficult for most women to understand much less emulate; men may view this as simply the way business is done. It is more representative of the win-or-lose games men have played since their childhood.

CURES

Learn to speak up and be heard.

If no one hears your ideas, you are losing out on missed opportunities and so are they. Within any group there are styles that work well and styles that do not work as well. Each group decides which styles work best within its framework to meet its particular needs, given their personalities and objectives. For men there is often a jockeying for positions of power within a group setting. Aggressive styles, loud, and interruptive styles may all be within the acceptable parameters.

For women, learning to adapt a style that works within the acceptable framework becomes more challenging. Men's styles do not work when mimicked by females. Instead, women need to find a more natural style that is acceptable and respected within their environment. Each group is different, so what works well in one setting may not work somewhere else.

If there are other females present in the meeting, take notice if they are being heard in the group. When you see that they are, try to identify aspects of their styles that allow them to be heard. Adapt those portions that you feel comfortable in adapting to get your desired results. Without being heard in meetings, you are fighting a losing battle.

If you are the only female present, look to other females such as outside mentors and formal network organizations. You may also consider a trial-and-error approach, knowing that each situation is different.

It is very important for a woman to realize that not being heard in meetings, while frustrating, can be suicidal for her career. Therefore, take every precaution about making certain that you are heard during these meetings. It is part of marketing your total image to management. It is how professional careers are made or broken. During the meeting, you may call attention to the fact that you had just made those same ideas. However, if they are not hearing you initially, it could easily sound like you are trying to take credit for someone else's ideas. Thus, the potential for backfiring and sounding whiny is great. See Sections 2.1, 2.3, 6.3, 6.6, or 7.1 for more information about changing your style to fit a particular audience. Also, Section 9.5 addresses making yourself heard.

Gain access to invisible microphones.

Within any organization you can find certain individuals who are given a sense of respect, authority, and credibility whenever they speak. Deciding who gets these labels can be arbitrary or it can be earned. This criteria varies: it may be politics, the result of a successful career, or you may be denied ever earning the honor because you're a woman.

Mike appears to have the attention of the other group members when he speaks. Even though he borrowed your ideas, when they came from his mouth there was a ring of trust and value that was immediately placed on his comments. If Mike is such a highly respected person within the group, work with him to get your ideas in front of others. Negotiate a method where the credit can be shared. This assumes that you trust and admire Mike and that Mike is willing to share the spotlight.

To find out if this is so, approach Mike after the meeting. Knowing his style will help you to approach him in a nonthreatening manner.

> *Mike, your ideas in the meeting today were great. I am always amazed at how your comments are received with such respect and authority. And I didn't mind the fact that you borrowed my sugges-tions because we were both able to win. What I'd like to do is learn from you how I can eventually get my ideas heard since you have that down to a fine art. Maybe we can find a way to work together.*

This style may not work with Mike. He may become defensive, espe-cially if he doesn't want anyone to know that they were your ideas original-ly. Your comments, while well-intended, may still threaten his group status. He may go so far as to make you look like you are trying to ride free on his coattail. Proceed carefully.

Play the game to win during territorial wars.

When there are threats of downsizing in a company, either real or per-ceived, it is not uncommon to see jockeying for positions of power. Women are often less equipped to fight these battles because of their inclusive style and their need to be connected with others and liked by all.

Keep your eyes open; do not be naive about what is going on. Because each person's future may be at stake, expect each person to market himself or herself aggressively to upper management. It is not uncommon to see people create a sense of indispensability about themselves and their positions.

The choice is yours as to how you want to play the game and if you want to play at all. Accept responsibility if you choose not to market yourself aggressively.

There is nothing wrong with finding ways to market yourself aggressively though. For example, you may want to write a memo to the Vice President of Sales, sharing ideas that you have designed. This allows your name to be associated with your ideas. When you communicate with other departments, or perhaps collaborate on a special project, again make sure that the Vice President is aware of these events, your role, and successes. You may write up a summary report to the department manager you worked with, and send a copy to the Vice President.

It is critical to your professional future that you get credit for your achievements. Do not feel that it will happen automatically; it won't. Do not feel that taking credit is being boastful. Part of being a successful manager will be marketing your professional image to those who make decisions. The sooner you learn to play this part of the game, the sooner you will see positive results.

7.6 | The Problem: You have been offered a promotion that you do not want to accept.

THE SCENE

You have recently been offered a promotion that you do not want. This particular department continues to be faced with a lot of problems from production, sales, and personnel. No manager has lasted there longer than six months in the past two years.

Each department is viewed as a profit center, but the losses this department generates continue to penalize its managers. Bonuses and promotions are based on department results; if you don't make budget, you are penalized financially. Taking this job will require a lot of work and would equate to a pay cut when you consider the hours, elimination of overtime pay, and the additional responsibility.

Although it is a big honor to be offered this position, you also know that it comes with a great deal of risk. It looks to be a revolving door—or a trap door—for managers whom the company wants to eliminate. You feel you may be set up to fail, and that no one can make the department profitable. You are also afraid that if you say no, you won't be offered another management opportunity. It may end your career before it starts.

POSSIBLE CAUSES

Politics makes strange bedfellows.

The extent to which politics influences your career varies from company to company. It is always important to identify these influences and use them to your advantage. Learn about politics and how to make it work for you.

Declining this offer may limit your career.

Some companies only give you one opportunity. To decline a promotion in such an atmosphere means that there is a great deal at risk. It may be a lose-lose situation, in your mind. Try to determine what effects your decision may have on your future career with this company.

You may be doubting your own abilities.

You may not believe that you are ready for this promotion, especially when you have seen so many managers fail. Because others have failed does not mean that you will fail. You may fear success as much as failure. While a part of you may want to be in management, another part may be holding you back. It is important to know why you are afraid of taking this risk.

CURES

Accept politics in the workplace.

Politics is a natural part of any organization. While it may conjure up images of back stabbing and dirty game playing, this is just the way some people play. The game itself is a matter of who you know, how you are perceived, and how you are able to persuade others. Politics often has to do with the unofficial manner that decisions are reached.

Assuming politics doesn't exist is naive. Assuming politics is evil is myopic. Politics is neither good nor bad. It is the people and the power employed that gives politics its bad name. Politics is simply a natural occurrence within any organization.

Understanding politics within the organization can better assist you with your decision. You should know what is expected of you, what support will be provided to you, and how much autonomy and time will be given to reach the desired results. Being direct may be your best avenue.

> *I am very interested in this position. It will be a great challenge for me and I appreciate your confidence in believing that I can do the job. Because there has been so much turnover in this department, and with its continued losses, I do have some reservations. I need to have some additional information to make my decision.* (Ask questions you feel are vital to your decision. The following are some suggestions.) *First, what exactly do you expect me to do with this department? Is it possible to be profitable? Has it ever been done? How long do I have to turn the department around, and what results are you expecting? Is it possible to take this position as a temporary assignment, and if it doesn't work out then place me in another position?*

These answers should help you decide whether this is the best move for you or not. It is important to make well-informed decisions based on your findings as well as your intuition.

If you believe that you can do the job, then accept it. Before you decide, you may want to talk with previous managers of this department to see what actually happened in their situations.

Learn to deal with missed opportunities.

Sometimes opportunity only knocks once. A missed opportunity may be something that you cannot recapture. The door may be closed permanently. Other times you will not be penalized for declining an offer, and the future will remain promising. Deciding which situation this one is may be difficult; ultimately rely on guesswork and intuition.

Observing what happens to other managers may shed light into how this organization operates. For example, do you know of others in the organization who have declined a position? If not, it may be because it is perceived too risky. On the other hand, if you are able to identify individuals who have declined promotions when offered, look at their careers today. Have they been demoted or passed over for other considerations? Did they get a second chance?

Finally, do you want to continue working for a company that penalizes you for your choices? This makes them no "choice" at all, but a heavily mandated request with strong consequences for refusal. The determination is yours.

Gain confidence.

Doubt can often hold you back from taking risks. Why do you doubt your ability to handle new situations? Is it because you fear failure? Is it because you fear success? Is it because you know your limitations and strengths, and this opportunity goes beyond them?

Women are inherently less risk takers than men. Women have been raised to nurture and be the caregivers, while men have been raised to be aggressive, courageous, and gamblers. Going beyond this socialization trap takes a great deal of courage, fortitude, and patience. Don't let others limit your ability to dream, nor your potential.

When you reach a crossroad where you do not believe you are ready for the next step, look inside of yourself for the answers. Listen to your inner voice, and be willing to take calculated risks. How else will you grow? No matter what the outcome, risks present opportunities to learn and to grow. Learn to reach inside yourself and follow your heart wherever it leads you. There are no limits, only dreams waiting to be fulfilled.

7.7 The Problem: There is an internal promotion that you applied for, and you blew the interview.

THE SCENE

You applied for a new position within the company, one that represents a promotion for you. There are several other employees interested in the position, but you feel you are the most qualified.

Since this is an internal posting, you believe management should already know your qualifications and agree with your assessment. Your past reviews have all been positive and very complimentary.

Everyone was asked to go through a formal interview process. Interviewing always causes you to become nervous and give stupid responses under pressure. During this interview you were asked about your current position and accomplishments. You knew that they were looking for quantifiable facts that they could compare, but you stumbled around and tried to change the subject. You had many accomplishments, but at that moment you couldn't think of a thing to say. You're sure you blew the interview and any chance of getting the promotion.

POSSIBLE CAUSES

You may not know how to promote yourself.

Women have difficulty accepting that doing good work is not enough, that marketing oneself is expected in this competitive environment. Everyone else is marketing themselves, which only makes you look less qualified because you are not speaking up with equal enthusiasm. Modesty will work against you every time.

Your style may be in question, not your abilities.

People respond to different styles in different manners. Most people have a favorite style, often the one they practice. Knowing who the decision maker is, and what style he or she is looking for will be helpful. Styles have little to do with ability and everything to do with perception. Some styles blend well together in certain situations, while the same style may find resistance in a different setting. First you must know what is expected of you, then you can decide if you want to fulfill those expectations.

You were not prepared for the interview.

Preparing yourself before you go to an interview can make the process less disruptive, ease the tension, and produce more positive results. It is your responsibility to be prepared ahead of time. Lack of preparation makes you look bad, and can suggest that you are not ready for the promotion. Being prepared means assuming nothing. Preparation does not stop with the interview process, but should become a normal operating criteria, especially for women.

CURES

Learn to promote yourself.

Women continue to equate promoting themselves with bragging. Little girls are taught about modesty and its ladylike virtue. These images continue to be quietly reinforced in females, until breaking those rules seems wrong. For men, promoting themselves is both natural and acceptable.

Stereotypes are difficult to break. Being self-assured and confident does not mean that you are egotistical. Instead, learning tactful ways of letting others know your accomplishments will allow others to judge you more fairly.

The best way to learn different methods of self-promotion is by observing men and women within the organization. See how they market themselves. Is it by having lunch with their superiors? Brown-nosing their boss? Taking the afternoon to go golfing with a customer? Once you have identified common and acceptable practices within the organization, then you can decide if these avenues are accessible for you as a woman or if you even want to participate.

Next, create your own opportunities. For example, call informal meetings in your office to elaborate on an idea you had, write memos, copy the powers that be, with results or changes you are implementing. When the department succeeds, there is a time to share the glory with all the players and there is a time to step up and receive the award. Both are acceptable, and both are equally as important. One style does not negate another; actually they work well together.

It is not a matter of right or wrong. It is a matter of adapting your comments to fit a particular audience and to gain your just rewards.

Find a style that works.

A variety of styles work for different situations. Finding a style that works with those who make the decisions is important to your future career. Advancement and promotions will come more easily with styles that are considered acceptable.

The element of finding a style that works for you as well as within a particular setting is of paramount importance to your career potential. The match must be on both levels if it is to work and be well received. You can pattern your style after someone you admire, but make sure that it is comfortable for you.

As a female, finding a style acceptable to the male majority and one that is comfortable for you to practice is often challenging. The acceptable range may be limited because of your gender. By the same token, there are many aspects of style that are more natural for women to emulate.

Do your homework.

Being prepared is the motto of both girl scouts and boy scouts. It is a lesson that bears repeating often. As an adult, its presence will continue to make your life run more smoothly. Not that it eliminates all the bumps, but being prepared is just sound business advice, especially for a manager.

Because women are judged more than their male counterparts, are assumed not to be as experienced, and are watched more, women must always be prepared. Women are expected to fail in management. Your presence is contradictory to the normal and acceptable stereotypes.

If you were caught off balance for whatever reason, and had not done the appropriate foundational research before the interview, you can still salvage the experience. Write a brief memo to the person with whom you just interviewed outlining your accomplishments. Even if you had verbalized them before, seeing them written down can make a strong statement. Learn to state events in quantifiable measures whenever possible. This would be a perfect time to reiterate why you are the best person for the position. Interviewing well is like sales; you are selling yourself and your qualifications to the person who is doing the hiring.

The final decision is not yours. Be willing to accept the outcome, whatever it may be, and learn from the experience.

7.8 | The Problem: You are getting into a loud, heated, verbal discussion with a senior executive.

THE SCENE

While you do not report to the Vice President of the company directly, there are many occasions when you need his approval for projects. You followed the appropriate chain of command, and with the blessing of your supervisor sought Robert's approval. Usually this action is like a rubber stamp. It has been researched and defended quite a lot before it gets to this level.

You need his approval on a special project you have been working on for the past month. He listens to your request and conclusions, but he disagrees with your recommendation. You suspect his decision is based on feelings, not facts, and proceed cautiously. Again, you present your findings, and are convinced you are right. Robert doesn't back down either.

Quickly the discussion becomes loud. Your voice is getting louder as you reiterate the facts and your conclusion. You feel very strong in your beliefs, and know this material inside and out. His arguments are vague and unspecific. You both stand your ground.

It appears that you are at an impasse. Reluctantly, you give both yourself and him an out. *"Robert, I will change it if you want it changed. But I still believe that is not the best solution."* He seems stunned by your strong position. He concedes with stipulations that give him a way out as well. Finally, you have reached a compromise, but you are not sure at what cost. You wonder if that discussion just shortened your career.

POSSIBLE CAUSES

This may be another of your many tests as a manger.

Women encounter many tests throughout their management careers. This may be a test to see how strongly you are willing to defend your position. Men enjoy this game because they have played it many times themselves. Yet when women enter the picture, the rules often change. You must adapt a style that does not cause you to lose, and can allow you to win. Sometimes the line between winning and losing is drawn very closely.

Do you have the reputation and experience to back up your claims?

Without this foundation, your words can falter easily. After earning the respect of your many colleagues and superiors, this may be the final test of acceptance. Do you have the courage to stand up for what you believe in? Are you willing to reach a compromise when you disagree? Both are excellent learning tools, that often come at the expense of wounded players. It takes skill to maneuver this exchange. Make sure you are already standing on a strong foundation before you jump in.

No one may be willing to concede.

Reaching a consensus doesn't mean that you lost the battle; in fact, it may be the best way for both parties to save face and move forward. The art of knowing when to push and when to concede is an important lesson to learn. Sometimes, pushing solely for your solution will make your opponent look bad. Therefore, in assuming a defensive posture, he may fight to make you the loser of the game. Learn how and when to compromise without threatening the game or alienating its players completely.

CURES

Learn how to defend your position.

Men are very adept at playing aggressive, combative games. They are more comfortable going head-to-head in a heated argument and seeing who backs down first. It is all part of how many organizations make decisions. It is representative of how these games are played in some companies.

For women, this is often an unnatural and uncomfortable style to incorporate. Learning how and when to defend your position can be confusing, not to mention intimidating.

If you believe in your position and feel very strong about the findings, a major part of winning any game is convincing others that you are right. There may be times when your recommendations are dismissed quickly, and unless you are willing to stay and fight, your ideas will fade away just as fast.

The first thing is to have a strong commitment to your findings. Believing in yourself and your answers can catapult you into defending that position. Adopting the style of your combatant is usually the best way to be heard in these heated discussions. If he is loud, being soft-spoken will not cause him to stop and listen. Instead it will give him the edge because you are drowned out by his voice. Not being heard could possibly cost you the game. When he is loud, the only way to be heard is to be just as loud.

In the early stages of your career, this situation could cause you to be labeled difficult, bitchy, hard to get along with, or combative. It may be better to lose one battle along the way than to risk your career.

However, if this style means your survival in the company, it would definitely be to your advantage to learn to play hard and learn quickly! Watch and learn from those who play the hardest and have the best winning record.

Build a strong reputation.

Without establishing a strong and reliable foundation, this situation encompasses a great deal more risk than should be undertaken. When built on a strong and proven track record, it can become just another test into your registry of management ranks.

If your solution fails, you will also be risking the reputation that you worked so hard to build. While you may not have to start over completely, you will lose significant ground. It is the risk of getting ahead: sometimes you don't make it.

Yet, if you are never willing to take this step, you are conceding an important element of courage that is necessary to succeed in leadership. Stand firm on your convictions and your reputation when you feel called upon to do so.

Reach a compromise and save face.

Confrontations are often uncomfortable for women. Men have learned to control these situations whereas women are more apt to avoid the conflict if possible. In business, as in life, conflicts will constantly be a part of its natural fabric. While men have learned through their many sports triumphs to either win or lose, women prefer seeking a win-win proposition. Finding a win-win proposition is the basis of compromise.

First, it is important to find those areas in which you both agree. Then look at where you do not agree and determine the differences that are the strongest. Focus specifically on "what if" scenarios. Be willing to give up something in order to get something. During this process it is important to know which points are negotiable and which are not.

Another important lesson is to know when to back down. If your adversary feels threatened or cornered, he or she will likely assert stronger power and a more aggressive style over you. He does not want to lose face in front of anyone, especially a woman.

Part of the art of winning is making the other person feel as if he did not lose. Watch others in action to find out what particular methods and styles are more acceptable within this particular organization. If other women have already reached upper levels of management, observe them in action whenever possible. There is no need to reinvent the wheel when others have already created it. Use your energy to improve on what they have found that works and to modify it to fit your style comfortably.

Chapter Summary

Bosses can create some of the most difficult obstacles to overcome for any manager. Sometimes they present problems or dilemmas that cannot be countered. For example, the glass ceiling research has determined that the primary reason men exclude women from the inner circle is because they feel uncomfortable beside them.

During the most difficult of times, when you feel caught in the middle, it is helpful to stop and list your options. You will always have options; some may be more advantageous and pleasing to you, but there are still choices to be made. In some instances you may seek other employment, choosing to completely remove yourself from the environment. In other instances, finding another employer is not a realistic option. When changing jobs is not logical, you may focus your energy on those things that you *can* change, including your attitude and perceptions. In other words, if you cannot change something, then change the way you look at it. Admittedly, the difficulty in this option is knowing when you cannot change something; it is important not to give up this battle too soon, otherwise you cannot expect to see attitudes or policy ever change.

On the other hand, once you realize that change often comes along very, very, slowly, then changing your own attitude makes a lot more sense. Otherwise you will continue to live under a great deal of anxiety and frustration, which is not recommended. Changing our own attitude takes time and practice. But it can happen.

Unfortunately, you may find yourself in the middle of a situation which includes the option of filing a lawsuit or complaint against your employer. While this may remain an option, you should evaluate what you win in the end by following this path. Then consider what you have to lose.

Risk is always a factor to be considered in these situations. Is it worth the risk? Will you lose your job? Will you be forced to work in an environment that holds resentment and animosity toward you? Will work become a hostile environment for you? Will you be labeled as a disloyal employee or troublemaker whom other employers do not want to hire? Also consider what happens if you file charges but lose. You may be forced to continue working but feel very uncomfortable in those surroundings.

The final decisions are personal choices. Each of us must evaluate the options, weigh them according to our own expectations and needs, and decide what is best for us. Whether our future with a particular company is at stake, or whether the problem lies with only one individual, we still must proceed cautiously and with the proper information to make the best decision for ourselves.

Troubleshooting Tensions Between Upper Management and the Staff

Overview

At times you will have more control over a situation than at other times. This chapter focuses on those problems created by situations that are outside of your control. Your management ability will be tested as you intercede and try to resolve tense situations. This chapter places you as the person in the middle, forced to operate between the employer and employees.

Sometimes your loyalty to the employer can complicate your answer to the staff. It could require you to misstate an event so that you protect the best interest of the company. For women this can be especially troubling, because of their strong bond to individuals and their need for connection. When forced to choose, women place less importance on hierarchy, rules, and procedures than on the individual welfare of people. Conflicts may arise when priorities differ.

This chapter addresses the following problems, possible causes, and cures.

8.1   The Problem: Rumors of the department being downsized are spreading, interrupting the office routine.

Possible Causes: This is just a rumor; there may be a conflict of loyalties; should you tell the truth?

Cures: Deal with rumors; manage conflicts of loyalty; honesty is the best policy.

8.2   The Problem: You have been told to reduce the staff size by one third.

Possible Causes: Are staff reductions absolutely necessary?; certain options lead to more problems; do not make decisions based on fear.

Cures: Understand the reasons; identif your options; address fears.

8.3   The Problem: You are unable to get a promotion for a deserving employee because you lack authority, not because of her qualifications.

Possible Causes: You may not have followed the proper procedures; the politics of an organization cannot be ignored; you will not always win.

Cures: Prepare presentations; deal with office politics; become a gracious loser.

8.4   The Problem: You are trying to bring the salaries of staff members closer together.

Possible Causes: Follow all the regulations; there is confusion as to who is making the decisions; understand your motives.

Cures: Follow the law regarding salary issues; identify who is in charge; choose your battles carefully.

8.5   The Problem: Other managers are assigning special projects to staff members without your approval or knowledge.

Possible Causes: There may be power plays within the company; you may not be well respected; your authority and role as manager may not be defined clearly.

Cures: Handle power plays; earn respect; define roles and responsibilities.

8.6   *The Problem: An employee is personally involved with the boss, and their relationship is creating problems around the office.*

Possible Causes: You may be giving an employee special consideration; there may be a problem in communicating expectations and authority; you are being controlled and manipulated.

Cures: Respond to individual needs; establish boundaries and open communications, avoid being used.

8.7   *The Problem: A corporate merger has caused the department to lose some of its independence, and the employees are very frustrated.*

Possible Causes: Office routines have been disrupted; you may have to start over to prove yourself; things may work out in time; your reactions may be based on fear.

Cures: Understand the effects of mergers; regain your voice and reputation; have patience; minimize fear.

Know your audience. Accept the political boundaries under which you must operate. Also, communicate in a style that is accepted, appreciated, and understood by all parties involved.

8.1 | The Problem: Rumors of the department being downsized are spreading, interrupting the office routine.

THE SCENE

Several staff members have asked you about whether or not they should start looking for another job. They are concerned about their future with the company, if there is a future.

One employee voiced concern about buying a home because both his and his wife's incomes are necessary to qualify for the mortgage. He asks for some assurance from you that his job is not about to be phased out; that buying the house is a smart financial decision for them. Another employee questions how much debt she can afford to incur over the holidays. She is seeking some guarantee that her job will be protected for a few months, giving her time to pay off this debt.

You have heard that the department might be sized-down or even completely eliminated. Nothing has been confirmed, but several colleagues have shared the grim stories they have heard as well. Someone heard that the department may be merged in with another area and both staffs reduced. Someone else heard that they were going to contract outside the company to provide that service. There is no job security for you either. In management meetings, all that has been mentioned is that changes will be introduced within the next few months. You want to avoid setting off a panic button, because nothing has been confirmed. You also do not want to be naive to what seems very possible.

In the past few years, similar rumors have been spread through the company and have died without action being taken. That knowledge brings you little solace. You are not sure just how to answer the staff's concern.

POSSIBLE CAUSES

This is just a rumor.

Rumors are just that: rumors, not fact. Whether rumors eventually become true or not may have little bearing on the morale of the department. Employees have already voiced their concerns about job security; it is time to reassure them as best you can, by whatever means necessary. Otherwise, these apprehensive attitudes will disrupt work.

There may be a conflict of loyalties.

As manager, there is a bond developed between you and the staff as well as between you and senior management. Conflicts arise for a number of reasons, including when you know more information than you are allowed to share. These situations are difficult for all managers, but especially female managers, because it suggests that someone else knows what is best. While information can flow both ways, it is often when information is withheld from employees that is most bothersome. Since that someone may not have the employees' best interests at heart, conflicts arise.

Should you tell the truth?

Assuming that you know information that can be helpful to employees in deciding their futures, should you share what you know or think you know? Honesty can come with consequences that may be explosive and even painful to accept. While you can deny any knowledge or speculation, you may feel uncomfortable lying to, or intentionally misleading anyone. When you have built a department based on trust and respect, it is important that you adhere to those same guidelines.

CURES

Deal with rumors.

Rumors may or may not become a reality. By their very definition, at the time they are being spread, there is no verification of the facts. Rumors are based solely on conjecture, speculation, and hypothesis.

Because rumors are not known to be factual is exactly why they must be stopped immediately. Offices cannot run efficiently and smoothly when they are constantly bombarded with taunts of rumors. Instead, rumors absorb the energy and time that would otherwise be devoted to work. Their presence benefits no one.

Your speculations will only add fuel to the rumor fire. Speak from what you know to be fact. When employees are asking for assurances that cannot be made, then say so. Job security is a thing of the past, even for you. It no longer exists in today's competitive marketplaces. You cannot promise job security even under the most positive and encouraging of situations.

Because these rumors are affecting the office, deal with them immediately. Time will be your worst enemy. Talk to the employees and share your concerns:

> *I know that several of you have questions about whether or not we are being downsized. The answer is that I do not know, but I do know that there is a lot of worrying and talking about things that none of us can control. This is not the first time that these rumors have made their rounds. That is not to say nothing will happen this time. No one is guaranteed job security, including me. This compa-*

ny is no different than other businesses; every company, every industry, and every position is at some risk. That should not stop us from doing the best job we can do every day that we are here. In fact, we can do our best to secure our jobs by our strong performance. If we allow these rumors to impede our job progress, we would be lame ducks waiting to get axed. It stands to reason then that we need to continue working hard and do the best we can. Probably the greatest fear and consideration we all have is about money. It is never wise to live from paycheck to paycheck, but I know most of us do it anyway. If you would like, I can have someone come to one of our meetings and talk about various savings plans and personal financial planning. Because of the competitive job marketplace of today, research suggests that we need to have a minimum of six months living expenses in our savings account. This has nothing to do with downsizing, and everything to do with being prepared financially for the unexpected. Would you like me to invite someone, perhaps a professional financial planner, to a staff meeting?

Individual employee requests should be taken up with that employee in private after a group meeting. For the employee who is buying a home, he and his wife must make their decision based on what is in their best interest. They are the ones responsible for that decision as well. For the employee concerned with overspending during the holidays, talk about financial planning and being prepared for the unexpected. You may even suggest ways to make the holidays less commercial.

See Section 5.4 for more information about building morale during these tenuous times. If these rumors are the effects of a recent merger or acquisition, see Section 8.7.

Manage conflicts of loyalty.

If you know more than you are at liberty to tell, you may feel torn in how you handle this situation. When restricted by upper management, you must respond as directed. If you were to inform the staff about upcoming changes before other employees had been notified, you would be creating turmoil, ill will, and jeopardizing your future, all of which could be avoided by following your directives.

Whether or not you agree with waiting is much less important than respecting and honoring your commitment to management. If you feel a bond and closeness to the staff, lying to them may be difficult and seem wrong. Even lies by omission may not make you feel better; it may be difficult for you to justify this action to yourself under any circumstance.

Share with the staff what you can. Do not go beyond that line:

> *Many of you have asked me about the possibility of our department getting downsized. Management is continuing to review its options and will make its final recommendation soon. Something has to change for us to survive in this competitive marketplace. Here is what I do know: If you do not maintain your current high production levels, that will not look good, especially to management. If you are truly concerned about your job future, protect your job by being the dependable and reliable employees that you have always been. I cannot stop you from looking around if you feel it is necessary. But if you are looking for job security, you will be disappointed. It just doesn't exist anymore. If you are looking around for other reasons, that is your choice.*

Downsizing is the one subject that tends to be handled poorly in most organizations. It is not uncommon for someone in senior management to decide that those employees affected by staff reductions are not able to handle the information before management is ready; therefore they wait until the very last minute to spring it on them. Often this is done for senior management's benefit, not the employees. This action only adds to the suspicion and mistrust that already exists in many hierarchical structures. The fear that production might decline if the employees are told about their job futures rarely occurs. Management is less concerned with the psychological well-being of the employees and more concerned that the work gets done.

To motivate employees under these stressful circumstances is difficult if not impossible. Do the best you can and be sensitive to the needs and feelings of those around you.

Ultimately, you must make the determination of what to tell, who, when, and where. If you defy senior management's orders, your job may be in jeopardy and severe consequences may ensue. Those may be consequences that you can live with, and that you are willing to accept. It is your choice.

Honesty is the best policy.

Is honesty always the best policy? There is no easy answer to this question. There are costs and consequences associated with telling the truth or not telling the truth. Much depends on whose understanding of the truth you are telling, and why.

We live in a society where others protect our feelings by lying. We live in a society where harmless lies are tolerated, even widely accepted. We live in a society where many feel that they are above the rules or laws that govern the masses. We live in a society where mistruths and intentionally misleading someone *may not even be considered a lie.*

Crossing the line between truth and a lie has become blurred and difficult to determine. Whose truth and how much truth you want to reveal can be a very individual decision. When you seek justification for your actions, you can usually find it, no matter what action you decide to take.

Speaking the truth is not always easy. Feelings may get hurt or someone may become angry because of the information you shared. Yet speaking the truth allows for the recipients to evaluate the information and decide for themselves how to respond. It shows that you respect the individuals enough to be honest.

Speaking the truth is one way to defuse conflict. Time and time again, it solves more problems than it ignites. Establishing boundaries and guidelines can add some stability to a tenuous situation. Since others will be taking the lead from you, be sure to clarify your position:

> *You have asked me about what is going on in this company and how these changes may affect you. I think those are very legitimate questions and I will try to answer them as best I can. Before I start, let's try to establish some guidelines. What we discuss in this meeting is to stay here. If you have a concern, I want it brought to my attention, not gossiped about throughout the department. Also, it is important that each of us do the best job that we can; we must keep a positive attitude. Nothing has been decided absolutely. First, what have you heard? I will try to respond to those things as best I can.*

Guiding this dialogue takes skill. It is important to have built a foundation of respect and control within the group, otherwise the group can ignore any boundaries that you have established. The conversation may get out of control and become volatile; be prepared to pull the reigns in tighter if this occurs.

Section 1.3 discusses society's acceptance of little lies and the blurred lines we often cross.

8.2 The Problem: You have been told to reduce the staff size by one third.

THE SCENE

You have just left a very intense managers' meeting where staff reductions were the primary topic. Everyone was uneasy with the news. Drastic price cuts, competition, and industry changes mean that employee reductions are absolutely necessary in order for the company to survive.

Each manager is to recommend changes for their staff. Each staff must be reduced by one third. Senior management will have the final approval on who stays and who goes.

Your decision may be based on either seniority, experience, or contributions; the decisions produce very different results. You hate to let anyone go because the department is running smoothly right now. Any reduction will cause disruption, but you have no choice except to recommend who it should or shouldn't be.

Note: Key to making staff reductions work is minimizing the fear in the remaining employees that their jobs are in jeopardy. Keeping morale up as well as productivity will be your indication as to how successful you have been in implementing these changes.

POSSIBLE CAUSES

Are staff reductions absolutely necessary?

If you feel that staff reductions are not the best solution for the problem, it may be harder to make these recommendations. The reason why a company is downsizing may affect your ability to make these decisions. You may not know or believe any of the underlying reasons that have been given by senior management. Some of the more common reasons used to support the need to downsize include: needing to post a profit (the company is currently showing a loss); trying to meet the industry changes (often having to do with technological advances); preparing for industry changes (based on trends and future expectations); saving more money (greed). Some reasons are easier to sell than others. Management typically uses one of the first two reasons with greater frequency, while the last one is often the culprit.

Certain options lead to more problems.

There are three primary methods used for employee reductions: employee seniority, individual productivity and skill, or voluntary resignations. One is subjective; another factors out subjectivity, but fails to reward those employees who do the best job; the final one removes the decision-making process from your control completely. Before you can make a recommendation, you must have a clear understanding of the future. You must know what you need to accomplish after these changes are implemented to make certain that you are as prepared as possible. Letting employees go because of general staff reductions is never easy, especially when they are good employees.

Do not make decisions based on fear.

During these uncertain times it is common to be motivated by fear. The staff may be motivated by fear if they know or sense what is going on. You, too, may make decisions based on the fear for your recommendation that you create a larger problem than already exists, or that you are not a strong enough manager to lead the department through this critical stage. Making these tough decisions is what management is all about. Fairness may or may not enter into the equation. Before making a stance and defending your action, seek the advice of those more knowledgeable about downsizing and building employee morale.

CURES

Understand the reasons.

How you address this problem may be based on your understanding of why the company is downsizing. It may be harder to recommend a plan if you believe that downsizing is being used to pad the pockets of the top managers or shareholders, and is not in the best interest of the employees. It may also be difficult for employees to accept and move beyond this hurdle if they believe that is management's objective.

At some level you must accept that you may never know with complete certainty why staff reductions are necessary. Answers that are given may contradict what you know to be the truth. Still, you must do the best you can given what you know.

While the reason should not affect your recommendations, it would be naive to think that it won't affect your ability as a leader. Women may have a more difficult time promoting something that they believe is wrong. On the other hand, men are more likely to accept the statements offered by senior management as fact.

Identify your options.

While variations may exist, the three most common methods of deciding who to keep and who to let go are: using a seniority-based system, evaluating each employee's skills and contributions separately, or asking for voluntary resignations. The first method produces fewer complications and the least amount of argument. The downside is that it can cause you to lose some excellent employees while keeping only adequate ones. The second method, evaluating each employee's performance, skills, and ability to handle the additional workload, is more subjective and open to dispute. Feelings are more likely to get bruised during this process because it suggests some employees are more valuable than others. The final solution, asking for voluntary resignation is the riskiest of the three. It completely takes the responsibility away from you and allows the employees to decide for themselves. It often produces a random selection of both good and adequate employees remaining with varying levels of seniority.

Most employers recommend using a seniority-based approach for large-scale downsizing. If the reductions are to be small, then you may consider eliminating a position altogether as well as the person who occupies that position. While this provides some ability to evaluate employee performance, it is viewed as less argumentative by those affected by its outcome. It works best for small-scale reductions though; otherwise like evaluating individual performance, it becomes open for subjective interpretations and creates controversy.

Asking for volunteers assumes that someone will volunteer, that enough people will volunteer, or that not too many people will volunteer. Results are often tied to an incentive for volunteering, usually monetary. If any of these elements are missing, it is likely to fail miserably.

When you prepare your recommendations, look at each position carefully and see what jobs can be reassigned with the least amount of training. Then make a list of all the employees including their length of employment, special training, job performance, and replacement ability. In this list you will want to note items that may influence your decision beyond length of employment such as special degrees or if only one employee can handle specific equipment. Review this information carefully.

There are no easy answers. If the process is extremely grueling and difficult, then you are approaching it correctly. Be ready to defend your recommendations to both senior management and to the staff. Reaching a decision is only the first step. Implementing that plan takes even more courage and fortitude.

Respond according to the tone the employees set. If they prefer direct communications, deal directly with them. However, if they are afraid and need reassurance from you that things will be able to function properly after these reductions, then softly and gently begin rebuilding their confidence in you, in each other, and in the company itself.

The road ahead will be bumpy. Supporting and encouraging the employees will be essential to making downsizing become rightsizing. It can succeed if you believe that it can succeed.

Address fears.

No one enjoys working for a company that is in the process of downsizing its staff. It is a difficult and trying time for everyone. The emergence of fears is not uncommon throughout the company. These fears can produce a multitude of side issues and problems to deal with.

Feeling overwhelmed and inadequate during the process is natural. You may fear that you are not the best leader for the job, and your insecurities and self-doubt may begin to emerge. The best defense for these fears is to look inside yourself and remember your accomplishments and strengths. Know that the best person for the job is someone who is sensitive and caring. Because women operate in such a strong mode of connectedness, rejection and anger can be interpreted personally; but they aren't personal. Find ways to share your pain, perhaps with other colleagues or a mate. Your pain is real and it is normal.

You may fear that you are not making the best decisions, or that senior management doesn't accept your recommendations. Separate out those things that you control from those things that you don't. Your defense for making the best choice is research and evaluation of your particular situation. Senior management's acceptance or rejection of your plan is beyond your control. Do the best job that you can, with what you have. Make a strong, positive presentation, and include specific details whenever possible. Then be willing to accept whatever decision is rendered by senior management and implement it to the best of your ability. If you cannot do that, you need to find another employer.

You may fear employee revolt. Again, you cannot control the employee response; however, you can give some guidance by how you frame the events. Anticipating problems can provide an excellent foundation for solving many problems before they happen. Have a variety of plans ready to implement on a moment's notice. Look at different "what if" scenarios, and create possible and probable solutions.

The lack of job security remains a major fear to most employees. Job security is not something that you can promise; it rarely exists today. Additional work is often expected without any additional compensation. Employees often feel used, as if they are nothing more than a number on an expense account, easily eliminated if need be. Be prepared to deal with these situations directly.

Create an atmosphere where everyone can share, without fear of ramifications. Make this a place where employees are encouraged to offer suggestions for improvement, and a place where they are listened to, valued, and appreciated for who they are and what they contribute.

See Sections 5.4 and 8.1 for more information about managing during times of downsizing and restructuring.

8.3 The Problem: You are unable to get a promotion for a deserving employee because you lack authority, not because of her qualifications.

THE SCENE

Pamela is an excellent employee who has taken on many responsibilities beyond her job description. Recently she came to you for a salary increase, one she deserves because of her increased duties, and one that would put her within industry standards for what she does.

There is no question in your mind that Pamela should get a salary adjustment, however, it is not your decision to make—only to recommend. The salary review committee approves all salary increases that are recommended outside an employee's annual review. Despite your declarations concerning all Pamela's accomplishments and contributions, the request was turned down by the committee.

The declination surprised you because several requests were presented by other managers at the same time, and most were approved. You failed to see differences in the requests. You suspect they declined your recommendation because it came from you, a young female still earning the respect from colleagues and superiors, and not because Pamela wasn't qualified.

Now, you are not sure what to do. You haven't told Pamela yet, but you know you must.

POSSIBLE CAUSES

You may not have followed the proper procedures.

Whether the guidelines are written or not does not lessen your responsibility to follow them. If you have deviated from these policies, you can find yourself facing defeat, no matter how deserving or thorough a request you have made. As a new manager, many of these procedures may be completely foreign to you. In fact, you still may believe that justice is always given to the most deserving, although you are quickly learning otherwise.

The politics of an organization cannot be ignored.

Politics cannot be factored out; it is in every organization. Politics is not evil, though people who abuse the power of politics are evil. Women often underestimate the power and influence that political systems contribute and control. As a new manager, this is a major part of learning how to play the game within your particular organization.

You will not always win.

Don't take it so personally. The more risk you take, the more chances you have for facing defeat. Courage will go a long way toward getting you ready for your next attempt. How you rebound may be one of the most critical aspects of establishing a leadership role for yourself. Consider the defeat as just one of many tests you must undergo to gain the respect and appreciation of fellow managers.

CURES

Prepare presentations.

As a woman manager, you will be judged on many aspects of your job performance, including presentations. You will most likely be assessed more critically than the male colleagues. Women are forced to be more thorough and careful in making requests; the playing fields are not equal, nor will they ever be. Accept this difference as an obstacle or challenge, but never let it be your defeat.

Do your research *before* you play the game. Research includes knowing the facts, the risk, and how to present the information so that it is received by a particular audience. Women are more comfortable asking a lot of questions which can help during the research phase. Use this benefit to your advantage, ask a lot of questions, and find out as much as possible before making your presentation.

A mentor can provide some friendly advice of the do's and don'ts for getting your request approved. A mentor can be a welcome ally, if he or she is willing to share and is available for the commitment. Without access to a mentor, you will need to learn more information on your own.

Your style of communicating is also a factor. You will be judged as much or more by how you say it instead of what it is you are saying. If you come across too strong and aggressive, the other managers may want to prove to you how limited your power really is. A soft, weak voice can be just as devastating to your cause when management is looking for someone much stronger and louder. Women must consider the pitch of their voice, especially when they become excited or angry.

Stay focused on your objective: getting Pamela's salary adjusted. If that means asking for advice from those holding the power, then do so. If it means appearing less knowledgeable than you really are, then what's the harm? In the end, Pamela gets the raise she deserves, you know how smart you really are, and colleagues are not threatened by your presence.

Deal with office politics.

Every organization is a political system. Yet, politics is just one of several factors affecting your ability to succeed. Women often approach management in an innocent fashion, believing good things happen to good people and that justice will always prevail. Businesses operate politically; goodness and justice may not influence the outcome.

Learn about the politics in this organization. Politics is key to how things get done. It is less a matter or choice of playing the game as it is how well you work in this environment. You cannot avoid playing the game, it is everywhere.

Find out from others, preferably a mentor, how to play political office games. Although it is never discussed directly, subtleties can be picked up on by watching the game in action. Observing others may be one of the best indicators for what works well and what doesn't. Another way to learn is through networks and outside organizations. These may provide some insight into general rules and situations that can be adapted to your particular environment.

Remember that the style adapted by males may not be available to you as a female. Try variations until you find one that works comfortably for you. Section 7.6 also discusses politics in the workplace.

Become a gracious loser.

Learning how to accept defeat is never easy, especially when you feel the defeat was rendered for unfair or unjust reasons. How well you learn to accept defeat and move on to the next game is a critical step in how well you acclimate to the role of manager.

Some people will face more defeats than others because some people take more risks, calculated or otherwise. Everyone will face defeat at some time. While risks should be minimized, they should never be factored out completely. Eliminating risks suggests that you are too conservative and protective in your style, are not moving forward, and are not open to change.

Because you have been confronted with defeat does not mean that you are defeated. Surrendering means defeat. Losing one battle means that you are learning, compromising, regrouping, playing the game—any number of things—but not defeated!

Other Considerations: You should talk to Pamela. It does not get easier. Besides, you owe her that much out of personal respect for her. Putting it off is not in anyone's best interest. The sooner you talk to her, the sooner the healing process can begin and everyone can move forward to new issues.

While it doesn't have to come immediately, waiting will only aggravate an already tense situation. The exception would be if you were still working on getting her salary adjustment passed, perhaps through another avenue. However, you should still keep Pamela informed of where you are in the approval process.

> *Pamela, I am not going to be able to give you the salary increase you requested right now. What I would like to do is to*

reevaluate your situation in three months and see where we are then. I don't want to sound overly optimistic at that juncture either, at least not yet. Typically these adjustments are only done during annual reviews. Yours comes up in May, so that may be the best time to look at making an adjustment. You have done a remarkable job since you have been here and you have a great future with this company. I appreciate all your hard work, dedication, and enthusiasm. In fact, I am writing a memo to your personnel file stating just that. I'll give you a copy for your personal records as well.

Be careful not to promise more than you can deliver. It can divide your relationship with the staff members if they begin feeling used. Continue to compliment and praise Pamela whenever her actions and accomplishments warrant it.

8.4 | The Problem: You are trying to bring the salaries of staff members closer together.

THE SCENE

You are managing a staff that has a wide range of salaries. This staff is a combination of several departments merged together, plus a few transfers. The department has been in operation approximately six months. You want to bring the salaries within a closer range, based on current positions, and with less disparity for the same duties. When you mention this to your boss, he suggests that you might meet with personnel first. He gives you neither his support nor his objection.

You schedule a meeting with the personnel manager to discuss these much-needed adjustments. The personnel officer asks the chief financial officer to be present at this meeting. The CFO is quite fiscally conservative, and she suggests ways to minimize expenses and reminds you of the bottom line effect of each adjustment. Cost is her only concern.

The meeting doesn't go well. This is going to be an uphill battle, and you are not sure if this war can even be won. You are not sure if it is wise to fight this battle because you are new to the position. You know you lack a solid and proven reputation to lean on.

POSSIBLE CAUSES

Follow all the regulations.

Both Federal and state labor regulations impact salary structures. You always want to comply with the law, especially when it comes to discrimination, but not every injustice is illegal. There is a big difference between unjust behavior and illegal actions, and it is incumbent upon you to know the difference and to be able to support your claims. By the same token, no company readily admits when it has violated the law.

There is confusion as to who is making the decisions.

Knowing who the decision maker is will help you speed up the approval process. Whether the chief financial officer is more important than the personnel officer is not known. Expect one person to have power and control over the other though, equal decision making is rare in most organizations. The red tape and game playing can be annoying, but it is part of the equation. Ignoring it or not playing does not make it go away; you are simply participating with a disadvantage.

Understand your motives.

Choose your battles carefully. Not every disagreement has to be confronted. This lesson is often learned at the expense of many battle wounds. By evaluating and weighing various aspects of the situation, you will decide whether it is worth your time and energy, assessing the cost and risk involved.

Note: Equalizing salaries is an honorable task. Make certain that you are doing it for the benefit of the employees, and not just to get a feather in your cap. Good workers should be rewarded with competitive salaries. Are employees unhappy with the current salary structure? Or are they even aware that there are discrepancies? Because of the importance of timing, you may decide to wait a few months (if no one is pushing you right now) and gain more ammunition to defend your recommendations while you continue to build a strong record.

CURES

Follow the law regarding salary issues.

The law is very specific about pay discrepancies based on patterns of discrimination. The Equal Pay Act of 1963 prohibits pay discrimination based on gender. Other discrimination patterns are also included in this act such as race, religion, and age. However, pay differences based on seniority or merit system or on a system that measures earnings by quantity or quality of production are permitted.

First, understand how these discrepancies originated. The history may be able to explain why the discrepancies are so large. Next, try to identify if there are any patterns. Patterns are an indication that laws may have been broken, whereas random discrepancies are more representative of bad management.

Learn how these salary differences originated. Either the personnel officer or employee personnel files may provide you with sufficient details about this background information, including employee training, experience, and education. Those working in one department may have gotten higher salaries than those in another department simply because one boss was a better negotiator.

If there are patterns of discrimination, bring them to the immediate attention of personnel. Patterns can be identified with things such as: men are making more than women, all minorities are paid less than nonminorities, and so on. If patterns are identified and brought to the attention of senior management, hopefully everyone will move quickly to bring them more in line with each other.

It is important to know which practices are prohibited by law, and to distinguish these from actions that may be unjust, but not unlawful. If the discrepancies are random, where no consistent pattern can be identified, then discrimination would less likely be an issue. This would be more representative of unjust behavior, not unlawful behavior. Not that it is right, only that the law doesn't prohibit it.

Unjust actions do not demand your immediate attention. Before you fight this battle you want to know why it exists and who you are fighting. It may be representative of injustices that management allows or supports.

Chapter 9 addresses numerous conflicts arising out of corporate policy differences, while Section 7.3 looks closer at pay discrepancies.

Identify who is in charge.

Within any hierarchical organization some individuals will have more power than others. Title may have little to do with the actual decision-making authority granted a person. Once you have determined who the decision maker is, you can tailor your presentation to a style that is acceptable or receptive by the decision maker. For example, if the chief financial officer is the primary decision maker, numbers will be the focal point in her discussions. Or if the personnel officer is the decision maker, the human element may play a more significant factor. Prepare your presentation accordingly. If you are still unsure, be prepared for both: include sound reasons for both the financial and moral decisions.

Within any organization, certain individuals are more powerful than others. These are the individuals who can make decisions without being questioned, who are automatically provided time to discuss their ideas, and who must be convinced that your recommendation is worth their stamp of approval.

There are several methods you can follow for identifying these individuals. First, if you have a mentor within the organization, he or she may be able to provide some insights and directions as to the power certain individuals wield. Don't feel lost if you do not have a formal mentor within your organization, you can still learn a great deal by observation, particularly through group interactions.

Once identified, find a style that this person respects and responds to positively. Don't create more problems for yourself than is necessary by ignoring his or her concerns.

Choose your battles carefully.

Deciding *when* to fight a battle and *which* battle to fight is the result of numerous considerations. Ultimately, it is a personal decision that you control. There are both costs and consequences associated with these actions that should be taken under careful consideration before you jump in.

Taking up various causes against the beliefs or traditions of management or colleagues is a time-consuming responsibility. Decide why you feel this cause is important and what you wish to accomplish. Is it for your own benefit, to get another feather in your cap? Is it for the benefit of the employees? Have some of the staff members complained about salaries and brought these discrepancies to your attention?

Also, make sure that what you want to happen can happen. If your expectations are unreasonable, you will be disappointed. If you are starting out with room for negotiation, know what concessions you are willing to make, then find out who the individual is who has the power to negotiate.

Once you have decided to fight this battle, proceed. Be willing to go the distance once you begin. Going the distance shows that you have perseverance, stamina, and determination, which are all positive leadership qualities. Even if you lose the battle, never surrender your pride.

8.5 The Problem: Other managers are assigning special projects to staff members without your approval or knowledge.

THE SCENE

During weekly staff meetings, employees update you on the status of their outstanding projects. This is the time to review workloads and assign pending projects. No one gets penalized for not completing projects; the purpose is to maintain open communication and to make reassignments if necessary so that workloads are balanced. Both production and attitudes have improved significantly since these meetings began.

According to last week's meeting, Jeff and Betsy should be near completion of their current projects and ready for new assignments. You have a report that needs to be handled immediately that you want to assign to them, and they are perfect for the project.

As each employee updates you on the status of their projects, you are surprised to learn that Betsy is in the middle of another assignment. She is working on a special report for next week's board meeting. You knew nothing about this project. All assignments are supposed to come through you before they are assigned, but some managers ignore that request. In particular, Steve, your boss, often goes directly to his favorite employees with projects, completely bypassing your authority. This means that Betsy will not be available for this assignment, one you really needed her to work on.

You have talked to Steve about the need to bring the projects to you to be assigned. In the past, he simply apologized and said he had forgotten. But nothing has changed. Steve and other managers are making it difficult to control work flow in the department. They are affecting your ability to manage.

POSSIBLE CAUSES

There may be power plays within the company.

If you are without power or have only limited power, there may be little that you can do to remedy this problem. Power plays can destroy a workplace. Absolute power corrupts absolutely. The game no longer is equal or fair; instead you will be set up to lose every time. When power is a factor, advance cautiously.

You may not be well respected.

Gender may or may not be a factor causing the disrespect, but the result is the same. A lack of respect can cause managers to ignore your requests, to want to cause you to fail, or to simply be a constant source of irritation in your life. Respect must be earned. If someone does not want to respect you, there is little that you can do to change them. Conserve your energy; instead focus on those things that you can control and affect.

Your authority and role as manager may not be defined clearly.

Without establishing clarity in your role, there could emerge numerous misunderstandings and obstacles. These differences can grow to become an even greater source of conflict between you, your boss, and staff.

CURES

Handle power plays.

Power can be a dangerous tool within the confines of management, especially when you are faced with a boss or other managers who enjoy asserting power over you. These roles can be frustrating as well as hazardous to your professional career.

Power is seldom discussed openly. Even though there is nothing to gain by addressing it head-on, there is still a lot that you can do. Once you have identified the main cause as stemming from power, you must be prepared against future attacks.

Keep communication open and positive within the department. This is a confusing time for the employees, be sure not to punish them for the awkward situations in which they have been placed. If Steve refuses to follow the procedures you have established, have the staff come to you directly when they have been asked to work on special projects.

In a conversation with the employees, you might say something like:

> *I understand that sometimes you receive special projects directly from another manager. While generally these come to me first, that is not always the case. If you receive a project that I haven't assigned, I'd like for you to let me know about it. This way, I will have a better grasp on each person's work schedules for future assignments.*

While you may not be able to change their actions, at least you would know what was going on in the department. The element of surprise would be eliminated.

Earn respect.

Respect is something you hope to receive. Respect must be earned, it is not given freely. There will be times that no matter how hard you try, and no matter how good you are, respect is never offered. In these cases, there is little you can do, except continue doing your best. You can still respect yourself.

You may not have earned someone's respect because they are still testing you and building trust. Because women managers are tested more than their male colleagues, this situation can be seen more frequently along gender lines. You will not know which tests are necessary to win someone's respect and approval, nor will you know at what point you will no longer be tested. Don't give up; set your own standards to do the best job you can. Trying to please everyone else all the time can become exhausting and benefits no one.

In situations where one individual does not respect another, confront the individual. Respect is an important and necessary ingredient for trusting, and honest relationships to develop:

> *Steve, when you have some time I would like to discuss what you expect of me in this position. I want to know exactly what I am*

responsible for and what I have authority over. It helps me if we agree on these areas and take out the ambiguity. How does your schedule look for later today?

Establish footings, expectations, and specific details up front. Your style in handling this problem should be the path of least resistance. Another consideration is that perhaps Steve cannot respect any subordinates because he doesn't respect himself. If this is the case, you cannot change Steve or make him respect himself. You can only change yourself. Do not define your successes and image according to Steve's respect of you. Consider respect on its own merits.

Define roles and responsibilities.

When you have vague or undefined roles, it is important to establish clarity on the situation. Without clarity, the roles will become even more confusing. Improving communications can solve many problems.

Steve, as your boss, is the most logical person to approach about clarifying your role as manager. When you talk with him be sure that you do not appear threatening, condescending, or as if you are making personal attacks about him. Try something like:

Steve, there seems to be some confusion about what my job is. I have a weekly meeting with my staff where we discuss workloads and assignments. That is where I hand out the new projects. I have asked that all projects go through me for distribution, as you know. You have gone to employees with requests on several occasions directly, as have other managers. It makes me look bad when I try to make assignments only to find out someone is working on a project that I knew nothing about. I think it will help both of us to outline exactly what you expect of me, and how much authority is given in my role.

Realistically, nothing may change. Steve may apologize again but continue doing what he wants to do. Work on changing those things that you can and work around those things that you cannot change. Learn to be more flexible; not all battles are worth fighting.

See Section 7.1 for more information about defining your roles and conflicts with a boss.

Other Considerations: Additional problems may occur if managers are hand-picking certain employees for special projects. Not only does this take the top employees out of the circulation pool, but it can create resentment by the other staff members because they haven't been chosen. These situations require handling more aggressively to preserve the cohesiveness of the department. Act immediately to regain control.

8.6 | The Problem: An employee is personally involved with the boss, and their relationship is creating problems around the office.

THE SCENE

Sandy, one of the department secretaries, has recently started dating your boss. In theory you do not have a problem with them dating, however the relationship does interfere with work.

Other employees in the department have complained about her special treatment. You are limited in your ability to control Sandy because she will just run and tell Anthony, your boss and her boyfriend. She has already done it on several occasions. When she does this, Anthony comes to her defense, contradicts your comments, and aggravates the situation more than it already is.

Sandy is less than a stellar employee. You have considered placing her on probation, and have had several heart-to-heart talks with her about her performance. You are supposed to discuss personnel problems with your boss before placing someone on probation. Each time you have tried to bring up Sandy's poor performance Anthony thinks she is doing fine, and that you are too hard on her. You feel very frustrated with the whole situation. Since other employees have noticed her lax work habits, there needs to be something done to regain control.

POSSIBLE CAUSES

You may be giving an employee special consideration.

You may have decided that Sandy's situation warrants special consideration, and it may. But if you are treating Sandy differently without realizing it, the situation needs to be reviewed carefully. It may not be fair. Fairness is subjective; it does not mean equally fair to all parties. If you feel that it is uncalled for, then regain control by managing the situation, not avoiding it. Otherwise, adopt an exception to the policy and move beyond this situation. If the treatment of one employee begins to interfere with the office routine, and other employees are complaining, you cannot ignore their concerns.

There may be a problem in communicating expectations and authority.

Boundaries are important. You should agree on what type of authority you have to carry out your responsibilities as manager. The problem may have little to do with their relationship, and everything to do with clarifying roles, power, and personality conflicts. Sandy may just be caught in the middle.

You are being controlled and manipulated.

Sandy may be using you to further her own personal gain. Whether she wants to advance her own career or to see you fail at her whim, she may enjoy the power she currently holds by sleeping with your boss. She may like making you squirm. It may be part of her game to have an intimidating presence. It is critical that you reestablish boundaries and authority between yourself and Sandy, otherwise the resentment felt by the rest of the staff could cause worse problems to erupt.

CURES

Respond to individual needs.

Managing people on an individual basis takes courage and the blessings of those around you, both management as well as those you manage. Without the support for your individualized treatment, it can fail if you are not careful. Proceed cautiously.

First, determine why you are treating Sandy differently. If you are the one treating Sandy differently than the other employees, it is something you have chosen, and something you control. You may either allow or disallow these actions to continue. Be sure to review the possible consequences of your actions, and follow the path that produces the most positive results and the least amount of resistance.

Talk to Anthony and establish some guidelines and boundaries for you to operate within. Anthony may be trying to show his power and control to his "woman." Neither he nor Sandy may be handling the relationship very professionally, and you are caught in the middle. Unfortunately, no one usually admits that they are not handling their personal affairs in the most professional manner. Confronting the situation would be counterproductive.

Follow the plan that makes the most sense. If you choose to make an exception to the guidelines, that is fine. Assuming, of course, that your management style is one of flexibility and responding to individual needs. However, do not blame Sandy or Anthony for something that you are allowing.

On the other hand, if politics is clouding the issue, you still have a choice. There will be times when your best choice is to let it be, and try to work around these obstacles as best you can. Build stronger relationships with the rest of the staff. Do not let them feel left out. It will be up to you to make each of them feel special and appreciated.

Establish boundaries and open communication.

You will operate in a better environment if you know and understand where your parameters are drawn. Know exactly what you are allowed to do and how much freedom you have or don't have when doing it. Also determine the appropriate protocol to follow when exceptions arise.

Anthony will probably be the one to establish and measure your ability to adapt to those boundaries, so discuss this matter with him directly.

> *Anthony, whenever it is convenient for you, I would like to go over my job description, duties, and responsibilities. It is always useful for me to have these roles defined clearly and agreed upon. I think we both benefit when we know exactly what I am supposed to be doing. This way we are working toward the same goal. How does your calendar look this week?*

During this discussion, allow Anthony to define his role for you first. You should come to the meeting prepared with some guidelines that you would like, somewhat like a wish list. Some managers do not like establishing formal boundaries. He may say something like: *"Oh, you are doing just fine. Is there a particular problem about something that has happened that you want to discuss?"* It is better to keep the conversation focused on generalities, not specifics. If, however, he does not cooperate, list the boundaries you have or need and ask that he either confirm or deny each one.

Determine what the consequences are for not following these boundaries. There may be times when you want to go directly to a source to solve a problem, even if it is against policy. Know what the costs of that approach are before you undertake it.

Avoid being used.

Absolutely nothing can be more frustrating or aggravating than feeling manipulated by an employee. Whatever her reasons (assuming that she even has them) Sandy may enjoy holding power over you. Part of her game may include controlling you. Accept that she may do almost anything to reach this position of power.

Talk immediately to Sandy. You will need to establish control; be firm but receptive.

> *Sandy, over the past few weeks there has been some friction between us. Each time I ask you to do something you do not want to do, you run to Anthony to get out of it. If your problem is with me, I would like for us to be able to sit down and talk about it right now. This situation is causing some hardships with other employees; it is interrupting the office. Do we have a problem? If so, let's try to work it out. I do not have a problem with you and Anthony dating, but in the office, I am the manager.*

While this dialogue sounds dictatorial and very autocratic, that is the exact approach to take in order to limit her manipulation. Anything less would be ignored easily by Sandy, or even trivialized. Document meetings carefully. Make sure that a clear and complete paper trail is maintained. This may be beneficial later on, so consider it preventive medicine. Take it, do it, and hopefully you will never have to use it. Be prepared for the unexpected.

8.7 The Problem: A corporate merger has caused the department to lose some of its independence, and the employees are very frustrated.

THE SCENE

Because of a recent company takeover, departments are being merged and many procedures have been centralized at the home office. Despite the success of the department, you must implement numerous changes that have come down from the corporate office. These changes have resulted in delays, mistakes, and frustration. It now takes twice as long to get a new order processed if it misses an arbitrary cut-off date. Customers are complaining to the employees, making everyone uneasy.

No longer can an employee make decisions or order products directly for customers. Now, everything must be approved at the central location, which means another state, and another group of decision makers.

Although these changes look good on paper, no one thought through how they might affect individual departments or work flow. When you spoke to your boss, he was just as frustrated about it as you were. He offered no words of encouragement; instead he basically left you alone to fight your own battle or to conform.

POSSIBLE CAUSES

Office routines have been disrupted.

Mergers, takeovers and acquisitions can produce tension, frustration, competition, and even resentment between the companies involved. It is important to know and to believe in the direction the company is now headed. Changes are often justified by financial savings, not employee morale or customer goodwill. Unless you share your concerns with the new decision makers, how will the corporate office know that a problem exists?

You may have to start over to prove yourself.

Decisions are easier to make when they are based on a reputation and a proven track record. Because new players have been introduced, though, you no longer can rely on your previous record. Instead, you may find your-self starting at the very beginning having to prove your abilities to gain their respect and trust. Gaining your voice requires preparation, research, and an ability to adapt to the audience.

Things may work out in time.

Your ability to be patient and to weather the storm can provide the sta-bility and security that is currently lacking in the workplace. Patience does not mean that you agree with the methods and the changes that are current-ly going on. During times of transition, change is often replaced by more change, until things quiet down and find an acceptable routine. Reacting to the first round of changes may be premature.

Your reactions may be based on fear.

Both you and the employees may be responding more to the fear rep-resented by the takeover, including the possibility of future staff reductions. It may have little to do with changes in job duties, and everything to do with a lack of control and the probability that additional changes are yet to be felt. Your ability to minimize the effects of fear will directly correlate to the suc-cess of the department during such times.

CURES

Understand the effects of mergers.

The effects of mergers can be felt on a multitude of levels. Often those who feel they have no voice are the ones who feel affected worst. As a man-ager, you will need to defend the changes and promote and support senior management's position. You can still voice concerns quietly to the appropri-ate individuals. If these complaints are causing additional confusion or lost revenue, then make certain they are heard by the corporate office.

Know what you are fighting before you go forward. Mergers are mar-riages between companies. These blended families take some time working out the details and adjusting to each other. It is important to know if it was an equal merger, or if one company is the minority partner (more like an acquisition). Most takeovers are considered hostile, where the minority com-pany did not want the marriage to take place. The company that holds major-ity interest may be concerned primarily with its own agenda, something you may not be privileged to know.

Do the best you can with what you have. Learn to adjust. Keep communication open with the staff, allowing them to share concerns and ideas.

If the employees (or you for that matter) are concerned about downsizing and employee reductions, see Sections 8.1 and 8.2 for more specific information about how to handle this situation.

Regain your voice and reputation.

According to the basic hierarchical structure, the staff comes to you to have their voices heard. They expect you to take their concerns up the line of command. They expect you to get results. Your ability to achieve the necessary changes for them will directly affect the staff's belief and respect in you.

Gender may play a role in how your concerns are heard. Unfortunately, all the stripes you had earned in your previous management tests are nearly washed away. You may feel voiceless through this process.

Before taking on this battle, determine why the changes have been enacted. It gives you a place to start and allows you to present your recommendations aimed at addressing the concerns of a specific market.

Try to understand the benefits of these changes. Keeping certain functions centralized may produce more consistency throughout the company. It may provide greater buying power, thus affecting the bottom-line expense, or it may be because of power.

In any case, by knowing exactly what you are up against, you can focus on the repercussions of these changes. After you have voiced your concerns and provided supporting documentation, you must show that you are a team player. Work within the confines of the group dynamics to regain control over whatever else is left.

Complaining will change nothing. Write your memo, then accept the obstacles that you now face. Learn to work around these challenges. Document the situation, in case management calls for more information. Address facts, not feelings, when making your presentation to management. Be sure that you are not just whining because you feel like big brother is watching over you, but that you have some legitimate concerns and recommendations.

Have patience.

Patience is never an easy thing to have. Time and time again you will be tested on how patient you are during a particular situation. Know your own limitations as well as your ability to manage stress. Both play heavily into how patient you are.

However, when you are confronted with situations that do not appear to be permanent, the healthiest, safest and most logical response is to be patient. Such may be the case when mergers are first enacted. The first wave of changes may not be permanent. Some will remain the same, others may go back to how they were before, and still others may change to a different method altogether.

Patience does not mean that you accept the way things are. In fact, I would recommend just the opposite. A memo making senior management aware of the problems these changes have created is important. How else would it know that there is a problem? But patience does mean that you learn to go with the flow, and that you withhold final judgment for a period of time while allowing the kinks to be worked out.

Whining accomplishes nothing. In fact, it may actually cause you to lose a few notches down the road. During these times of change, everything in the company is available to be looked at, analyzed, reviewed, and ultimately affected by change. Including your position; nothing escapes notice.

Minimize fear.

Fear is a natural response when one is faced with change. Mergers represent change, and this represents the unknown. Fear is our response to the unknown.

The staff may be afraid of many things, not the least of which is job security. Because mergers often implement changes in different stages, it is logical to expect more changes to be introduced later. Those changes could include employee reductions.

Focus on what you know as fact, on attitudes, and on those things that you can control. Avoid letting the rumors dictate your responses. See Section 8.1 for handling rumors about downsizing.

Denying fear exists does not make it go away. In fact, the opposite is normally the result. The less you talk about fears the more they may grow and overpower you and the staff. Instead, allow the staff to talk about their concerns. By keeping the conversation focused on individual feelings, you are able to help employees become empowered. Remember, you cannot empower someone, you can only offer him or her an opportunity to grow. He or she must be willing to accept empowerment along with its responsibility.

Set the stage for weekly meetings. Create and support open dialogue. Let the staff members know that you care. And let them know it is okay to be afraid.

I know that there are a lot of changes going on that are troubling to you. Some of those changes affect how I am able to manage this department as well. So, believe me when I say that I understand your frustrations. But, we have to accept these changes and work within the boundaries that are being established. What I would like us to do is to have a weekly meeting to see how everyone is doing. This is not a bitching session; it is a time when you can openly share your concerns, a time when we will listen to one another. I may not be able to solve your problems, but together we can learn better ways to work within these confines. Let me start with something that has been brought to my attention. Several of you have already voiced concerns about what is next. I do not know and I suspect the corporate office hasn't decided. No, I cannot guarantee that they will not consider staff reductions. At the same time, let's focus on what we can do and what we already know. There is no sense worrying about what might happen next. Instead, we already know we have changes in this department that are affecting how we operate today. How are those changes working out?

You will probably need to set the tone and the parameters at each meeting. Answer and respond as best you can to each person's questions. Realize that there is a great sense of power when everyone supports each other. It may not create job security, but at least the staff members will know that they are not alone.

Chapter Summary

Some days managing will be more challenging than it is other days. Being caught in the middle and feeling tension and loyalty to two colliding forces can produce a very difficult situation, especially for females. For women, management is built on a foundation of honesty, respect, and trust. Any one of these aspects may be in jeopardy when you are caught between the demands and expectations of upper management and the needs of the staff.

Sometimes there are no easy answers. Each situation may need to be analyzed and evaluated on its own merits. You will need to determine the risk, the importance of honesty, and whose loyalty is the strongest.

These are the times when you have little input into a situation, except to execute someone else's command. For example, should you inform your staff about the possibility of downsizing when you know it is coming but have been told not to discuss it with employees yet? Women do not see truth so clearly defined. It is not an absolute, but more the spectrum of shades of gray. It includes whose truth, what truth, and how much truth.

Men, feeling the importance of status and loyalty to the corporate structure, are more often comfortable in denying information they know to be fact, assuming the lie is justifiable for the good of company. Whereas women may prefer telling the truth, even though it is painful right now. You must carefully evaluate the risk for telling the truth; ultimately, it could cost you your job. You may decide it isn't worth the risk, and that is an understandable conclusion.

For a woman manager to be placed in a situation by upper management that suggests she lie or provide untruths about what she knows to be fact is tantamount to saying that each individual employee is less important than the company itself. Women value the importance of each person and often have great difficulty when forced to make these choices.

Upper management may interfere with your ability to do your job. Its interference may be for a number of reasons, including that it does not feel you are capable of autonomous rule. Other women who have broken through the barriers in a company will make your role easier. However, if you are still in a significantly minor role, expect to be scrutinized and evaluated more closely each step of the way.

Some companies accept and even advocate a feminine leadership style. If you are in such a surrounding, you will find a great deal of support and flexibility within the management ranks. But when the feminine leadership style (the kinder, gentler, more inclusive style) is still rejected in the upper ranks, management is likely to interfere a great deal with your ability to do your job.

Many women are caught having to prove their abilities again and again to both senior management as well as to the staff. If staff members feel you are not able to respond to their needs sufficiently, they are likely to circumvent you and go to someone they trust—someone who can get them results. Open communication with all parties concerned is imperative to avoiding this pitfall. These interludes can be quite annoying and distressing if they occur.

Troubleshooting Corporate Policy Conflicts for Women

Overview

Corporate policy represents the bureaucratic structures that exist in every organization. It is the ebb and flow of what may or may not be permitted. Some organizations are swamped with written policy and procedures for each step taken. They stress uniformity and conformity at every turn. Other companies rely less on formal policy and procedures, while there still remains a great deal of restriction on acceptable operations.

Policy conflicts can create a lot of unwanted stress in your personal as well as professional life. Yet policy conflicts generally include those things that happen beyond your immediate control. They simply exist as part of the corporate structure, and have been established by more powerful individuals than yourself.

This chapter addresses the following problems, possible causes, and cures.

9.1   The Problem: You are unable to interview or hire a staff.

Possible Causes: Previous problems may have led to this decision; the problems in the department may have little to do with interviewing and hiring procedures; you have been given responsibility without authority.

Cures: Understand the history behind this policy; solve internal problems; adjust to your boundaries.

9.2   The Problem: You are caught fraternizing with a colleague. You get reprimanded, but he does not.

Possible Causes: There are consequences for your actions; the situation is both unequal and unfair; gender biases may decide your fate.

Cures: Accept responsibility for your actions; overcome obstacles; work with sexist policies.

9.3   The Problem: You feel the company policy and procedures are limiting your ability to manage effectively.

Possible Causes: You may have to prove yourself first; this may be a new game; you may just be a rebel.

Cures: Pass the test of time; play by new rules; quiet the rebel within.

9.4   The Problem: You disagree with the mission statement of the company.

Possible Causes: There may be differences in moral judgment; it may be a poorly written mission statements; nothing has really changed.

Cures: Assess understandings about morality; interpret a mission statement; now it is up to you.

9.5   The Problem: You find that the decision-making process is convoluted, complex, and too slow for you to manage comfortably.

Possible Causes: Different styles of managing may be colliding; the boundaries may be drawn very close; no one understands your perspective or reasoning; this battle may not be worth the fight.

Cures: Understand micro vs. macro management styles; work inside the defined boundaries; practice your powers of persuasion; choose your battles carefully.

9.6 ***The Problem: For those women who have made it into management, the line that separates the men from the women continues to be drawn wider and with more disparity.***

Possible Causes: This may be a case of sexism; you may feel left out; these actions may be sporadic, and random.

Cures: Combat sexism; try to fit in; do what you can.

9.7 ***The Problem: Recent corporate changes and restructuring have left you feeling alone, and uncertain about your own future.***

Possible Causes: You may be overreacting; your morale may be a problem; there is a natural resistance to change; it may be time to leave.

Cures: Put things in their proper prospective; improve your morale; become more tolerant of change; say goodbye.

At first glance, there may seem to be no easy solution when conflicts in policy arise. But after reviewing your options, responsibilities, and consequences, the choices may become more defined. Remember, even though you do have choices, this does not mean that an easy solution exists.

9.1 | The Problem: You are unable to interview or hire a staff.

THE SCENE

As a new manager, you feel strapped and unable to perform your job duties. The company policy dictates that personnel or designated senior managers interview and hire all employees. The company has been experiencing very high employee turnover rates and is trying to rebuild unity into the system.

Instead of building a cohesive work unit and improving morale, you find yourself putting out fires and having to train new employees who do not have the job skills necessary for the work required. Some employees have even complained about being misled during the interview process only to find out the job is very different than they had been told.

You believe interviewing and hiring the staff is integral to creating a strong department. Since you are new to the position, you do not want to appear pushy or demanding. Should you ask about changing this policy just yet or wait until you've been in the department longer?

POSSIBLE CAUSES

Previous problems may have led to this decision.

Understanding the previous problems that management has had to clean up can help in determining if this is a good time to suggest change. For example, if the policy is the result of poor interviewing and hiring practices from previous managers, then training and education may be logical remedies. However, if the company has had to answer several EEOC complaints in the past few years, perhaps even pay damages, then they may be more skeptical and gun-shy about repeating those mistakes.

The problems in the department may have little to do with interviewing and hiring procedures.

High employee turnover can be the result of improper training, poor work conditions, personality conflicts, tension, unreasonable expectations, and low pay, to name just a few. Interviewing and hiring may or may not be a factor in this situation. Since you may not be able to change the policy, look for other areas that you can control that are more likely to produce positive results. Assuming that you are not given that authority, there is still a lot that you can do to create and build a cohesive and strong department.

You have been given responsibility without authority.

When this happens, it produces a great deal of frustration and anxiety among managers. Results are expected, yet you have very limited control over these events. Realistically, gaining authority may or may not be something that you can change with time. It is important to know and understand the boundaries that you are working within. If you can't change something, then change the way you look at it.

CURES

Understand the history behind this policy.

Before you can change anything, you must first understand *why* management has implemented such a restrictive policy. If it has been the practice for many years and never been questioned before, it may be difficult to find the underlying answers. However, if it is a relatively new policy, then answers should be easy to uncover.

This history will help you plan a better defense or decide if you even want to challenge it. Some policies are so entrenched in politics and history that they are not going to change easily, if ever. When you find such a policy, you must accept that there is great risk to you personally and professionally to try to rock the boat. Consider all possible outcomes carefully before you proceed.

Some of the more challenging reasons for this policy include creating stricter controls on the interviewing process because of sloppy practices in the past, monetary costs associated with mistakes (EEOC filings, court costs, attorney fees, and so on), and a lack of consistency within hiring practices. You cannot change the past. Convincing senior management that a manager should be able to hire his or her own staff can be a win-win proposition if presented carefully. It means convincing senior management that this action can save them money, create consistent hiring practices, and provide stricter controls.

If corporate history provides vague and unchallenged findings, then your case may be easier to present. You will need to convince senior management that you are capable of handling this function by knowing the law, the paperwork trail required, and how to interpret the data. You will need to sell your abilities as well as the benefits the company receives if you participate in the process. It is important to realize the time involved in the interviewing process, time that will take you away from other responsibilities. This is not necessarily a bad thing, only a factor you need to consider. If you are already pushed on time constraints, it may place you under additional pressure.

After observing the dynamics of an organization, decide whether or not you are willing to pursue a change. If you decide yes, do your research and proceed. If you choose no, then learn to accept the employees you are given and do the best job with them that you can. Remember the old saying: When life gives you lemons, make lemonade. It definitely applies here.

Solve internal problems.

Blaming the high employee turnover rate and poor morale on the interviewing and hiring policies may be your way of shifting blame and not taking responsibility for your own actions. Within the department there is a great deal of input and contribution that you can interject.

If your problem is a high turnover rate, look at a variety of factors that may be influencing this rate. High employee turnover rates could be because of low wages, personality conflicts, or poor working conditions. Even your style and leadership abilities may be adding to the problem.

In every situation there will be some things that you control, and many things that you have absolutely no control over. When you are identifying and working through a problem, it is always important to stay focused on these two areas. What do you have the ability to change or affect, and what areas must you simply respond to that are outside of your control?

You control your research, presentation, and managing the staff. Each of these areas requires that you are doing all that you can to create a positive, safe, and fun workplace. It is easier to blame someone else for problems instead of finding ways to solve them. You do not control policy, politics or management.

Concentrate on those things that you can control. Create a sound and thorough training program for new employees. You may consider offering ongoing training programs, making it part of the weekly routine. You may consider frequent meetings with the department, allowing them the opportunity to voice their concerns, offer suggestions, and share in accomplishments. You may consider creating a suggestion box for welcoming more and more new ideas from the staff. However, if you implement a suggestion box, make sure that you either reward the suggestions or create boundaries around what can actually be changed. If employees make numerous suggestions but fail to see any results, the process becomes nothing more than lip service and can weaken their trust in you.

This may be your first test of being able to build unity—by being given disharmony. Continue to create a cohesive department at every opportunity that presents itself. Chapter 5 addresses many of these concerns, specifically, Sections 5.1 and 5.2 provide insight into personnel problems within a team.

Adjust to your boundaries.

Sometimes you may feel that you are operating with your hands tied; you are responsible for certain results but you do not have the authority to make the changes you feel are necessary to achieve them. Having responsibility means your successes and failures are measured by how well you achieve certain results. Authority is the ability to do what you feel is necessary to accomplish that end. Sometimes these limitations are annoyances; other times they hinder your ability to do your job effectively. In either case, the results may be altered.

Adjusting to those boundaries can be challenging and at times very frustrating. The sooner you adjust, though, the sooner you can find your own confines to work within. Fighting against the system is generally a losing battle; a battle that consumes energy and may even cost you your career. A frequent test for new managers is to see how well they adapt to a particular situation. Instead of focusing on the authority that you do not have, your energy should be focused on creating ways around these obstacles. Throwing in the towel too early is also a strong statement on your ability to lead or *not* lead well—a statement that you do not want to make.

Whether or not authority will be relinquished gradually, as is typically the case, is less important than how well you adapt to the defined boundaries. Seldom is authority given carte blanche. More likely, you will see different boundaries drawn from time to time. These boundaries may change for any number of reasons including having a new boss, a change in company policy, or as a form of reward/punishment.

There may be times when being allowed to interview is considered a right of passage. As a new manager perhaps you may not have earned that right yet. Whether the right of passage is gender-related is really not an issue here; there is no indication that gender is a factor. Determine at what point if any you will be allowed to interview and hire your own staff. Then work aggressively toward achieving that goal.

During the period of waiting, learn techniques and advice about how to interview from the experts. Perhaps you will be allowed to sit in during some of their interviews and observe the process in action. This is a great time to learn, especially if you have not interviewed before.

What If: You perceive these limitations as personal? Review the situation carefully before making such a judgment call. No one benefits from crying wolf. If you cannot identify consistent patterns of behavior, then assume they are not there. Not everything that happens to you happens because you're a woman.

What If: All the men in various management positions interview their staffs, and the females do not? Do the best you can given those limitations. It is not uncommon to have to prove yourself at every turn. Realistically, not all playing fields are equal. Refer to Sections 6.5, 6.7, and 9.6 for more information concerning gender biases in management.

9.2 | The Problem: You are caught fraternizing with a colleague. You get reprimanded, but he does not.

THE SCENE

The company discourages fraternizing, especially between managers. Even though there is no formal written policy you know that it is strongly discouraged.

You knew the risk involved when you and Doug began dating. Things just happened. You are managers in different departments but had to work together on several projects, so one thing led to another. Since you are both single it seemed harmless. Besides, the company expected you to work such long hours—where else were you going to meet any available men?

Keeping the relationship away from the office was agreed upon by both of you. However, someone found out about it and the word began to spread quickly. You were called into the personnel department alone and told to either end the relationship or quit. It was reiterated that fraternizing was not allowed. When you discussed this conversation with Doug, you discovered that he had not been admonished for the relationship. No one had even mentioned it to him.

Needless to say, that didn't sit very well with you! Why were you the only one doing something wrong? Two people had been involved, but only you got punished. Maybe it was because you hadn't worked at the company as long as Doug had, you didn't have as much clout, or you didn't produce the high sales volume that he did. That shouldn't matter, should it?

POSSIBLE CAUSES

There are consequences for your actions.

Before you got involved with Doug you knew that the company discouraged fraternization between employees, especially managers. Despite that fact, you chose to follow your heart and pursue the relationship. You accepted the risk when you began dating; no one ever said the consequences would be evenly dealt. You must be able to take the punishment, when you have gone against the policy. While you may not like the situation, there may be little recourse.

The situation is both unequal and unfair.

No one ever said it would be fair, much less equal. At times like these, you may feel powerless and frustrated. Accepting the fact that these injustices are a reality can be difficult. Some women will want to fight back; other women will accept the consequences and decide their future accordingly. It is important to identify your options and proceed how you best see fit.

Gender biases may decide your fate.

You are not part of the good ol' boys club and you will never be a member. When you are able to identify gender as the basis for the action (as opposed to experience, expendability, or politics) then respond directly to these injustices.

CURES

Accept responsibility for your actions.

Accepting the responsibility for your action is not an easy lesson to learn. You knew the risk involved when you began dating, and you chose to proceed anyway. Now the time has come to accept the responsibility for those actions.

You could feebly argue that other people on the interstate were speeding and they didn't get a ticket, but that doesn 't justify why you were breaking the law. You are still responsible for your actions.

Basically you have three choices: end your relationship and stay with that employer, leave (whether or not you end the relationship), or continue with the relationship and wait to see if you're fired.

It is your decision, based on your value system, courage, and career future. There is no right or wrong answer. Instead, you have the ability to weigh all the factors and proceed according to your own best interest.

It is not Doug's fault he wasn't punished anymore than it is yours. Defying your superiors may also cause Doug to lose his job. If that happens, what have you gained? Whether or not others are also punished does not justify your actions.

Overcome obstacles.

Life isn't always fair nor is it always equal. When life isn't fair, it would be naive to think that work would be different. Work is a reflection of the world you live in. Therefore, you can expect to find the same injustices in both life and work.

Overcoming these obstacles in work, as in life, is risky and takes time. However, after evaluating them carefully, you may still choose to undertake this plan of action. First, determine who is responsible for the injustice. It may be one person or a collective voice, such as a personnel officer versus the policy board. If it is a single voice, talk to that person about why you are the only one being punished. Try to understand why the rule exists even though you may not agree. However, if the answer comes from a group, then it may be harder to take action. Your choice becomes to either talk with the person who delivered the message or to go directly to the top. Going straight to the top involves the greatest amount of risk, but it can work by eliminating the go-betweens.

Your conversation may sound like this:

> *I am confused by this situation and how it is being handled. I want to be sure that I understand it completely. It has come to your attention that Doug and I are seeing each other away from the office. Even though our work has not been affected by this relationship, you believe that we should end it. And, you are asking me to either end the relationship or leave this company. Is that correct?*

The remedy offered may then be to punish Doug as well. If that were the outcome, you would both lose. It may be too late to recapture a sense of fairness.

In the event that someone decides to make an exception to the policy, or to reevaluate the current procedures, you may be allowed to continue working. Expect to be closely and critically watched. Every stumble you have could be blamed on the outside relationship, whether or not it has any bearing on the situation. The relationship may become the easy scapegoat for all other problems.

Work with sexist policies.

Sometimes the differences can be isolated to gender inequalities. When this happens, it can knock the wind out of your sails. You cannot change your gender; you are being punished for being born female.

Depending upon how much risk you want to take, you may bring this to the attention of personnel. Doing so may jeopardize your relationship with Doug so be sure that you are willing to risk your relationship if you proceed. Accept that Doug may lose his job or that he may feel the relationship isn't worth the risk, and drop you.

Since personnel has called you in, the first place to start is with the individual who gave you the ultimatum. This individual may be the messenger or the author of the message; you may not know at this time. If you accuse someone directly of sexual discrimination, expect his or her response to be one of denial. No one ever admits that sexism really exists.

> *Yesterday you said for me to either end the relationship with Doug or to find another job. However, these same demands were not made to Doug, only to me. I hope you did not choose to punish me because I am a woman, but I admit that it does appear that way. Could you explain why I am the one being punished or asked to leave? Punishing Doug now is not the answer; it is too late for that. I am rather confused about the whole issue.*

This dialogue gives the other person several opportunities to defend him- or herself and yet does not blatantly attack his or her position. It comes across more conciliatory and leaves the door slightly open for other options.

Nothing may change. That is something you must consider before you try to affect change. Then again, you may not want to continue working for a company that has such stark differences in how they treat managers.

9.3 | The Problem: You feel the company policy and procedures are limiting your ability to manage effectively.

THE SCENE

While you have been with the company for several years, you were just recently promoted into management. As an employee, you felt a strong sense of self-worth through the organization thanks to the leadership abilities of previous managers.

Now, as a manager you are finding out just how difficult those ideals are to maintain. It seems that the company's policies and its procedures are very limiting for you. While your previous managers had gained a great deal of respect within the company, it appears they did not follow the rules. There is more accountability and pressure on you to conform because you are new.

Are you sure it is worth it? At times it is frustrating, other times you feel compromised and cheated. Neither are good feelings to have about the employer.

POSSIBLE CAUSES

You may have to prove yourself first.

As a new manager you can expect to go through many tests and challenges to prove yourself capable of handling a situation. As a woman, these tests are more rigorous and defining. Complying with these restrictions may be just another of many tests that you are required to take to illustrate your style, strengths, and abilities to work creatively around specific boundaries. Senior management may want to see your ability to handle the pressure before they allow you the freedom or flexibility to manage autonomously. When you cannot change something, change the way you look at it.

This may be a new game.

Depending on several factors, the conditions you are now working under may be different than when you were an employee. Whether the company has changed ownership, responded to increased competition, or is faced with financial constraints, the company has chosen to operate under different terms and policy guidelines. Living in the past will not help you adjust to the current situation. You must learn to accept the boundaries that you are facing and decide to play by those rules or move on to another place.

You may just be a rebel.

Why do you resist these policies and procedures? Are the policies obstructing your ability to do your job or are they simply an irritation to you? Your resistance to these policies and procedures may not disappear if you move. Instead, you may find that these policies and procedures are indicative of how most companies operate. And wherever you go, it will be necessary for you to adjust.

CURES

Pass the test of time.

As a new manager you do not have a proven track record or history to support your strengths and style. Your previous managers earned their reputation slowly, over time, after being put through many other tests and challenges. You were fortunate to work for someone who carried influence; someone who was respected and had a reputation to back up his or her claims.

Because you are new, though, you are not automatically given those stripes. They must be earned. Earning the respect of employees, colleagues, and superiors comes after passing numerous tests. It is slow and gradual. Yet there is a great deal that you can do to move it along.

First, seek the guidance and input from one or more of your previous managers. These individuals seemed to know how to make the system work for them, and they may be willing to take you under their wings and suggest ways to get the system to work in your favor as well.

These individuals have learned how to maneuver through the system. Of course, this depends on whether these managers are still employed with that company. If they are not, then try to find out why all the good ones are leaving. They may have paid a very high price for doing it their own way. Heed their warnings.

Another way of helping yourself is by learning how to promote yourself and your accomplishments. Observe what measurable things are important to senior management, then strive to reach those goals. Once you have reached them, it doesn't do any good if no one else knows it. You must make sure that you receive appropriate credit for your achievements. You should also fine-tune your management image. One of the most important tests as a manager is that you look, talk, and act the part. Image is extremely important, especially when you are new and even more so if you are a woman.

Expect to be judged by the standards of how men typically manage. Results may be less important than how the game is played. This is often difficult for women to understand. Women seek results, and the path to those results represent options and opportunities. Playing the game seems of minor importance to many women. But, men approach management very differently. Men may find the game equally if not more important than the results. It is all part of the total package.

Play by new rules.

Games change, causing rules to be altered to fit the new game. This is a dynamic world we live in; static rules are too restrictive in this environment. While knowing *why* the rules have changed may make it easier to accept, it really doesn't change the situation. Instead, you should review your choices. You may either play by the new rules, operate outside of the defined boundaries, or leave.

Choice one suggests that you play by the new rules. It reflects a willingness to accept the boundaries as you understand them, and to abide by those limitations. Assuming that you know what the rules are, it then becomes a matter of accepting them and agreeing to stay within those boundaries.

Choice two has you operating outside the defined boundaries. Obviously there is a great deal of risk in this solution because it may not be tolerated by senior management. However, the only way to create change is for someone to push the limits. Since you do not have a track record or reputation to fall back on, this approach could result in your immediate termination. Although, when it works it is another way to show management that you are a strong and focused decision maker, worthy of handling more authority. By proceeding down this path you are willing to accept its consequences.

And finally, the third choice includes leaving this employer and finding another one, hopefully better suited to your needs and less restrictive in its procedural style. However, what you may be looking for may not exist, maybe not for a new manager, at least. Instead, this desired self-rule may be something that can only be earned over time. You may not be able to get the rewards without paying your dues; others have paid theirs. But you were not privy to those learning years. You just witnessed the benefits that happened after a lot of pipers were paid. There may not be any quick answers or quick fixes for this problem. The respect and autonomy you desire may only come after years of hard work, sweat, and earning of respect. See Section 9.7 for more information on saying goodbye to your employer.

Quiet the rebel within.

There may be an inner voice wanting to buck the system, to be different, and wanting to play outside the rules. If that is you, proceed carefully. These qualities can be admirable in certain situations, but in business they are often viewed as negative traits. Being labeled a rebel can damage your professional image and career potential. Risk is seen as a positive characteristic within very restrictive boundaries. Outside those boundaries, risk can become a detriment to your career.

Concentrate on those things that you can change. Fortunately, you can change your own actions. Before you speak, draw battle lines, or fight back, look at why you are doing it. Take a moment to write down your own objectives. Then write down a list of reasons why you shouldn't jump in at this time. Stepping away from the heat of the moment may provide you with the necessary distance to see your actions in a different light and hopefully to change your current destructive patterns.

9.4 The Problem: You disagree with the mission statement of the company.

THE SCENE

The company decided it was time to rewrite its mission statement. A vague and basically meaningless statement had been guiding the company for the past 20 years. Even though the company practiced a very conservative moral code, you found ways to avoid causing conflict or disgrace. You did not agree with many of these viewpoints.

Only a few managers were involved in drafting this new statement. You were not included in this closed circle. The final product looked much like those managers who had input; it was very conservative and proclaimed various moral codes of conduct. It even went so far as to define what acceptable morality was and was not.

You were completely offended by the new mission statement. You felt it had gone too far by adopting a very narrow and closed-minded definition of moral conduct, influenced by conservative religious doctrine. Since this document was not in existence when you were hired, you felt betrayed. You are not sure if you will be allowed to stay. It does not offer ways of integrating and accepting diversity. Besides, what does it have to do with business anyway?

> *Note:* The purpose of a mission statement is to identify the goals of a company, to help create its personality and shape its philosophy, and to provide a foundation on which to grow.

POSSIBLE CAUSES

There may be differences in moral judgment.

When personal differences on morality contradict working relationships, a hostile environment may develop. It is important to know your moral code, and to identify where the differences are. Some areas may be more divisive than others. These differences should never be viewed lightly.

It may be a poorly written mission statement.

Simply because it is written does not mean that it is written well. In fact, it may still be evolving into its final stage. You may not be alone in your reactions to this mission statement; others may have similar objections. Mission statements should be broad enough to embrace a medley of ideas under a single umbrella. When they limit the company's potential, they may be doing more harm than good.

Nothing has really changed.

Since you already knew the company was operating under a very conservative policy, this statement may communicate the existing practices better. It may reflect what you have always known—that you are working in a conservative environment. You have learned to maneuver this course already, and nothing may be different.

CURES

Assess understandings about morality.

Morality remains a subjective issue. Some people feel the problems Americans face today are a result of a lack of moral teachings. There are some individuals who consider themselves to be moral police, determining exactly what is morally acceptable and what is not. Disagreements on morality are often born out of religious teachings.

Whose religious teachings are to be followed? Within the various Christian sects there are often wide interpretations, internal bickering, and little agreement, and less when you factor in non-Christian beliefs, and nonbelievers. The senior managers may be adopting a platform much akin to their personal religious doctrines, and they may be expecting all employees to accept and practice what they believe to be appropriate behavior.

Review the mission statement. Identify those areas that you object to, and that you feel uncomfortable adopting. There is a big difference between morality and integrity. While the latter is an universal goodness based on honesty, the first refers to virtue and lacks universal acceptance. Moral topics are frequently the most explosive and divisive topics around.

Next, you must decide if this new mission statement is so objectionable to you that you will not embrace or accept it at any level. If you say yes, then talk to your boss or to senior management and let them know your concerns before you respond. You may say something like:

> *I just received a copy of the new mission statement. There are some areas that concern me. Specifically,* (list what items you object to and explain why). *I am not sure how to resolve these feelings and conflicts. What do you suggest?*

But know that you may be asked to leave if you cannot agree to these principles. Then again, you may not want to work for a company that espouses such restrictive viewpoints anyway. You must be true to yourself and to your beliefs. When your beliefs collide with those of the company, it may be difficult to ignore. Follow your heart to find the path most likely to bring you joy and peace. Anything less is a disservice to yourself.

Interpret a mission statement.

Just because someone wrote it, does not mean that a lot of thought actually went into its creation. Badly written mission statements are difficult to follow. Instead of providing an umbrella for growth and long-term potential for the company, they may actually hinder development and leave a great deal of room for misinterpretation.

What are your options? First, determine if the mission statement is in its final form and already approved or if this is a working draft. Ask your boss to explain how this mission statement will change the way business is done and your ability to manage.

> *I was reading the memo on our new mission statement and there seems to be some big changes as a result. What differences, if any, in how we operate do you see as a result of this statement? Maybe I am overreacting, but it seems pretty drastic and restrictive. I am confused by it all. Is this the final form, or is it still open for discussion and suggestion?*

The authors of the statement will, undoubtedly, defend it to the end. Especially if it has already received the blessing of the president or chief officers. Therefore, if your conversation is with an author directly, try to make it more in line with *"I need more clarification"* and less of *"What is actually going on here?"* He or she would be more apt to respond to general questions. Suggesting that it is nonsense will accomplish nothing.

Research other company mission statements as well. There are books available at various libraries that outline a variety of company mission statements. If it is still a work in progress, and if you are really interested in the final form, offer your services to be involved in researching and rewriting the statement. While this will take an additional time commitment on your part, it is an excellent way of participating in the process, if accepted.

Now it is up to you.

Perhaps nothing has changed as far as attitudes and work environment. The only change may be that management has written down a mission statement that it has been advocating and following for some time.

When you find yourself in a management environment that makes you feel uncomfortable, you need to review why you are there, and whether it is in your best interest to remain. It may or may not be, depending on a lot of peripheral issues.

You knew the current management environment was far more conservative than you preferred. You accepted those working conditions and managed to work around them. By your own admission, this new statement just reiterates those values that the company has always practiced. Is it somehow more emphatic because it is written down? Or do you just give written words more power?

Talk to your boss or to the appropriate senior manager about your concerns and determine exactly what impact this new statement will have on business operations. Evaluate whether it has reached a point of intolerance, and if it is time for you to find other employment.

> *After reading the new mission statement, I am not sure that I fully understand what it means as far as business operations. Will anything actually change in how we do business? I must admit that I do have some reservations about the language. It seems rather restrictive.*

Unless meetings have indicated that certain practices will no longer be tolerated, it may be safe to assume nothing has really changed.

This may be a good time to decide, however, if you want to continue in this conservative environment. While you may have felt it had the potential to change before, the mission statement clearly indicates that the company is quite pleased with the reputation it has earned as being conservative. There are no indications that things will change any time soon.

9.5 | The Problem: You find that the decision-making process is convoluted, complex, and too slow for you to manage comfortably.

THE SCENE

Recently, an employee asked to work flexible hours. You reviewed the situation carefully and agreed to get approval from the appropriate levels. Even though it seemed like a logical and acceptable solution for this employee, you are not able to manage the department autonomously.

Reactions have not been favorable about approving an exception. There has been concern about what other employees will think if they are not offered the same benefits and opportunities that you are offering. Even though you remind them that this department is different, or that a particular situation warrants special consideration, management has been less than enthusiastic.

To gain this approval you must proceed through several layers of red tape. First you must gain the blessing at the general managers' meeting. And this, as you already know, will be an extremely difficult task. But, assuming that it passes this meeting, the next step is for it to be presented at a senior managers' meeting and then to the executive committee, all before it goes before the board for final blessing. Each of these steps presents a multitude of obstacles that you must overcome before moving to the next stage. Expect each step to take more than one presentation before it passes.

POSSIBLE CAUSES

Different styles of managing may be colliding.

Women are often more comfortable in a "macro," or big picture environment. They often look toward the long-term benefits beyond the short-term obstacles that may confront them. However, many male managers prefer the "micro" approach that replicates dealing with the most minute of details. The micro approach is more apt to avoid exceptions by focusing on each trivial and potential repercussion. When the universally accepted style within an organization is different from your management style, many problems and frustrations naturally occur.

The boundaries may be drawn very close.

How close the circle is drawn is less important than knowing where the line is drawn. If you know exactly what you are able to do, and the proper procedure for getting exceptions approved, then half the battle is won. Fighting tradition and getting approval for exceptions is often difficult when a company operates with restrictive policy guidelines. Establishing your boundaries is part of learning how to play the game by the accepted and practiced rules.

No one understands your perspective or reasoning.

No matter how hard you try, how well you communicate, how good the cause, nothing seems to be able to penetrate beyond these walls. No one understands you; they won't even listen. In fact, some will immediately vote no because it comes from your corner. If you continue on this path, you are creating a negative image; something that will be difficult to turn around.

This battle may not be worth the fight.

Not all battles are worth the time and energy it takes to fight them. It may not be a matter of winning or losing that is important but valuing the time and energy involved and protecting your own image. Evaluate the risk of both winning as well as losing each contest; both come with consequences.

CURES

Understand micro vs. macro management styles.

Micro managing refers to managing the smallest of details. Senior management would be involved in decision making to its most minute level. Few functions are delegated beyond these controls. Your ability to respond independently may be almost nonexistant.

On the other hand, macro managing refers to the broader scope and vision used in managing. It is sometimes referred to as the big picture because it emphasizes the future long-term benefits and lessens its reaction to the everyday obstacles found in the workplace. The macroperspective often comes with a higher price tag, at least on the front end, which is viewed as an investment in the company, a way to provide long-term capital gains. Long-term benefits and gains are often placed second to the initial costs.

Within the home, women have learned the art of macro managing without realizing it. Women over time have learned to categorize and prioritize events, then respond according to their relevant importance.

When your style is different from what management expects, and when those differences impede your ability to manage, then review your options. You can stay and adjust to a more acceptable style. You can stay and continue to manage in a style you are more comfortable adapting, even though there may be tension and conflicts which arise frequently. Or you may find a different employer more representative and appreciative of your style.

Work inside the defined boundaries.

Boundaries are just part of doing business. Boundaries exist within every organization, though some are more stringent and confining than others. Some boundaries are more concrete and closely monitored.

Identifying boundaries is critical in being able to stay within its confines. In this case, there are numerous policies and procedures that are written down. These are boundaries that you know exist. Even though you do not agree with their implementation, you still are able to identify them.

Once they have been identified, it then becomes a matter of personal choice whether you want to follow them or not. You can accomplish a lot more by working within a system than working outside of it. The policy may represent years of experience and hardships felt by managing in separate styles. The exception you are requesting may remind managers of the difficulties they faced before.

Practice your powers of persuasion.

No matter how hard you try to explain or defend your position, no one seems to understand. It completely escapes you how this could be happening, but you see it before your eyes. You know that if they understood the reason for the exception, they would agree with your recommendation. It seems so obvious to you. How could they miss it?

But in their confusion, they look at you like a rebel, troublemaker, or outsider. They see you as someone who wants to complicate the routine, cause problems, and work around the procedures that everyone else seems to abide by. You know that they just don't understand you; you are none of those things.

You have not been able to persuade others, but don't give up without a fight. There is still a lot that you can do to persuade others to support your ideas. Watch others who have great success in the art of persuasion. Take lessons from their style. Specifically try to find women who are very persuasive with their arguments and ideas. Is their style forceful? Strong? Knowledgeable? Nonthreatening? Conciliatory? Congenial? A variety of styles can work.

While you may not be a troublemaker, if you are perceived as one there may not be much difference. Once others have labeled you as the enemy, your role becomes disproving this, and the process can take up valuable time. This time should be used to manage the department; it is time that you do not have to waste.

Try to avoid standing alone too often. It can make for a lonely ride; shortening your career opportunities and future. It is not enough to be right if no one will listen. A very important part of managing and communicating is adapting to a style that will work in a particular environment. Otherwise, everything you say and do becomes wasted energy.

Choose your battles carefully.

Before you undertake a battle, you need to decide if it is worth your effort and what costs and consequences are attached. Not every battle is worth your participation, especially when you are judged by the number of battles as well as by your win/loss record.

Battles represent conflict with policy, procedures, or influential people. Conflicts are best resolved by sitting down working through them openly and honestly, trying to find a compromise or a place to meet. However, when these battles become more intense the odds are stacked against you. That does not mean you should avoid all conflicts. Only that it is essential to review your motives, what you might gain from this fight, and what you have at risk. Then you can decide if it is worth it.

It is never advantageous, no matter how correct, to be labeled a troublemaker or agitator. There is a great deal of respect within any system for one's ability to compromise and to get along. This may mean that certain conflicts are avoided, not because they are not worthy of your support but instead because you have already taken on several other battles.

Learning to accept your limitations is an excellent attribute for all leaders.

9.6

The Problem: For those women who have made it into management, the line that separates the men from the women continues to be drawn wider and with more disparity.

THE SCENE

There are few women who have reached the ranks of management with the company. Many of the practices dissuade women from participating, and several even exclude them. Because there are so few female voices, though, women are afraid to complain. You, too, sit quietly while you boil inside.

For example, management both supports and pays for the membership into several elite country clubs so that the men can go golfing and have lunch with their various business associates. In fact one of the clubs has an exclusive dining room for men, a place to quietly conduct business, and a separate room for families where wives come to relax after a game of tennis. The company sees nothing wrong with paying for these memberships.

You do not golf or play tennis. When you have approached the company about other activities, your ideas have been ignored or quickly dismissed. There is no question that the men close many business deals during these outings. You feel completely left out and do not know how to make the playing field more level.

POSSIBLE CAUSES

This may be a case of sexism.

When the upper ranks of a company practices sexism, it generally works its way to all levels. This "separate but equal" claim does not really mean equal in the sense of the same, but equal in the sense of maybe fair and hopefully not unjust. There may be other avenues for you to explore so that you can create more business opportunities. Learn to play a different game.

You may feel left out.

Whether your feelings are real or a perception is an important distinction. If, for example, you *choose* not to golf, then it is something you can control and change. But if management is intentionally excluding you, then it is in control, not you. In either case, you control how you respond to a situation.

These actions may be sporadic, and random.

Within any organization certain behavior is condoned while others receive preferential treatment. Not that it is a rational approach to business management, only that it is a factor with which you must contend. Your ability to accept and work within these parameters will help you succeed within the confines of the business world. Identify the parameters that you must operate within and then exercise all options you have available to you. Don't worry so much about what others are doing. Instead, show them that you can do it your way.

CURES

Combat sexism.

While companies are not people, they can emulate an attitude that is replicated throughout the walls. These attitudes start at the top and work their way down the management ranks. If the person at the top is sexist, given his or her strong influence on policy, procedures and business operations, you can expect to see many other chauvinists inside the organization.

If you are able to identify the cause of this separate treatment as one that originates in sexism, then at least you know what you are up against. Not that you will fight; nor if you choose to fight, will you necessarily win. But, at least you know what to expect as a response to your actions and your presence.

While you can talk to your boss about this isolating treatment, it will probably not change the situation much, if at all. It can even serve to make you look like a troublemaker if you are not careful.

If you know of other women managers in the company, talk to them to get their understanding of certain events. Perhaps together you can create other avenues to explore that are beneficial to women in management. These do not have to be exclusive options; instead you are looking for ways to find and close more business sales, and to create a relaxed environment for talking about business.

Look for avenues in which you can win. Whether or not men are able to join in this activity is completely irrelevant. If they can, it could be seen as a win-win proposition. Your primary concern is finding ways to promote yourself, not to fight back.

If the women within your organization offer little support or suggestions, try tapping into outside organizations. These can provide networking opportunities as well as opportunities for sharing concerns. A female-only group may be less intimidating for you and provide avenues that the company had ignored previously. Realize, however, if you feel more comfortable in a gender-exclusive setting that you cannot find fault with men who also feel more comfortable around other men.

Try to fit in.

Nothing can be more frustrating than feeling or being intentionally left out of the game. Unfortunately, it happens. When it does happen, you are apt to feel alone, with no where to run or no place to go.

An essential aspect of this equation is deciding whether the feeling is intentional or whether you are reading more into these actions than is meant. If the feelings are intentional, the company could be creating these opportunities simply to exclude you. If you are reading more into these actions, you could be making the situation much worse than it really is. In other words, do you feel the role of victim every time something happens that you do not like or do not agree with?

While none of us admits to playing the role of victim, just like some people do not own up to sexist attitudes, the reality is that both roles exist in life and in the workplace. Review your own motives carefully before pointing fingers.

Then, still don't point fingers. Finger-pointing never solved anything. In fact, it only serves to separate more than it will solve. Since the wall that divides is already there, you need to work at methods for removing the wall, not reinforcing its existence.

Work, instead, at trying to better yourself within your surroundings. Find ways to make yourself included. Create an inner circle of friends and confidants to share ideas and enjoy company. Rise above the loneliness that you feel in the office. While there is no easy solution to undertake for this problem, adopt and practice consistent behavior for the best results.

Do what you can.

There may be any number of reasons why you are excluded from whatever game they are playing. Gender may be a factor as well as length of employment, credentials, race, age, social status, common interests, or background experience. Preferential treatment may exist for those individuals included in the club. You may be excluded for reasons unknown to you, reasons you may never fully understand. When the deck appears to be stacked against you, do what you can, as best as you can. Control those things within your power and let the rest be someone else's worry.

You may decide to blow the whistle and call attention to the imbalance that currently exists. If so, what do you want to happen? Either the imbalance can be changed by adding you to the club or disbanding memberships altogether. If you do not want to be added, but are more jealous that they are receiving something you are not receiving, then you need to deal with those feelings. Punishing those who are currently receiving these advantages does not benefit you or the company. It becomes a losing proposition.

You may ask to be included. If you want to be included because you enjoy golfing or need a place to take your customers, that is one thing. But if your reason for being included is to burst their bubble and to be the first female to enter their ranks just to show them you can do it, you are not really winning anything—especially if you do not even enjoy the atmosphere. As a compromise, you may ask for a membership at a different club that doesn't exclude women.

You may decide to move on to other issues, including finding another employer. Leaving may not improve your situation, but merely transfer the problems elsewhere. However, it remains an option.

9.7 The Problem: Recent corporate changes and restructuring have left you feeling alone, and uncertain about your own future.

THE SCENE

During a recent managers' meeting, you looked around the table and were stunned by the number of new faces that were present. The company has been undergoing many phases of restructuring, and you had been shielded or at least protected from these cuts in the past. There is no comfort in knowing that you are the manager with the most seniority at these meetings. You begin to feel worried by this fact, as if your days are numbered and your time coming quickly to an end.

As you are well aware, no one's job is safe, and you might be next. Despite your years of service and your efforts, nothing seems to protect you from the fact that there is no job security for you.

You are not sure if you are reading the writing on the wall or reading more into the situation than is intended. But in any case, you are scared.

POSSIBLE CAUSES

You may be overreacting.

Panicking or overreacting to a situation can easily happen unless you constantly remind yourself to focus on the facts and try to stay objective. Has the company changed its direction? Why have there been so many changes recently? When answering these questions, try to determine your role in the future of the company.

Your morale may be a problem.

You may be the one who is down or has a bad attitude. Understanding the reasons that led to the reorganization should help you regain a sense of control over your emotions. It may be time for you to either move on or refocus your attention on the job. You must decide if you want to continue to play. If so, then give it your all; if not, move on.

There is a natural resistance to change.

While you may prefer routine, dependable, and predictable days, you may be confronted with anything but a routine and predictable life. When faced with change, your ability to remain flexible and open to new ideas and new people will be your greatest reward. It does not alter the fact that change is coming into your life, but it helps you cope with the situation better. When you cannot change something, change the way you look at it. Look closely at what it is you fear.

It may be time to leave.

There is a time to stay and reasons for staying. Other times, you may feel your best solution is to move on; the time has come to say goodbye.

Once you have decided to leave, often a painful and complex decision, then put the wheels in motion. Waiting will only aggravate the situation. This does not mean that you should respond irrationally to your feelings, but make sure that you are not procrastinating, trying to avoid the future. Moving on is a situation that provides you with a great deal of power and control if you are willing to use it.

CURES

Put things in their proper prospective.

You may be overreacting to the situation around you; that is something you must consider. It may be hard to avoid. First, how do you determine if you are overreacting to the situation or if it warrants quick and decisive action? You may not be able to determine this with complete certainty, and ultimately it may be decided by your gut reaction. Never underestimate your own intuition.

Find out why the other managers are no longer employed by this company. Did some leave on their own choosing? Were some less productive, and eliminated through natural attrition? Did anyone retire or find another job? Were some departments combined and staffs reduced? Review those facts which you have access to; accept that some coincidence may be a factor as well. Your reaction is probably to the cumulative effects of these changes, not to one specific event.

However, you must also accept that perhaps you are not overreacting. Perhaps your job is in jeopardy, and perhaps the company is slowly cleaning house, replacing all managers. Job security is a thing of the past, and your future may be tenuous at best. Actually, job security was eliminated long before this restructuring began. Before restructuring, you survived on the illusion of job security.

All is not lost, so don't despair. The quickest way to write yourself out of a job is by assuming the future doesn't include you. When you eliminate yourself from the equation, it will only be a matter of time before others will also eliminate you.

Assess the situation as best you can. Senior management may be able to answer some of your questions, although you must also be willing to accept that there may not be answers to all your questions just yet. In other instances, management may only tell you what they believe you need to know.

If you feel overwhelmed by stress, consider a vacation. If possible, talk with someone in senior management to get a clearer picture of what the future will look like, and at what the long-term effects of these changes means. You may determine that these cuts have been very specific and that you feel (relatively) safe for now. See Section 4.1 for ways of handling pressure.

Improve your morale.

During times of restructuring, the atmosphere in a company may be negative and apprehensive at best. It would be abnormal not to feel these tensions. If you are feeling less than supportive about the company, dread coming to work each day, and your mind is constantly drifting out to more serene places, your morale may need a boost.

There may be little that you control, yet there is much that you can affect. Know the difference. Make a list of what might improve your spirits. You are the only person responsible for your happiness, so don't blame others. What would you like to see done differently now? Is this a realistic list? If not, rewrite the list with both small and large goals. Work on changing yourself and your attitude.

Information is the best way to empower a person. When the situation around you is so unsettling, it is not uncommon to feel drained and undervalued. Empower yourself to get some of that lost energy back. Seek answers where they can best be found. Accept that most companies, when reorganizing, remain flexible. There are no guarantees. Answers may be changing as the situation warrants it. If you want guarantees, know that they do not exist during these tumultuous times.

Be as prepared as you can be. But in the meantime, continue to do the best job you can. See Sections 5.4, 8.1, and 8.2 for more information about employee morale and the effects of downsizing and restructuring within any organization.

Become more tolerant of change.

Change has a way of scaring most of us. Resistance is a natural reaction to a very difficult situation. No one denies that you are facing an uncomfortable and potentially frightening future. Your ability to adjust and respond may be critical to surviving through these conditions.

Look inside yourself to find those things that you fear the most. While you may not be able to change the circumstances, identifying your demons can allow you some control over them. Work on those problems that are within your ability to control, and try not to worry about those that you cannot control.

For example, your problem may appear to be the possibility of losing your job. But as you begin to look closer, you can to uncover what your underlying fears really are. They may be of finding another job because you hate the interviewing process, or of losing your insurance benefits during the time it takes to find reemployment. They may have to do with your age, and feeling it will be used against you, or they may be financial worries.

Once you have identified your fears, then begin to solve, educate, or empower yourself about each of your concerns. Seek information, internal strength, and network support to find answers to as many of these fears as possible.

Obviously it is in your best interest to plan for the future. This means assume what you would do if you lose your job, and prepare accordingly. However, during working hours it is imperative that you devote 110 percent of your time and energy to work. Otherwise, you could be speeding up the unemployment process. It can only make matters worse.

Say goodbye.

There may come a time when you decide you need to seek employment opportunities elsewhere. The writing may be on the wall and the days limited where you are, and the environment may not be as nurturing and supportive as you want, or you may be lured away in hopes of a brighter career future. Making these choices becomes the natural flow of life and careers, especially in volatile job markets created by massive corporate downsizings and mergers.

Even though you have decided to take this step, you may feel resistance and hesitation. Though you want to take control of your professional future, and you know this is the best choice for you, none of this will eliminate the fear you may experience as you begin the process of looking for another employer. Transition time is almost always a frightening experience.

There are several things you need to do as this process begins to unfold. If you participate in a company retirement plan, review the holdings as well as the procedures for rolling over those investments after you leave this employer. If at all possible, do not cash in your retirement account for living expenses. First, there are steep tax penalties when retirement plans are lost, but more important is the fact that retirement accounts are your safety net for the future. Women have a propensity for living in the moment and not planning for the future, especially the retirement years. Do not make that mistake. Next, look at your personnel file to see what reviews, letters, or commendations are in there. Make personal copies for your own records if you have not kept a copy of them previously.

Never burn any bridges. In other words, maintain a very pleasant and positive relationship with your current employer, even after you leave. You never know what twists of fate the future may bring. Whether you need letters of recommendation or are seeking reemployment, burning this bridge can come back to haunt you later in your professional career. No matter how bad they are, no matter how dishonest or chauvinistic you see them, keep the channels of communication open. In other words, do not tell them off even though that is exactly what you want to do and exactly what they need.

Start by taking inventory of your personal qualities, experience and accomplishments. Update your resume, if you haven't already. If you need help in writing a resume or cover letter, go to a professional. Many organizations now offer numerous workshops and training sessions on these topics; take advantage of what is available. Collect letters of recommendation from a variety of sources (personal acquaintances, co-workers when appropriate, former employers, and depending on the circumstances, perhaps even customers). The more information that you are able to present to a potential employer to document your statements adds credibility to what you are saying and lessens their required research after you leave.

If it has been a while since you have looked for a job, times have changed. Know how the system works in today's marketplace. Make sure that you feel confident about interviewing. Find a person who will let you practice interviewing; use your family and friends until answers flow smoothly and naturally from you. The art of successfully interviewing is based on being well prepared. This includes anticipating many common questions that are likely to be asked and having logical and comfortable replies.

Concentrate on your strengths and create a vision of where you want to go. This will help you to focus on how to find that perfect place to continue your career. What are you looking for in that perfect job? Write down what you want to do as if someone gave you a blank job description form and said to fill it out. Don't be shy; don't be afraid to list your strengths. This is your chance to dream and envision your future.

Then look at various types of companies. Determine if there are certain industries you want to work for, or certain size companies that you prefer.

Make a list of as many companies that you see which fit this description. List your salary range expectations and the total benefits package that you are looking for so that you can focus on negotiating to your advantage. See Section 7.2 for more information about learning how to negotiate during the interview process.

Next, start networking. Most jobs are gained through the networking mazes instead of through want ads or job placement firms. You will be surprised not just by who you know, but by all the people they know, and on and on. That is the depth of networking. Contacts are not made just in the first layer; it is in the multitude of layers upon layers of who knows whom that produces such astonishing results. Use every advantage you can think of to get your foot in the door. Otherwise, you are only limiting yourself.

Finally, match all your lists and begin the arduous task of seeking a bright new career opportunity. If you approach this task from being forced to do so, it becomes a negative. But, when looked at as new opportunties, it becomes a positive challenge.

Expect the process to take time. Know exactly what it is you want and go get it! Be creative, aggressive, and positive. Know that it is out there somewhere—it is simply up to you to find it.

Chapter Summary

Conflicts may arise at work for several reasons. They may be the result of the company stressing different priorities than are important to you. For example, when family is a primary priority for you, but the company places work first, you may expect policy conflicts to occur from time to time based on these distinct differences.

Women are faced more often with policy conflicts because of differences in priority compounded with a basic lack of knowledge about how the game is played. Or more accurately, a blatant disregard for the system itself.

Everyone accepts that businesses must make money to survive. Another avenue of conflict may arise when the means for making that money differs. Some businesses may say cut expenses first; these businesses typically view employees as easily dispensable items on the expense ledger. On the other hand, a company may look for ways to increase productivity with the same number of employees, thereby increasing sales and retaining a greater profit margin. Both (presumably) net the same bottom-line results, but they are very different means for achieving those results.

In addition, conflicts may be born out of gender stereotypes, tradition, and outdated philosophy styles. Women are slowly finding seats on major corporate boards, although still in a minority. These women will be able to affect change and help rewrite corporate policy by their very presence. But change takes time.

When addressing policy conflicts, it is important to accept that when you can't change something, then change the way you look at it. By concentrating on those solutions which you retain some control over, you will begin to grow stronger and more confident as a manager.

There will always be bumps in the road ahead. Actually, those bumps are what create new opportunities for you. Not that they are easy and they are rarely planned, but by growing through these experiences, you are becoming the manager you always wanted to be. Someone you would enjoy working for.

Learn from the many lessons in life. And have fun, no matter what challenges await you. Because without having fun, what's the point?

Bibliography

Megatrends for Women, by Patricia Aburdene and John Naisbitt.

Life and Work: A Manager's Search for Meaning, by James A. Autry.

Love and Profit: The Art of Caring Leadership, by James A. Autry.

Letitia Baldriges's Complete Guide to Executive Manners, by Letitia Baldrige.

The Professional Image, by Susan Bixler.

The Manager's Troubleshooter, by Clay Carr and Mary Fletcher.

Thick Face, Black Heart: The Path to Thriving, Winning, and Succeeding, by Chin-Ning Chu.

Women Who Run with the Wolves, by Clarissa Pinkola Estes

In a Different Voice, by Carol Gilligan

Men Are from Mars, Women Are from Venus, by John Gray, Ph.D.

The Female Advantage, by Sally Helgesen.

Becoming a Manager: Mastery of a New Identity, by Linda A. Hill.

Louis Rukeyser's Business Almanac by Louis Rukeyser.

Failing at Fairness by Myra and David Sadker.

Mismeasure of Woman by Carol Tavris.

Talking from 9 to 5, by Deborah Tannen, Ph.D.

You Just Don't Understand, by Deborah Tannen, Ph.D.

Index